Mary Jo Muratore

EXPIRER AU FÉMININ

Narratives of Female Dissolution
in French Classical Texts

University Press of the South
New Orleans

2003

Published in the United States by:
    University Press of the South, Inc.
    5500 Prytania Street, PMB 421
    New Orleans, LA 70115 USA
E-mail: unprsouth@aol.com   Fax: (504) 866-2750   Phone: (504) 866-2791
Visit our award-winning web page:
                      http://www.unprsouth.com
Visit our partner's web page: http://ww.punmonde.com
Acid-free paper.

Mary Jo Muratore.
Expirer au féminin. Narratives of Female Dissolution in French Classical Texts.
First Edition. French Studies 3, Women's Studies 2.
vi + 184 p. cm.
Includes Bibliography and Index.

1. Neo-classical. 2. Seventh Century French writers. 3.   *La Princesse de Clèves*.
4. Literary Protocols. 5. *Horace*. 6. *Phèdre*. 7. *Athalie*. 8. *Mariane*.
9. Corneille. 10. Les Lettres portugaises.

ISBN: 1-931948-14-3(pbk.).
Library of Congress Catalog Card Number: 2002115841.

CONTENTS

ACKNOWLEDGEMENTS

I would like to thank the Research Council at the University of Missouri–Columbia for assisting with funding for this project. I would also like to thank my colleague Richard-Laurent Barnett, for his encouragement, his brilliant insights, and his exemplary scholarship.

Finally, I would like to thank Susan Ferber for her invaluable assistance in preparing the final copy. Her patience and extraordinary talent were much appreciated.

CHAPTER 1

Theoretical Resistance;
Hypothetical Compliance

In seventeenth-century French literature, both the tenor and vehicle of the work were constrained by theoretical rules, a combination of synthesized and refined concepts derived from a variety of Ancient, Renaissance, and contemporary musings on the subject. It is precisely the number and indispensability of these regulations and restrictions that particularize French neo-classical discourse. Most writers submitted willingly to precepts established by a wide variety of commentators on the matter: political leaders with literary aspirations; literary hacks whose desire to create exceeded their talent for poetic production; established writers; ever-vigilant theorists and critics. However, this steady barrage of aesthetic pre-requisites imposed upon the writer could not fail to affect textual representation. In *Expirer au féminin,* I argue that the writers' conflicted attitude toward aesthetic conformity revealed itself in a number of "gendered" conflicts found within the works. What distinguishes this book from other "gender" studies currently in great supply is that gender is here transformed into an ideological marker of distinction. In the works under review, the battle lines are drawn between a male hero or heroes willing to comply with political mandates or historical traditions, and a dissenting heroine whose violation of established regulations or behavioral codes provokes either surprise, or hostility, or both. It is to be expected, perhaps, that in the political context of seventeenth-century France, a heroine's refusal to embrace the reigning ideology would result inevitably in her punishment, dissolution, or excision from the text. Such elimination underscores the importance of conformity, and lays stress on the necessity of supporting the prevailing political viewpoint. But what is less apparent and more intriguing is how the death of the rebellious and outspoken heroine serves a contemporary aesthetic cause as well. In these analyses, the heroine's non-conformity is linked to an aesthetic protocol, and the death of the rebellious heroine becomes the means by which the text can be "purged" of its non-regular (baroque) elements. In consequence, the heroine's elimination serves to justify and validate the more submissive and disciplined posture manifested by her masculine counterpart(s), those loyal to the principles of mimetic fidelity and patriarchal order. The death of the heroine represents a victory not only for political, but for aesthetic conformity as well.

The triumph of conformity is not effected without leaving behind a few traces of authorial resistance. Indeed, in the works under review, the dissolution or nullification of the dissenting heroine is not cast definitively as a political or aesthetic triumph. Often it communicates either an ambiguous or a contradictory message regarding the necessity of conformity. More often than not, the writer slants the readers' attitude toward the rebellious or aberrant heroine and against the obedient or conformist hero. This textualized bias offers the reader an initial point of access into a more comprehensive understanding of how obsessively the neo-classical writers wrestled with the need to serve both an ideological and an aesthetic master, and how conflicted was their attitude towards the perceived political necessity of blunting the creative impulse.

Richelieu and his *Académie* established early on that aesthetic perfection was located in the past and that France's literary aspirations could be achieved only by following closely in the footsteps of ancient forefathers. Reverence for the masters of Antiquity was so absolute, theorists believed, that it demanded works of seamless homage to them, not so much in subject matter, as in form and substance. For the most part, writers conceded (intellectually, at least) that the surest way to literary canonization was to imitate these masterworks of the past, to incorporate the proven literary strategies of Antiquity into their own textual creations. The deliberated and aggressive focus on form and theory led ultimately to the regularization of all literary practices, and succeeded happily in containing and eliminating the aesthetically displeasing excesses of what we now refer to as the "baroque."

The writers' desire for success, coupled with the growing political influence of Richelieu and his *Académie,* ensured widespread ideological conformity, even in the absence of total conviction or genuine faith. In the age of Richelieu, a writer's aesthetic survival depended on the degree to which a text remained faithful to established literary protocols. As Corneille's *Le Cid* demonstrated, even minor breaches would suffice to unleash the vitriolic wrath of the prime minister's academic watchdogs. In such a highly politicized literary arena, open rebellion against imposed regulations would constitute nothing short of aesthetic suicide. Yet, we know from a variety of treatises, prefatory remarks, letters, and argumentative discourses that there was significant and widespread debate regarding the interpretation and application of established literary protocols. *Expirer au féminin* adds another dimension to the debate by including evidence from the texts themselves.[1] While the rational side of writers generally conceded that the regularization of literary practices was a requisite, even constructive, development, *Expirer au féminin* suggests that underneath the disciplined overlay of the well-constructed neo-classical text smoldered an unspoken fear: Could the over-regulated text ultimately be perceived as too predictable, too safe, and too comforting to matter much at all? Might not such formal perfection jeopardize the very legacy that motivated the writers' aesthetic sacrifices in the first place?

For Tristan l'Hermite, the poetic reforms of the early seventeenth century *"rhétoriqueurs"* generated conflicting reactions. A malherbian disciple in some respects (his rhythmic perfection, for example), Tristan clearly believed poetry involved more than technical mastery. In his poetry, the valorization of poetic technique does not diminish its fundamentally lyric quality. The distinction between linguistic manipulation and aesthetic purity is, I argue, a central theme in *Mariane,* a tragedy that opposes the sincere Mariane to her deceptive and opportunistic King and husband Hérode. Hérode's political survival is linked initially to his ability to distort linguistically the reality around him, to mask his genuine motives in more appealing

---

1. Richard Goodkin's study of Racinian tragedy, *The Tragic Middle: Racine, Aristotle, Euripides* (Madison: University of Wisconsin Press, 1991), 5, argues for a theoretical model using the text to explain the work's context. This approach establishes the autonomy of the text, while keeping the historical context well in evidence. "What the text says, it says as only a work of literature could say it. And it is only once we have established what we believe the text to be saying—and, at least as important, how it is saying it—that we can make fruitful connections to the extraliterary domain."

garb. Mariane, on the other hand, insists that words and emotional reality coincide, a conviction for which she is ultimately executed. Her refusal to subordinate sincerity of expression to Hérode's political fictions does, however, serve a redemptive purpose in the end. After her death, a grieving Hérode confronts the error of his poetic past, and in the end pledges allegiance to the ideal of aesthetic authenticity that cost Mariane her life.

Corneille's resistance to theory is well-known and documented. What is striking, however, is his consistent use of the heroine to express his reservations regarding the state's attempt to bracket creativity within narrowly prescribed ideological limits. After the *Académie*'s reaction to *Le Cid,* Corneille offered the public *Horace,* a tragedy that was in many ways an act of aesthetic defiance. In the wake of the *Académie*'s review, he set out to prove that his rather loose conformity to doctrine in *Le Cid* was not the result of incompetence or ignorance, but of deliberate aesthetic choice. He was, as *Horace* would demonstrate, fully capable of writing a tragedy in perfect compliance with dramaturgical doctrine. What is most compelling in *Horace,* however, is not the tragedy's regularity, or even the play's representation of a fanatical hero who appears willing, even eager, to place abstract ideology and obedience to authority on a higher plane than humanity itself. What is most interesting in *Horace* is how the values defended by the hero mirror, even allegorize, the aesthetic principles mandated by Richelieu and his *Académie.* Roman values, like those championed by Richelieu, are predicated on a theory of mimesis, on an ideological premise that defines "progress" as a devolutionary concept. This unquestioned allegiance to precedent is opposed in Corneille's tragedy by Horace's sister Camille. Her betrayal of patriotic principles results in her elimination. The problem is, her murder in the name of the state, however politically rational, is morally and aesthetically displeasing to all who must confront it. Horace may remain technically exculpated for his action, but his exoneration satisfies no one. Consequently, the unexamined reverence for precedents that motivates Camille's execution is called into question, metatextually re-opening the debate between theory and practice unleashed by the "*querelle du Cid.*"

A similar repudiation of blind fidelity to past protocols can be seen in *Rodogune,* a tragedy featuring a defiant heroine in active rebellion against all manner of discriminatory practices, most of which are justified on the basis of historical tradition alone. Like Camille, Cléopâtre falls victim to those who defend the traditional order of things. Her death, like Camille's, serves ultimately to undermine that tradition when her elimination from the public arena leads not to the anticipated restoration of order, but rather to unintended scenic disorder and collapse.

The thematic repudiation of adhering to precedents in Cornelian theater reaches a climax in *Tite et Bérénice,* a tragedy penned when Corneille was in active rivalry with fellow dramatist Racine. Racine's tragedies (unlike Corneille's) were hailed for their aesthetic regularity. Although much has been made of the motivation behind these authors' dueling versions of *Bérénice,* one of the more interesting contrasts to be found in the competing dramas is the antithetical attitude toward aesthetic conformity that is revealed by the respective authors. Corneille's version, created at precisely the same moment in time as Racine's, portrays the rejection of authority as a moral, political, even an aesthetic imperative. Consequently, when the senate votes to suspend the interdiction barring the Roman emperor from marrying a foreign queen, Bérénice defies its authority in order to affirm her independence. In so doing, she exchanges finite happiness for literary eternity. By refusing to obey the senate's order, she hopes to become an icon of independent resistance for future generations to admire.

Racine's *Bérénice* demonstrates precisely the opposite viewpoint: there is no salvation outside the parameters of established regulations. Racine, it has been noted, had no difficulty creating tragedies in perfect consonance with dramatic theory. Not surprisingly, the necessity of dramaturgical regularity is affirmed in a number of metatextual references and thematic examples in his tragedies. In particular, Racine's *Bérénice* depicts respect for tradition and precedent as a sacrosanct and inviolable tenet. Consequently, his tragedy closes with a submissive Bérénice accepting the senate's verdict upholding the prohibition against marriage between a foreign queen and the Roman emperor. In contradistinction to Corneille, Racine elects to end his tragedy with the principal characters all pledging allegiance to political necessity and historical precedent. In an interesting parallel, Racine's heroine, like Corneille's, anticipates that her sacrifice will earn her a place in the more permanent realm of literary legend.

In the mythological tragedies *Andromaque* and *Phèdre,* Racine's defense of conformity is prominently in evidence. In these tragedies, initially rebellious heroines renounce ultimately their non-conformist stances via a very public suicide. In the early scenes of the tragedies, both Hermione and Phèdre attempt to script scenarios that violate historical, political, even aesthetic traditions. Hermione labors in vain to sever the emotional and political bonds that weld her fiancé Pyrrhus to the recent past; Phèdre commits several breaches of moral, political and aesthetic protocols in her attempt to escape her pre-destined demise. In the end, both heroines surrender to the necessity of precedent and take the stage one last time in order to commit suicide, a self-sacrifice that constitutes a repudiation of their non-conformist past, and a metatextual surrender to aesthetic protocols.

Whereas most of Racine's tragedies appear to offer a metatextual affirmation of the need to submit to established authority, one of his last tragedies, *Athalie,* reveals a kind of theatrical conversion on the part of the dramatist. In *Athalie,* the conflict between the more progressive-thinking Athalie and the traditional orthodoxy of the Israelites can be read as a textualized allegory of the battle between the Ancients and the Moderns. In *Athalie,* however, Racine appears to be on the side of the Moderns. His heroine's rebellion is clearly portrayed as admirable and heroic; the religious fanatics who seek to destroy her portrayed as narrow-minded, illogical, and surprisingly cruel. Moreover, the cause for which they fight is divinely proclaimed as a failed quest, rendering Athalie's death wholly gratuitous. Additionally, the fact that Joas' resurrection/revelation at the tragedy's close is one of the most deliberately theatricalized scenes in all of Racine's theater suggests that Racine's focus in this tragedy was as much on aesthetic issues as religious ones. Athalie's defeat at the hands of moral and political inferiors, coupled with the announcement that Joas, the king intended to validate the Israelites' unblinking faith in precedent, will fail to fulfill the Messianic promise, convey the distinct impression that mimetic fidelity is not necessarily synonymous with triumph, and may in fact be a flawed initiative after all.

In narrative, the heroine's withdrawal from the text can be seen as a triumph for the art of fiction. In *Les Lettres portugaises* and *La Princesse de Clèves*, the heroine's departure constitutes an affirmation of the pleasures of fictional inventions. In Guilleragues' work, the contradictory drift of Mariane's identity renders the notion of a grounding reality problematic, if not untenable. In the end, the heroine denounces definitively the necessity of linking tale to truth at all, and closes her text by proclaiming literary independence. For the Princesse de Clèves as well, fiction proves far more alluring than reality. More significantly, however, it proves more reliable than historical facts as a means to discover truth. Whereas the reality-based and detail-rich historical text, grounded by the compelling virtue of historical exactitude, might logically be expected to represent the privileged narrative component, it is in this novel portrayed as a fundamentally parasitic and static narrative form, one destined to remain ever subservient and inferior to the reality it passively re-constructs.

The profusion of works and of forms, the very stuff of seventeenth-century French literarity is no less compelling than the disparateness embraced. This is an era marked by pretensive creation: an outwardness of hegemony subsists in relentless if muffled confrontation with an inwardness of difference. The Barthesian and Derridean principles of otherness slake, prematurely, preemptively, in some sense anachronistically, into and well beyond the margins of classical discourse until such alterity finds its way to the very core, a restless, insidiously playful center. In fact, this vast enterprise, fashionably termed that of the "grand siècle" is all about difference, difference raised a notch, difference to the second power. The texts birthed during that epoch of would be purity, of normalization, differ not only from the precepts to which they were to adhere but, in fact, from themselves, from their own ostensible being. They are neither what they are supposed to be nor what they contrive to be. Difference from other and difference from self, twice contrived: therein resides no doubt the most salient characteristic of this neo-classical literature of conformity: it simply does not, will not, cannot conform. Beyond a veil of sameness and adherence, it proffers a dismantling of codes, a challenge to prescription, a poetically intoned ode to *désobéissance.* In an era of prescriptive exactitude, of textual despotism, we witness the wiles of transgression.

Once we accede to the prevalent ruse, appropriate it, take ownership of it, we, as readers, are equipped to decode the operative mechanisms by which such duplicity comes to be, the manifestations of its investment. For our purposes, it is the awkwardly redundant refrain of female eradication, dissipation, dissolution, in all its subtle demeanors that will come to mark, representationally, semiotically, metaphorically the conflagration rampant within. The heroine is, whatever her plight, a cipher of some quest for, or reflection of, contrariness: she embodies the non-permissible vision, the unspeakable other, the essence of alteration or alternation or alienation. She either breaks with tradition or derides it by her satirical exploitation of it. Thus, by her presence in the work, the writerly covenant finds its mode of expression; by her demise or disenfranchisement, justice is rendered. She knows the fate of those who would taint the status quo and thus, ostensibly, all is reset in place. She is, then, woman, heroine, fictional icon, rendered essential by her presence, but quintessential by her absence. If her words or deeds or being elucidate, it is ultimately her suspension, only her suspension, its necessity and its realization, that illuminates truth. There is no second exit, sameness must triumph externally and to that end, the creatures of otherness must not perdure, but dissolve. In powerfully metonymic terms, one might posit that the exegetical key to French neo-classicism is fleshed out and flushed out by one unspoken imperative on which sustenance hinges. If the text is to survive, those who would violate a world and a word of man-made precepts and male dominance must "expirer au féminin." This work exemplifies the process of such eradication and captures the orthodoxy of life that art must overcome.

CHAPTER 2

Tristan l'Hermite's *Mariane* and the Quest for Aesthetic Authenticity[1]

In his article, "Artifice and Sincerity in the Poetry of Tristan L'Hermite," Philip Wadsworth underscores how blurred was the line between poetic contrivance and emotional authenticity in seventeenth-century literary circles.[2] Claude Abraham, too, notes that in the seventeenth century, artifice and sincerity were not regarded as antithetical concepts.[3] He affirms further that all Tristan's poems tend to include a combination of technical skill and emotional sensitivity, although he does concede that Tristan's later poetry has a more personal, less rhetorical, edge to it, an evolution that if not exactly revolutionary, is nevertheless significant.[4] James C. Shepard also detects an aesthetic shift in Tristan's art, and suggests that in later poems, Tristan appears to rely less on mannerist techniques and more on those that we typically identify with the baroque or even the *baroque dompté.*[5] Consequently, if it is true that for Tristan l'Hermite, stylistic technique and heartfelt lyricism go hand in hand,[6] it is no less true that the poet was consumed throughout his career with finding a perfect balance between these competing demands. *Mariane,* his first play, sandwiched as it is between emerging and sophisticated poetic accomplishments, holds a pivotal position that makes it ideal terrain for examining how Tristan managed to fuse technical tropes, theatri-

---

1. A primitive version of this article entitled "The Gender of Truth: Rhetorical Privilege in Tristan's *Mariane*" appeared in *Papers on French Seventeenth-Century Literature,* ed. Francis Assaf 102 (1997), 145–53.
2. *Modern Language Notes* 74 (1959), 422–23.
3. *Tristan L'Hermite* (Boston: G. K. Hall, 1980), 31.
4. *Tristan L'Hermite,* 32–33.
5. *Mannerism and Baroque in Seventeenth-Century French poetry: The Example of Tristan L'Hermite* (Chapel Hill: North Carolina Studies in the Romance Languages and Literatures, 2001). This work establishes a particularly fine distinction between these two literary trends and examines Tristan's poetry in light of both. Philip Wadsworth, on the other hand, believes it is a mistake to speak of Tristan's "early" and "late" periods because the chronology of his poems is too difficult to establish (423). However, even he concedes that Tristan's later writings manifest less artifice and reveal a more elevated style (428).
6. Philip Wadsworth suggests that the constant mixture of artifice and sincerity is what makes Tristan such an innovative poet (423–26), an opinion shared by Claude Abraham (*Tristan L'Hermite,* 32–33).

cal flair, and unvarnished sincerity into one poetic whole. Indeed, *Mariane* can be said to track Hérode's own aesthetic evolution from a discourse of fictional contrivance to a discourse of the poetically sublime, a transformation motivated and effected by the death of the heroine, Mariane.

For many dramatic figures, death establishes that liminal boundary between mortality and legend. Dying grandly is in fact the surest means to acquire a larger than life silhouette within the world of tragic drama. For the heroine in Tristan's *Mariane,* however, no hyperbolic magnification results from her tragic demise.[7] At best, she is "rehabilitated," returned to her former stature by the elegiac *mea culpa* of the husband who ordered her execution. In fact, Mariane's image remains largely unchanged throughout. She is at the end, as she was in the beginning, an accessory to Hérode's rise to power in life, and in death, the agent of his redemption. Indeed, within the drama itself, it is Hérode whose grandeur continuously augments in the eyes of his public, often in proportion to the suffering he claims to endure as a result first of Mariane's coldness, then her alleged infidelity, and finally her death. In other words, it appears initially that Mariane's function, both dramatically and thematically, is limited to promoting the ascendancy of a male counterpart who is inferior to her both in political rank and in moral character. And just as her royal heritage legitimizes her husband's political status while she lives, her death validates his heroic posturing by endowing him finally with an authentic tragic dimension. Arguably, Mariane remains Hérode's victim no less in death than she was in life. Marginalized by a final exit that has import only as a measure of her husband's grief and suffering, Mariane appears little more than a convenient pretext, the means by which Hérode can achieve a variety of self-serving ends. The hero's goal of securing power, respectability, and finally, a kind of classical tragic stature, all require the participation of the reluctant heroine

7. The issue of feminine heroism is discussed at length by Carol Pearson and Katherine Pope in *The Female Hero in American and British Literature* (New York: R. R. Bowker, 1981). For a general discussion of heroism, see Joseph Campbell, *The Hero with a Thousand Faces* (New York: Pantheon, 1949); Dorothy Norman, *The Hero: Myth, Image, Symbol* (New York: World, 1969), and F. R. S. Raglan, *The Hero: A Study in Tradition, Myth and Drama* (New York: Vintage, 1956).

who is then sacrificed to political necessity, or so it surfacially appears.

Mariane's isolation and final elimination invite feminist attention to two familiar socio-political dilemmas: a) the manner by which women are consistently absorbed and oppressed by a patriarchal society in which they have no part, and b) the degree to which the continued existence of the female depends on the value she is accorded by masculine needs and desires. But in addition to these feminist concerns, a more subtle gendering process can be detected, one that yields consequences of a more literary nature. In *Mariane,* the struggle for textual supremacy is fought in the name of competing views on the relationship between discourse and representation. Divisions between the sexes fall here not only along familiar fault lines (oppressor/victim; active/passive; brutal/gentle; primary/marginal; etc.), but delimit as well contrasting views on the relationship between language and reality.[8] Mariane believes that words and reality are intrinsically linked, that there is an integral connection between reality and representation. For Mariane, the goal of language is to reveal authentic states; words are intended to reflect rather than distort reality. Mariane upholds this aesthetically naive affirmation even when it is detrimental to her survival.[9] Counseled to feign affection for her own protection ("C'est vn art excellent que de sçauoir bien feindre" [352]),[10] Mariane still refuses to use language subversively, to modulate the tenor of her outrage to suit the nature of her audience:

8. Communication, or rather, the inability to connect discursively with the world, is a fundamental component of Tristan's tragic vision according to Daniella Dalla Valle in *Il teatro di Tristan l'Hermite* (Torino: Giappichelli, 1964), 293. Claude Abraham in *The Strangers: The Tragic World of Tristan L'Hermite* (Gainesville: University of Florida Press, 1966), 19–28 and 52–57, locates the tragic focus within the communicative chasm that separates Hérode from Mariane, a gulf that leaves the heroine isolated in a world of alien values.

9. "The greatness of Tristan's heroes lies in their total lucidity: fully aware of the worldly absurdity, they refuse the balms of unconsciousness no less than those of compromise. Like Corneille's *Suréna,* Tristan's protagonists die because they willfully choose not to live a lie," notes Claude Abraham in *Tristan l'Hermite,* 80.

10. All verse references are to Tristan l'Hermite, *La Mariane,* ed. Jacques Madeleine (Paris: Nizet, 1984).

le sors de trop d'ayeuls qui portoient des Couronnes,
Pour auoir la pensée, & le front differans,
Et deuenir Esclaue en faueur des Tyrans. (364–66)

This unbridled spontaneity serves to distinguish Mariane from nearly all the other characters in the drama, those who accept the machiavellian necessity of manipulating discourse for political ends, even self survival. Her own mother feigns contempt for her falsely accused daughter, a charade designed primarily for self protection:

Inhumaine, traistresse, assassine perfide,
Qui voulus laschement attenter sur ton Roy,
Ie ne te connois point, tu ne viens pas de moy,
Car de ces trahisons ie ne suis pas capable. (1388–91)

But it is clearly Mariane's husband, Hérode, who has most fully mastered the art of fictional discourse. Hérode, a fundamentally political animal, uses linguistic artifice to create a reality wholly unrelated to historical truth. As the play opens, he appears to have effectively refuted the necessity of linking empirical reality to its rhetorical rendering. Language is for Hérode primarily a manipulative tool, the means by which to construct a series of identities as the situation requires. Unlike Mariane, Hérode sees no need for language to be constrained by historical truth. With the aid of borrowed discourses and mimed reactions, Hérode intends to bury the memory of his tyrannical past, and to project a more favorable image of self, to construct a persona based on the example of successful historical models. Indeed, Hérode's atrocities are known to the reader only through Mariane's testimony. Hérode himself refuses to acknowledge his role in the commission of past vile deeds. He refutes aggressively Mariane's accusations, feigning incredulity that she would dare accuse him of such grisly misconduct. It is, he asserts, Mariane who is distorting facts:

Ie me ris de ta rage, & par ces vains blasphemes,
En pensant me picquer, tu te blesses toy-mesmes:
Ce reproche insolent choque la verité,
Et fait voir clairement ton animosité;

Par là ta perfidie est assez descouuerte,
Cette confession suffira pour ta perte. (827–32)

Refuting Mariane's characterization of him as brutal tyrant, Hérode presents himself to the public as a heroic warrior ("Ie suis assez muny de force & de valeur" [174]) and diplomatic statesman. His material largesse and rhetorical cunning have solidified his reputation in the political world:

Ie sçay bien quel support Auguste m'a promis,
Me voulant receuoir au rang de ses amis;
Et i'ay tant de faueur auprés de son Genie,
Que i'y suis asseuré contre la calomnie:
Ceux qu'il aime le mieux d'entre ses Courtisans
Font cas de ma vertu, comme de mes presens:
Et i'ay mille secrets par où le Iourdain libre
N'a point à redouter la colere du Tybre. (165–72)

In fact, so successful is Hérode at manipulating public opinion that Mariane appears alone in opposing him, a stance she maintains despite his histrionic demonstrations of affection for her. Indeed, the only crime to which he readily admits is that of having fallen in love with a woman who does not reciprocate his feelings, a rather common misdemeanor among those of his rank ("L'amour est tellement fatal à la valeur, / Qu'il n'est point de Heros exempts de ce mal-heur" [245–46]). This unrequited passion condemns him to bemoan Mariane's coldness in tortured antitheses ("O bon-heur imparfait! ô rigueur importune" [211]; "Que son coeur soit de glace & le mien soit de feu?" [238]), mannerist lamentations intended primarily for public consumption.[11]

Although his efforts to portray himself as a love-stricken suitor are, by all accounts, quite studied and relentless ("Il souspire tousiours quand vous estes absente, / Il vous nomme à toute heure, il compte tous vos pas; / N'est-ce pas vous aimer?" [444–46]), his sentimental posturing fails to impress or persuade Mariane. She dismisses his emotional vent-

---

11. James Shepard demonstrates persuasively Tristan's evolution from a more playful mannerist style to the more serious register of the baroque in chapters six through nine of his book *Mannerism and Baroque in Seventeenth-Century French Poetry.*

ing as the hyperbolic theatrics of an opportunistic hypocrite:

> On connoist à ce stile, & doux, & deceuant,
> Comme en l'art de trahir ton esprit est sçauant.
> C'est auec trop de soin m'ouurir la sepulture,
> Pour me perdre il suffit d'vne seule imposture. (917–20)

Mariane's refutation of Hérode's emotional authenticity serves to undermine repeatedly the hero's deliberated identity, and threatens to explode the legitimacy and credibility of the "masculine" narrative entirely. Her repudiation of his Petrarchan similes that mime authentic sentiments establishes the central conflict between the heroine's discourse, based on a truthful, unadorned rendition of sentiments, and that of the hero. Hérode's discourse is dependent on the power of highly stylized embellishments and linguistic manipulation, often at the expense of sincerity. Hérode, Mariane argues, is only playing the part of the smitten suitor; he loves not Mariane, the individual, but rather the status and power the marriage confers upon him. Even Hérode's own assertions suggest that his love is more motivated than spontaneous ("Ie n'ay pas des desirs que l'on puisse blasmer: / Car i'aime seulement ce que ie dois aimer" [257–58]). Moreover, his rather ostentatious displays of emotion seem expressly marketed for garish display ("On n'obserue en vous deux que plaintes & que pleurs" [230]; "Vous voulez que par tout on ait pitié de vous" [242]).

Mariane remains unmoved by his histrionic performances, and refuses to accept the verbally constructed façade Hérode so dramatically overstates. Her weapon of choice in the destruction of his credibility is the documented record of dishonorable actions that belie Hérode's rhetoric. Despite his denial of a criminal past, history reveals Hérode to be nothing but a vulgar tyrant, an uncivilized barbarian who murdered Mariane's family in cold blood for political gain ("I'ay mille trahisons, & mille cruautez, / Le meurtre d'vn Ayeul, l'assassinat d'vn Frere" [818–19]). The gentler, kinder Hérode now posturing before the public is a self-created fiction. He has not "evolved" because he cannot evolve. He therefore must rely on discourse to change what nature cannot. Hérode is, and will ever remain, a savage murderer. Sooner or later, his fundamental nature will reveal itself. His verbal denials of past misdeeds can cloud, perhaps, but not quite cover, the abhorrence of the crimes he committed in his quest for power. His attempt to poetically reconstruct himself as Mariane's devoted lover and husband, lacking any grounding in fact, constitutes little more than an act of rhetorical accessorizing. Because his discourse is so divorced from substance, Mariane is certain that his "impassioned" tirades will never fully dupe his audience. His plaintive utterances, no matter how well-chiseled, cannot continue indefinitely to convey meaning because ultimately, meaning depends on a relationship between stance and sentiment that his discourse fundamentally and deliberately lacks.

Mariane's revolt, her attempt to override a set of textual practices designed specifically to suppress voices of opposition, is a politically subversive activity. As the victor, Hérode enjoys the usual spoils of triumph, including the power of subjugation and the prerogative of rhetorical privilege. The vanquished have few options but to remain silent, thereby corroborating the authoritative discourse by default. Discourses of opposition, that is to say, verbal utterances that contradict or undermine the hero's articulated version of events, are destined to be silenced. However, in order for Hérode's scenarios of legitimately acquired power and domestic tranquillity to appear more plausible, he believes he needs the rhetorical collusion of his victim. Mariane's participation is required to provide credibility to his elaborate fictions. To accomplish this goal, it is not sufficient that Mariane merely enact the role of forgiving partner by remaining his wife and by caring for their children. These functions constitute important visual indicators of support, but images can be easily destroyed by words. Hérode, as much a theaterician as a politician, demands that Mariane complete her role by providing discursive corroboration as well. For Hérode, all reality is rhetorical. Consequently, for his masquerade to be wholly convincing, Mariane's discourse must conform to his, or cease altogether ("Son meilleur est d'auoir tousiours la bouche close" [701]).

Hérode's fears are not wholly unwarranted. Mariane's consistent repudiation of Hérode's linguistic version of "truth" appears even to Hérode's loyal followers as evidence of treason. Mariane's counter-discourse, they argue, threatens the very security of the realm ("Et de mille raisons anime son courroux, / Pour faire sousleuer les peuples contre vous" [317–18]). It is Hérode's duty to recognize and neutralize the destructive power of the enemy within ("Vous faites vanité d'aimer vne ennemie, / Qui pour recompenser vn traictement si doux / N'aplique son esprit qu'à mesdire de vous" [264–66]).

When confronted initially with Mariane's persistent and public refusal to reiterate or be silenced, Hérode attempts a variety of strategies designed to neutralize her contrariness and rationalize her linguistic behavior. He at first dismisses the significance of her inconsistencies by maintaining that her vitriolic and derisive verbal assaults are but the result of her excessive prudery rather than definitive expressions of unbridled contempt ("Toute ceste rigueur, vient de sa chasteté, / Mais son humeur hautaine est plaine de bonté" [281–82]). He argues further that her rhetorical attacks are but an embarrassed ruse to mask her impassioned attachment:

> Ie deus ma deliurance à son conseil fidelle:
> Sans cet insigne effet de sa secrette amour,
> Ie perdois à la fois, & le Sceptre & le iour. (284–86)
> . . . .
> Cette obligation me touche tendrement,
> Et me fait excuser ses desdains aisément. (289–90)

Because he believes Mariane to be too prudent to be as outspoken as her enemies report ("Ie connoy Mariane, & sçay qu'elle est trop sage / Pour s'estre abandonnée à tenir ce langage" [323–24]), he underestimates the danger Mariane's counter discourse represents.

It soon becomes clear, however, that Mariane's rhetoric cannot continue to counter publicly his own without undermining and eventually destroying the linguistic façade he is laboring to construct. In order to suppress Mariane's contradictory view of the recent past and his role in it, Hérode has only one sure-fire remedy: silencing her oppositional viewpoint. Hérode's desire to rewrite history depends on his ability to persuade others to repeat only his authorized view of events. He can neither acknowledge nor allow competing versions. As Hérode's obsession with maintaining discursive control intensifies, language and voice become overwhelming preoccupations. In essence, his regal survival depends on his ability to provide a rhetorical alternative to lived experience, to project a heroic self while rhetorically discrediting contradictory perspectives. Moreover, Hérode believes the act of speaking constitutes a right of office, a validation of his authoritative supremacy. The act of listening passively is the duty of his subordinates who are to submit willingly to his authority, both political and linguistic. His obsession with discursive control is reflected in his despotic need to have the full attention of his audience. When Hérode speaks, he imposes a rigorous silence on listeners ("Ne m'interromps donc pas quand i'auray commencé" [86]; "Escoutez donc le reste, & me laissez parler" [110]), as if to ensure subordination and eliminate contradiction through vocal dominance. This need to oppress verbally extends even to the realm of the seemingly insignificant. He opposes angrily Phérore's "medical" justification for a recent unpleasant dream (47–62) because it opposes the more grandiose explanation he wishes to put forth instead. He prefers to interpret the nightmare within a more noble and "mimetic" context, and places it within a historical tradition of similar warnings to celebrated "dreamers":

> Ces expositions ne me contentent gueres,
> Ces principes communs ont des effets vulgaires;
> Et tu sçais qu'autrefois l'Egypte remarquoit
> Aux songes importans que Ioseph expliquoit,
> Qu'il en est, dont l'image est heureux ou funeste,
> Nous annonçans la grace, ou le courroux celeste. (75–80)

Within the dream itself, Hérode's preoccupation remains with the elements of sound and voice. A disembodied call beckons Hérode to the corpse of Aristobule whom Hérode recognizes, significantly, by voice alone: ("Ie ne l'ay reconnu qu'à la voix seulement" [117]). Significant too is the fact that Aristobule's speech is the catalyst that provokes Hérode's violent response:

Il m'est venu charger de maledictions,
M'a parlé de rigueurs sur son pere exercées,
M'imputant tous les maux de nos guerres passées:
Bref voyant qu'il osoit ainsi s'emanciper,
A la fin i'ay leué le bras pour le fraper. (130–34)

Hérode's physical counter-strike in response to Aristobule's verbal assault underscores the hero's intolerance for opposing viewpoints, his impatience with perspectives that do not mimic with reverent exactitude his own. What Hérode fears most is contradiction, the articulation of documentable examples that contradict the elaborate fictional scenarios of self he so labors to construct. Indeed, the primacy of rhetoric over truth is part of his larger political strategy, a way to mold events of the past to conform to his current design. For Hérode, "truth" is a rhetorical construct and a political strategy. Credibility depends not on the factual status of what is articulated, but on the speaker's ability to inspire belief in the utterance. What matters is the ability to convey an impression of truth, to establish a credible semblance of reality that can overshadow completely reality itself. In other words, Hérode believes that illusions and facts have equal status in principle. Reality is not a privileged entity in and of itself but rather a function of popular consensus. Truth is essentially in the eye of the beholder. In persuading his audience to accept fictions for facts, Hérode relies heavily on rhetorical excess and linguistic ornamentation. He is in this sense the embodiment of a mannerist poet.

Hérode's reliance on verbal façades to disguise reality makes him particularly eager to suppress the emerging fact that he ordered Mariane killed in the event of his own death during a recent military campaign. Hérode's secret order provides irrefutable evidence that his moral transformation is nothing but a rhetorical sham, that his love for Mariane is nothing other than linguistic artifice. If Hérode's plan to have Mariane killed were publicly revealed, it would expose the purely rhetorical supports on which his love rests. For the politically obsessed Hérode, discursive betrayal constitutes an even far more serious threat to his survival than Mariane's plot to poison him. The threat of corporeal destruction, he reasons, can be neutralized with aggressive surveillance ("Estant assez instruit de sa mauuaise enuie, / Ie l'empescheray bien d'attenter sur ma vie" [689–90]). Confident he can defend himself against Mariane's poison, Hérode remains ready to forgive Mariane if she will simply alter her discursive manner in public:

> Fay qu'à iamais son coeur repentant de son crime,
> Responde à mes bontez auecque plus d'estime;
> Qu'elle quitte pour moy cét insolent orgueil
> Qui pourroit quelque iour nous ouurir le cercueil. (887–90)

Malevolent discourse, however, once unleashed, can never be wholly contained. Hérode fears Soesme's revelation far more than actual poison because it can destroy not just Hérode the man, but his entire fabricated reality. Hérode's secret order to have his wife executed in the event of his death belies his affirmations of love, and in consequence, undermines the rhetorical coherence required to maintain the integrity of his fictions. Any crack in the verbal façade threatens his political and rhetorical legitimacy. In the past, he managed to neutralize Mariane's repeated attempts to discredit him by simply re-scripting or re-interpreting her version of events. Soesme's revelation, however, exposes the hero's own rhetorical duplicity, and breaks, as it were, the consistency of the illusion of reality his discourse is intended to create. He cannot at once claim to love Mariane and at the same time justify her elimination for no other crime than surviving him. Hérode's own words now render him inconsistent, and the original conflict between Hérode's discourse and Mariane's counter discourse is transformed into a conflict between two Hérodes, one real and one counterfeit. Since Hérode's survival depends on his ability to promote a coherent image of self, the polyphonic potential of Soesme's revelation constitutes a mortal threat. For Hérode to remain linguistically consistent, that is to say, for his discursive illusions to remain free from the contaminants of ugly reality, both Mariane and Soesme must be eliminated.

Hérode hastily constructs a self-serving scenario designed to discredit both his wife and his closest advisor. Accusing Mariane and Soesme of adultery, he orders their execution in order to suppress the contradictory content of his own enunciations. For the narcissistic Hérode, the corporeal Mariane is no longer of any use at all. The visual sign of support she provides by playing the role of wife and mother will only serve to accentuate the odiousness of his earlier call for her death in the event of his own. Hérode's purposes can now be served only by transforming his uncooperative partner into a totally absent and silent signifier. Her death will at once allow him to suppress the evidence of his prior communiqué, and then to fill the physical void with poetic narratives bemoaning her loss. Mariane will no longer be able to counter his discourse. Consequently, he can finally transform her political enmity into silent acquiescence. Only then will Hérode be free to represent events from his own self serving perspective and to suppress wholly the evidence of his self centered motives. In death, Mariane will be transformed into a rhetorical accomplice, an unresponsive addressee to whom he can articulate fictionalized and formulaic expressions of undying affection. Mariane's execution eliminates the corporeal being and leaves in her place a malleable void, a blank canvas on which Hérode can reconstruct a past based on pure fictions and selective truths. In other words, Hérode elects to eliminate the real Mariane in order not to betray the lie of art.[12]

Hérode's sacrifice of Mariane to the necessity of protecting and prolonging a constructed image of self appears to encapsulate the all too familiar role of women in traditional forms of representation.[13] The locus of others' projections and desires, they acquire and are then made to convey meanings that remain wholly exterior to their real selves. Mariane's attempt to repudiate the authenticity of the

---

12. This thesis ties in nicely to an observation made by Jane Marcus in "Still Practice, A/ Wrested Alphabet. Toward a Feminist Aesthetic," in Shari Benstock, *Feminist Issues in Literary Scholarship* (Bloomington: Indiana University Press, 1987). Elaborating on the marginalization of women's texts, she argues that we "are at the very least forced to recognize that the suppression of women's writing is historically and psychologically directly related to male sexual violence against women, that men have cut out the tongues of the speaking woman and cut off the hands of the writing woman for fear of what she will say about them and about the world" (80–81).

13. See Marianne Hirsch, "Spiritual Bildung: The Beautiful Soul as Paradigm," in Elizabeth Abel, Marianne Hirsch and Elizabeth Langland, *The Voyage In: Fictions of Female Development* (Hanover: University Press of New England, 1983), 27: "Faced with the break between psychological needs and social imperatives, literary convention finds only one possible resolution: the heroine's death."

masculine narrative, no matter how falsified, is deemed an act of subversion, and swiftly punished.[14] It is Mariane's insistence on conveying her own truths that results in her textual elimination. Deprived of the power of voice while alive, she remains no less rhetorically impotent in death, leaving Hérode with the power to write his and her story. Hérode's preoccupation with rhetorical consistency makes the manner of Mariane's death (her throat is slashed) particularly significant ("Puis elle offrit sa gorge, & cessa de parler" [1550]). Embedded within a series of final *mea culpas*, Hérode, too, is quick to acknowledge the role voice played in Mariane's demise:

> Ta bouche a prononcé l'Arrest de son trespas,
> Et comme criminelle, & comme condamnée,
> On l'aura promptement au suplice menée. (1418–20)
> . . . .
> Ah! ie suis l'autheur de ce meutre inhumain,
> Ma bouche à son boureau mit le fer à la main:
> Ma bouche complaisante à ma rage animée,
> D'vn seul mot pour iamais rend la sienne fermée. (1589–92)

Unfortunately for Hérode, the decision to have Mariane executed does not bring the desired closure to his narrative. On the contrary, her execution creates as many problems as it resolves. Hérode cannot both destroy his wife and preserve his reputation as a loving and devoted husband. His own self protective strategy, the silencing of Mariane, can be used now to discredit him, leaving him with neither legitimizing partner, nor respected legacy:

> Cependant le desir que i'ay de me venger,
> Va mettre mon Salut dans vn autre danger,
> Ie m'aigry contre moy lors que ie la menace,
> Ma perte est enchaisnée auecque sa disgrace. (1121–24)

Hérode is quick to realize that Mariane's execution will require

14. See Mary Anne Ferguson, "The Female Novel of Development and the Myth of Psyche," in *The Voyage In: Fictions of Female Development,* 229: "Women who rebel against the female role are perceived as unnatural and pay the price of unhappiness, if not madness or death."

even more elaborate manipulation if he hopes to retain his current political status and influence. In a face saving gesture, Hérode dispatches messengers in order to present a plausible self-defense designed to mask the real motives behind the double execution:

> Il sera necessaire incontinent aprés
> D'en auertir Cesar par vn courier exprés,
> De crainte que l'Enuie, auec ses artifices,
> Me rende prés de luy quelques mauuais offices,
> Et me fasse passer, la verité celant,
> Pour vn Prince ombrageux, iniuste & violant. (1233–38)

But even as he scrambles to create ever more redemptive fictions and develop new linguistic strategies, Hérode begins to repent. Exhausted by the never ending need to distort reality, he surrenders ultimately to it and adopts the principles of linguistic fidelity espoused by Mariane. In a sincere and wrenching *mea culpa,* Hérode speaks finally with genuine sincerity and with less reliance on ostentatious poetic effects. Political salvation no longer his singular preoccupation, he directs a belated (and politically irrelevant) apology to the absent Mariane, now nothing but an ephemeral illusion and no longer in a position to influence events:

> Mais oubliant tes maux de qui ie fus l'autheur,
> O bel Ange! pardonne à ton persecuteur. (1781–82)

Hérode condemns emphatically his past hypocrisy, and calls upon all who witnessed his actions, both living and dead, to condemn him as well:

> Vous, peuples oppressez, spectateurs de mes crimes,
> Qui portez tant d'amour à vos Roys legitimes,
> Monstrez de ceste ardeur vn veritable effet,
> Employant vostre zele à punir mon forfait. (1599–1602)
> . . . .
> Tesmoins de sa bassesse & de ma violence,
> Cieux qui voyez le tort que souffre l'innocence,
> Versez sur ce climat vn mal-heur infiny. (1615–18).

Mariane died believing Hérode's love for her to be nothing other than a political pose designed to legitimize his royal status. In the aftermath of her execution, it appears his feelings, if not his rhetoric, may have been authentic after all. Arguably, his preoccupation with form and his heavy reliance on stylistic effects undermined the authenticity of his message, making it appear if not fraudulent, at least politically motivated. Hérode almost admits as much by his defensive assurances at the play's close. Now, he insists the sentiments he articulates are genuine ("Ne t'imagine pas que mes douleurs soient feintes" [1796]). In his monologue of bereavement following the death of Mariane, it will be noted that his lyrical regrets are without the formulaic tropes and predictable metaphors that rendered his earlier expressions of love so superficial, so precious, and so unconvincing. As if taken by surprise by his own sincerity, Hérode seems initially unable to navigate this new discursive terrain where rhetoric and reality coincide. Unaccustomed to speaking with any degree of sincerity, he seems hopelessly incapable of closing his own tragedy, of locating a suitable posture that will punctuate appropriately his feelings. He three times laments Mariane's death, each time as if it were the first, leaving spectators with the impression that he has wandered into a poetic cul-de-sac from which he is unable to extricate himself. This long and rambling farewell to Mariane, though somewhat disordered, represents his finest poetic achievement for it provokes finally the full attention and compassion of his listeners. It also renders him worthy of the status of tragic hero, and the play ends with an expression of sympathetic support for this self-destructive hero. His singular, or at least his most memorable, failing, we are led to conclude, was an excess of passion. His fate merits more pity than chastisement:

> O Prince pitoyable en tes grandes doueleurs!
> Toy mesme és l'Artisan de tes propres mal-heurs,
> Ton amour, tes soupçons, ta crainte & ta colere
> Ont offusqué ta gloire, & causé ta misere. (1805–08)

In *Mariane,* Hérode's initial concerns were political survival and theatrical showmanship, goals accomplished primarily through discursive manipulation and the suppression of competing or contra-

dictory viewpoints. His final preoccupation, however, is to render
publicly a faithful account of his feelings for Mariane. Upon the painful
realization that Mariane is dead and forever silenced, Hérode abandons his efforts to reconstruct his political identity, and elects instead
to commit his efforts to an aesthetic purpose: the faithful representation of Mariane. He also moves from a perspective of baroque egocentrism to that of self-sacrificing artist. Renouncing his past reliance
on the manipulative strategies of trompe-l'oeil and metaphoric excess, Hérode appropriates Mariane's practice of blending reality and
rhetoric into poetic congruence. Sacrificing political strategy to poetic sincerity, a reformed Hérode now subordinates the self to the
task of reconstructing poetically his subject ("Sujet de mes pensers,
obiet de mes desirs, / Ministre de ma joye, & de mes desplaisirs"
[1773–74]) . He orders that a temple be built in honor of Mariane's
memory ("Il faut que l'on construise vn Temple à ceste Belle" [1727]),
and he commits his discourse to expressions of love and regret:

> Et troublé toutefois d'vne aueugle furie,
> Ie t'ay vrayment traitée auecque barbarie.
> Mais à tout l'Vnivers ie m'en viens accuser,
> Et l'ennuy que i'en ay te doit bien apaiser,
> Si mon forfait est grand, si mon crime est horrible,
> I'en conçois vn regret bien vif & bien sensible. (1787–92)

Hérode's final articulations render him sympathetic not only
because they portray him in the classically tragic dilemma of a man
imperiled by his own devices ("Toy mesme és l'Artisan de tes propres
mal-heurs" [1806]), but because his discourse is now more aesthetically pleasing, more tinged with genuine pathos than were his previous
self-serving and overly-contrived articulations. It is in this sense that
the heroine's death can be read as the catalyst for poetic refinement.
Mariane's death prompts Hérode to reject the deceptive and overly
stylized discourse that served his concrete political needs, and to
dedicate himself to the more abstract task of reconstructing Mariane,
the woman he destroyed for political gain. In committing himself to
a representational, rather than a manipulative, use of language, Hérode
abandons functional artifice for poetic sincerity. Language becomes

for him no longer a tool of distortion designed to effect a variety of protean poses, but a means of objective and unmotivated aesthetic representation. In the end, rather than continue to distort language for personal gain, he elects to subordinate his discourse to the reality inspiring it. In imitation of Mariane, Hérode commits himself finally to making sentences and sentiments coincide. By making Mariane the revered subject of his discourse, he jeopardizes his political image in order to promote Mariane's. In death, she becomes the subject of his poetic lamentations, the muse responsible for his discourse. Belatedly, Mariane's narrative voice is recovered, as is her story which is communicated to the world via an intermediary (Hérode) committed to representing authentically and artistically his subject. Fittingly, it is Mariane rather than Hérode who provides the title to the tragedy. This titular designation, coupled with Hérode's final transformation into a more authentic-speaking poet, registers a metatextual defeat for textual artifice and a victory for the poetics of sincerity that Tristan's art so eloquently exemplified.[15]

15. For a fine and sensitive analysis of Tristan's poetry, consult Claude Abraham's *Tristan l'Hermite,* 31–77 and 120–21.

CHAPTER 3

Sacrificing Camille: The Wages of Invention in Corneille's *Horace*[1]

The link established between discursive audacity and political treason established in *Mariane* re-emerges in Corneille's *Horace*. It will be noted, moreover, that the heroines in both plays have much in common. Camille, like Mariane, is executed for articulating sentiments not sanctioned by the current regime. Camille's death, like Mariane's, ultimately serves to undermine the very cause in whose name she is executed. In Corneille's tragedy, as in Tristan L'Hermite's, a male discourse of artifice is pitted against a female discourse of emotional sincerity. In the early scenes of Corneille's drama, however, the female characters do not so much offer a counter discourse as refrain from stating a definitive position at all. Their reluctance derives from the fact that in *Horace,* the articulation of one ideological position is presumed to discredit and eradicate any and all oppositional viewpoints and perspectives. Consequently, rather than be forced to choose between the competing and irreconcilable values of love and patriotism, the heroines refuse to take a definitive verbal stance because to do so would oblige them to sever their emotional ties to political adversaries.

Whereas the heroines refuse to adopt a univocal posture and remain visibly and audibly torn between ideological and familial allegiances, the males, on the other hand, prove quite willing and able to conceal any trace of sensitivity by burying it with rhetorical panache. Their fanatical commitment to ideology and to the suppression of any natural feeling that might weaken their resolve results in Horace's indifferent slaughter of first his best friend and then his own sister.[2] What distinguishes heroine from hero in *Horace,* then, is

---

1. A version of this article, "Strategies of Containment: Repetition as Ideology in *Horace,*" appeared in *Romanische Forschungen* 109 (1997), 252–63.
2. Bernadette Lintz Murphy in "Du désordre à l'ordre: Le Rôle de la violence dans *Horace,*" *The Existential Coordinates of the Human Condition,* ed. Anna Teresa Tymieniecka (Dordrecth: Reidel, 1984), 435–47, uses René Girard's theory of mimetic violence found in *La Violence et Le Sacré* (Paris: Grasset, 1977) to explain the foregrounding of violence in *Horace.*

the former's refusal to re-affirm an imposed ideology, to proclaim what she does not believe. The hero regards this maverick repudiation of state-sanctioned platitudes to be nothing short of treason.

In tracing the signifying differences that produce or represent gender in *Horace,* we discover not only the obvious linguistic and behavioral distinctions that separate the sensitive females from their stoical male counterparts, but a feminine resistance to precedent. Camille and Sabine are reluctant to justify Rome's current quest for political dominance on the basis of some presumed historical entitlement. The heroines' repudiation of the masculine code of ethics valorizing repetition, conformity, and the suppression of natural sentiments serves ultimately to discredit, or at least, devalue significantly, established political protocols. Camille's execution reveals blind allegiance to conformity and mimetic duplication, two of Rome's most cherished principles, to be morally bankrupt. In the end, the King's intervention is required to salvage Horace's victory and justify his actions. Yet even royal intervention fails to rehabilitate the hero's character. The historical precedent of Roman matricide is insufficient to make Horace's performance any less odious to the public. Audience sympathy remains with the defiantly independent Camille, demonstrating that neither political power nor theoretical mandates can override the natural and sometimes inexplicable aesthetic response of viewers to the spectacle they witness. The murder of Camille in the wake of Rome's victory leaves the triumphant patriarchy with the ability to claim victory in principle, perhaps, but unable to justify morally the actions required for the ultimate triumph.

The ideological divisions depicted in *Horace* had a contemporary parallel.[3] Richelieu's politicization of the supremacy of Ancient writers put Corneille's *Le Cid* in the center of a controversy. The Academy's public airing and chastisement of the tragedy's flaws established a clearly drawn academic line that both aspiring and established writers feared to cross. The imposition of rules, and the writers' widespread acceptance of them, allowed the Academy to reconfigure

---

3. For a thorough analysis of the theoretical context underpinning and overdetermining Cornelian theater, consult the particularly illuminating study by Georges Forestier, *Essai de génétique théâtrale: Corneille à l'oeuvre* (Paris: Klincksieck, 1996).

the very elements of literary success. In Richelieu's "post-querelle" literary court, public approval no longer constituted the only, or even the primary, measure of aesthetic merit. On the contrary, the Academy's authority ensured that two separate but unequal juries would be henceforth responsible for determining the merits of aesthetic contributions: a) the unschooled consumers who responded emotionally and therefore, often inappropriately, to the dramatic representation and b) the learned theoreticians who evaluated intellectually and soundly on the basis of pre-established aesthetic principles.[4]

Corneille's response to the Academy's gauntlet was *Horace,* a play designed to demonstrate the author's uncontested ability to please both publics.[5] But if *Horace* illustrates the author's outward compliance with the theoretical demands of the Academy, the tragedy can be coaxed also to yield evidence that the triumph of *Horace* (both the play itself as dramatic manifestation of Richelieu's doctrinaire ideology, and the triumph of the hero within the play as well) is more apparent than real. Much of the evidence for such a claim is strategically located in the gendered attitudes around which the tragedy is structured. The masculine/feminine polarity so aggressively established from the outset serves to allegorize (and thereby partially conceal) an authorial protest against an arbitrary hierarchization that

---

4. "Ainsi *Horace* est-il le résulat direct de la querelle du *Cid,* Corneille ayant tenté de trouver la meilleure voie à prendre afin d'être à la fois fidèle à sa conception dramatique et, si ce n'est capable de plaire à tous ses publics—ce à quoi il ne parviendra qu'avec *Cinna*—, du moins garanti sur le plan de la théorie aristotélicienne" (Forestier, *Essai de génétique théâtrale,* 112).

5. "One important lesson he learned from the experience was how theoretical argument, once abstracted from the realities of performance, could gather such momentum that any consideration of audience response to the play itself receded into unimportance," notes David Clarke, *Pierre Corneille: Politics and Political Drama Under Louis XIII* (Cambridge: Cambridge University Press, 1992), 46. This commentary will achieve its full significance in light of the pardon of Horace in the final act, a verdict which valorizes aesthetic arguments over ethical ones and culminates in the exoneration of crimes committed in the name of theatrical necessity. Georges Forestier (*Essai de Génétique théâtrale*) asserts that this is his first real "tragedy" as the term was understood by Corneille's detractors (111). The observations of Philip Koch, "*Horace:* Réponse cornélienne à la querelle du *Cid,*" *Romanic Review* (1985), 161, are also quite pertinent here: "C'est avant tout une réorientation fondamentale de sa dramaturgie qui abandonne la tragi-comédie pour tragédie. Cependant, au moment de s'engager dans cette nouvelle voie, Corneille jette un coup d'oeil nostalgique vers ce qu'il quitte (Curiace) et un regard plutôt inquiet (cet Horace *imparfait*) vers ce qui l'attend."

locates perfection in the past and assigns victory on the basis of mimetic resemblance to historical precedents.

In *Horace,* the imitation of precedents is a sacrosanct imperative.[6] Roman males are particularly proud of their historical legacy, and eager for Roman conquests to continue. The primary female characters, however, are in rebellion against a political system intent on rewarding unexamined conformity, particularly when political allegiance is in conflict with natural sentiments. Sabine and Camille denounce Rome's insistence on privileging the reiteration of Roman values over the expression of non-partisan feelings.[7] Sabine, Alban by birth but Roman by marriage, is the first to express displeasure with Roman stoicism. For her, natural sentiments can be temporarily masked but never fundamentally altered by simple vocal assertion.[8] Confronted with the certainty of war between her native Alba and her adopted Rome, Sabine can do little more than control her outward countenance. Her conflicting emotions, however, cannot be held in check:

> Et, parmi les soupirs qu'il pousse vers lex cieux,
> Ma constance du moins règne encor sur mes yeux:
> Quand on arrête là les déplaisirs d'une âme,
> Si l'on fait moins qu'un homme, on fait plus qu'une femme;
> Commander à ses pleurs en cette extrémité,
> C'est montrer pour le sexe assez de fermeté. (9–14)[9]

6. "Chez Tite-Live, l'histoire est donc à la fois la récitation de la geste des héros et la reconnaissance de l'identité profonde de Rome au cours du temps. Les êtres sont à la fois les mêmes et ils sont autres, car ils ne peuvent agir qu'en référence avec ce qui s'est fait avant, à l'origine, qu'en répétant la fondation originelle," notes Jean-Marie Apostolidès in "Corneille, Tite-Live et la fondation de Rome," *Poétique* (1990), 209.

7. "The new Pandora who unleashes the strident notes of discord into what otherwise would be mimetic perfection is (a) woman," notes Mitchell Greenberg, *Corneille, Classicism and the Ruses of Symmetry* (Cambridge: Cambridge University Press, 1986), 67.

8. See Clarke, 183.

9. All references are to Pierre Corneille, *Théâtre complet* (Paris: Garnier, 1960). For additional insights into the "signs" of womanhood, see Susan Tiefenbrun, "Blood and Water in *Horace:* A Feminist Reading," *Papers on Seventeenth-Century Literature* (1983), 617–34, and Doreena Ann Stamato, "Le Renversement symétrique des rôles masculins et féminins dans les pièces de *Rodogune* et *Horace,*" *Papers on French Seventeenth-Century Literature* (1989), 529–40.

She repeatedly tries ("Prenons parti, mon âme, en de telles disgrâces: / Soyons femme d'Horace, ou soeur des Curiaces" [711–12]), but repeatedly fails, to resolve her internal conflict ("Flatteuse illusion, erreur douce et grossière, / Vain effort de mon âme, impuissante lumière" [739–40]). Despite aggressive efforts, her allegiance to family and country cannot be excised by oral proclamation. The legal bond that links Sabine to Horace fails to efface the residue of allegiance she yet feels toward brothers and country:[10]

> Je suis Romaine, hélas! puisque Horace est Romain;
> J'en ai reçu le titre en recevant sa main;
> Mais ce noeud me tiendrait en esclave enchaînée,
> S'il m'empêchait de voir en quels lieux je suis née. (25–28)

Sabine's perspective equating the masculine with stoical insensitivity and the feminine with internal emotional conflict is contextualized within a macrostructure linking male power and prestige with the destruction of all natural bonds to a maternal past.[11] The political conflict itself is a prime example of violence against both nature and motherhood at once. Rome, it is argued, can achieve its manifest destiny of universal mastery only through the destruction of its generative source ("Albe est ton origine; arrête et considère / Que tu portes le fer dans le sein de ta mère" [55–56]). From Rome's perspective, Alba, the mother country, must be destroyed in fulfillment of a higher mandate that has pre-ordained Roman supremacy:

> Je sais que ton État, encore en sa naissance,
> Ne saurait, sans la guerre, affermir sa puissance;
> Je sais qu'il doit s'accroître, et que tes grands destins
> Ne le borneront pas chez les peuples latins;
> Que les dieux t'ont promis l'empire de la terre,
> Et que tu n'en peux voir l'effet que par la guerre. (39–44)

10. Jean-Pierre Apostolidès, 207–09, notes that Alba is cast as the city of pathos, whereas Rome stands for the city of virility.
11. For additional insights into the matricidal nature of the Rome/Alba conflict, consult Guy H. Wagener, "*Horace* ou la pièce cornélienne des fondations: La Guerre entre Albe et Roma aura bien lieu," *Papers on French Seventeenth-Century Literature* (1987), 760–61.

From this initial metaphor of the mother as passive target of
inevitable and denatured male violence unfurls a sequence of gen-
der-based distinctions related to discursive practices. Women are
portrayed as orators of authentic sentiments and sincere expression,
natural beings for whom emotional thought and articulated pronounce-
ments neatly coincide. Indeed, the women's insistence on asserting
views grounded solidly in emotional reality is portrayed as a subversive weapon that threatens political stability. Frustrated by Curiace's
patriotic resignation, Camille endeavors to erode his convictions by
redefining the war in personal, rather than in political terms. Whereas
Curiace prefers to envision the conflict through a rhetorical prism of
impersonal political denominators ("Le choix d'Albe et de Rome ôte
toute douceur / Aux noms jadis si doux de beau-frère et de soeur"
[565–66]), Camille views it from a thoroughly subjective perspective. Unlike Curiace, she chooses to focus on the personal rather than
the abstract consequences of the war. The conflict will, after all, result in either the death of the lover or in the lover's unforgivable
murder of her brother. While a resigned Curiace finds some consola-
tion in the abstract value of patriotic self-sacrifice, Camille can envisage only the certain anguish of palpable evils. For her, this war
promises only corporeal destruction.[12] Despite her love for Curiace,
Camille regards his death as no less devastating to her happiness
than the death of her brothers. The metonymic exchange of her
brother's head for his assassin's hand in marriage is too barbaric to
consider:

> Tu pourras donc, cruel, me présenter sa tête,
> Et demander ma main pour prix de ta conquête! (567–68)

Like Camille, Sabine also sees war as a concrete evil entailing
but waste and destruction. The motivating force for such devastation,
she argues further, must not derive from the directives of disengaged
political authorities who call others to arms in the name of political

---

12. Mitchell Greenberg, *Corneille, Classicism and the Ruses of Symmetry,* 70–71, notes
that for men, death is always metaphorized, but for the women, it constitutes nothing
other than "bodily rot."

abstractions. Rather, the motive for mutual slaughter must be rooted in concrete (as opposed to abstract or ideological) sources. In consequence, she offers her body as the motive for conflict, and her death as the justificatory cause for retaliatory violence. In this way, violence, like feminine language itself, will be grounded in a concrete and palpable reality:

> Qu'un de vous deux me tue, et que l'autre me venge:
> Alors votre combat n'aura plus rien d'étrange,
> Et du moins l'un des deux sera juste agresseur,
> Ou pour venger sa femme, ou pour venger sa soeur. (631–34)

The feminine characters' insistence on expressing their natural sentiments is countered by a masculine tendency to create distance between linguistic signs and the things they signify. In contradistinction to their female counterparts, male characters have learned to suppress emotional conflict through rhetorical posturing. Indeed, masculine language in *Horace* is overwhelmingly ornamental and hollow; communication represents nothing other than a sequence of scripted responses designed to present an appropriately "Roman" attitude.[13] The hero speaks not to express internal emotions but to create an image of self wholly unlinked to personal realities. Old Horace, for example, demonstrates an extraordinary capacity to divorce sentiment and statement when informed that his son has survived his own defeat. Ostensibly unmoved, Old Horace launches a verbal assault against his sole surviving son:

> J'atteste des grands dieux les suprêmes puissances,
> Qu'avant ce jour fini, ces mains, ces propres mains
> Laveront dans son sang la honte des Romains. (1048–50)

He repudiates the oath just as promptly when the son's victory is affirmed ("Quand pourrai-je étouffer dans tes embrassements /

---

13. "All is spectacle, semblance, theatricality; and the histrionic mechanism is geared to deflect, re-route attention from a content un-present to a new found object," notes R. L. Barnett in "Of Discourse Subverted: Metonymic Dysfunction in Corneille's *Horace*," *Romanic Review* (1990), 3.

L'erreur dont j'ai formé de si faux sentiments?" [1145–46]).[14] Curiace, too, can be heard making statements diametrically opposed to his real feelings. Despite his emotional turmoil, he professes his eagerness to represent his country against Rome's representatives, the Horatian brothers:

> Dis-lui que l'amitié, l'alliance et l'amour
> Ne pourront empêcher que les trois Curiaces
> Ne servent leur pays contre les trois Horaces. (418–20)

Horace, of course, proves the most adept at using discourse to effect a total emotional cleavage. From his perspective, the sacrosanct nature of Rome's destiny requires that its citizens suppress personal sentiments in order to proclaim their unflinching, ideological commitment to country and thereby articulate a unified vision of Rome's manifest destiny. For Horace in particular, nomination is destiny. Once Curiace, his close companion, is chosen to represent the enemy, he becomes Horace's mortal adversary and nothing more:

> Et, pour trancher enfin ces discours superflus,
> Albe vous a nommé, je ne vous connais plus. (501–02)

Even in triumph, Horace continues to recreate linguistically the world. He betrays no twinge of regret for killing his sister's fiancé and his own best friend. Curiace's earlier transfiguration from Alban acquaintance to political adversary is permanent. After defeating him in battle, Horace manifests no compassion for his former friend, and in the wake of Curiace's death he reveals only the smug satisfaction of having successfully delivered his country from "un ennemi public" (1269). In similar fashion, Horace justifies the murder of his sister by rhetorically transforming her into a "monstre" (1334).

The hero's practice of articulating denatured sentiments derives partly from a preoccupation with discursive mimicry and behavioral imitation. In Horace's Rome, heroism does not consist in expressing

---

14. The first meaning of "faux" is undoubtedly "injustes" but the referential ambiguity (false or unjust) is alluring.

one's individuality, but in perpetuating a heroic tradition. Heroic behaviors are those that valorize resemblance over singularity; conformity over independence. Heroic language, like heroism itself, is
expected to remain faithful to discursive precedents. The hero is he
whose actions and assertions resemble those of heroes past. Any ab-
erration from imposed or prescribed models is cast as a character
flaw, a disdainful rejection of communally accepted values and precedents. For this reason, Julie scolds Sabine for exhibiting manner-
isms not in conformance with Roman values ("Bannissez, bannissez
une frayeur si vaine, / Et concevez des voeux dignes d'une Romaine"
[23–24]). Sabine is no less disappointed in herself, and she attempts
to correct her inadequate pose by a more focused imitation ("Imitons
leur constance, et ne craignons plus rien" [722]). Horace, too, affirms that the glory of one's reputation depends on a strict correlation between predictable expectations and witnessed performance
("Rome a trop cru de moi; mais mon âme ravie / Remplira son attente
ou quittera la vie" [383–84]). For all, the heroic standard is established in advance; worth is determined by degrees of resemblance
rather than examples of renegade non-conformity ("N'appréhendez
rien d'eux, ils sont dignes de vous" [686]). Rome's highest honors
are reserved for those whose accomplishments reflect most accurately predetermined expectations, that is to say, those whose performances recall the glorious deeds of heroes of the past.

Sabine's and Camille's refusal to embrace "Roman" values and
their venting of authentic outrage at the prospect of friends and family members mutually slaughtering one another, endow them with
subversive potential. Rather than focus on the separate history and
destiny of Rome and Alba, they prefer to underscore the contemporary blending of these two formerly separate societies. They no longer
regard Rome and Alba as polarities, but as intertwined entities, a
notion that jeopardizes partisan patriotism. Consequently, Camille's
and Sabine's evolutionary perspectives are increasingly perceived as
hostile threats to the national psyche. These dangerous renegades
eventually require social isolation lest their views contaminate those
of mainstream citizens. In point of fact, their sentimentality does prove
momentarily contagious. Even Curiace and the steely Horace prove

briefly susceptible to their seductive emotionality ("Courage! Ils
s'amollissent!" [663]). This brief surrender to emotional seduction
so alarms the male heroes that both Camille and Sabine are barred
from attending the final contest.[15]

> Mon père, retenez des femmes qui s'emportent,
> Et, de grâce, empêchez surtout qu'elles ne sortent.
> Leur amour importun viendrait avec éclat
> Par des cris et des pleurs troubler notre combat;
> Et ce qu'elles nous sont ferait qu'avec justice
> On nous imputerait ce mauvais artifice;
> L'honneur d'un si beau choix serait trop acheté,
> Si l'on nous soupçonnait de quelque lâcheté. (695–702)

The exclusion of Sabine and Camille from the battle arena is
their punishment for valorizing personal sentiments over state-sanctioned ideology, for investing emotionally in the political theater of
armed conflict.[16] The heroines' refusal to depersonalize the conflict
compromises their ability to appreciate, even comprehend, the battle
that is to decide whether Rome or Alba will triumph. Unable to view
the warriors as abstract representatives of separate and warring states,
Sabine and Camille focus instead on the familial links that bind the
warriors. This stubborn subjectivity threatens to distract the combat-
ants and risks compromising the final decision. Too emotionally over-
wrought to respond appropriately to the wrenching drama of a political
fight to the death, Sabine and Camille are forcibly separated from
the other spectators.

Given the female characters' propensity for interpreting events
through the prism of personal bias, their isolation is not unwarranted.
The women's insistence on decoding aural and visual messages from
their own subjective and emotional perspective results in their routine inability to assess accurately perceived events. Unable to divorce
sentiment and substance, they make a habit of seeing the reality they

15. On the necessity of fleeing "the contaminating emotionality of women," see Greenberg,
Corneille, Classicism and the Ruses of Symmetry, 69.
16. Representation, notes Mitchell Greenberg, *Corneille, Classicism and the Ruses of
Symmetry,* 67, is a masculine entity because politics is masculine.

desire rather than the reality that is. Camille, for example, assumes (erroneously) that Curiace's departure from the battlefield signals his willingness to commit treason in the name of love ("Curiace, il suffit, je devine le reste: / Tu fuis une bataille à tes voeux si funeste" [243–44]). An even more critical misunderstanding involves her faulty interpretation of the oracle's message. Elated by the apparent assurance of wedded bliss ("Et tu seras unie avec ton Curiace, / Sans qu'aucun mauvais sort t'en sépare jamais" [197–98]), she fails to take the riddle's ambiguity into account, and places her faith in misleading evidence. Like Camille, Sabine, too, is guilty of projecting sentimental bias onto witnessed scenarios. She mistakes Camille's animated conversation with Valère for erotic flirtation ("Pour ce rival, sans doute, elle quitte mon frère" [112]) when in fact Camille's high spirits result from her delighted reaction to the oracle's promise of an eventual union with Curiace. But perhaps the most significant quiproquo of the tragedy involves Julie's report that Alba is the victor over Rome. Her premature departure from the battle scene, it might be argued, reflects an unconscious desire to see what she wants to believe. Julie leaves the arena at a moment when happiness for the feminine cause is assured. Alba, the mother country, appears victorious; Sabine's brothers have survived and conquered; Sabine's husband, though wounded and defeated, is still alive. Julie reports what constitutes a best-case scenario for the female protagonists. The outcome she reports is one that is most pleasing from her subjective perspective as a spectator to the unfolding drama.

As it turns out, however, almost none of what she thought she witnessed is accurate. Rome wins the war, not Alba; Horace is a Roman hero, not an Alban prisoner. Julie's premature departure constitutes a rush to judgment based on wishful thinking. Her sentimental bias prevents her from objectively interpreting the situation at hand. Allowing personal desire to distort her judgment, she leaves before the true victor is revealed. Her false report proclaiming victory for the Albans exposes yet another female caught in the act of misinterpreting reality, a mistake that confirms the male prejudice that ensured Camille's and Sabine's expulsion from the theater of war in the first place. The female viewer, we are led to conclude, is unable to as-

sume the objective detachment required to make sense of difficult
and/or unwelcome scenarios. She is unable to appreciate the theoretical correctness (Rome's destined triumph) of a performance she
finds emotionally displeasing.

The emotionality of the heroines contrasts with the detached
neutrality of their male counterparts and alienates them from mainstream Roman citizens. But it cannot be denied that Julie's scenario
of desire is far more satisfying than the contrived outcome that actually occurred. In Julie's version, four warriors survive and Alba, the
mother country, triumphs. In actuality, five warriors die, and Alba is
subject to Roman rule. Moreover, Rome's victory is not the result of
its warriors' physical supremacy but of strategic cunning. For Rome
to triumph, Horace must manipulate events and synthetically re-create and re-engage the battle by feigning a retreat. When Horace flees,
Rome has already lost the battle as it was defined by the original
terms of the combat. This was to be a contest for physical supremacy
("Que le faible parti prenne loi du plus fort" [310]). When Julie leaves
the scene of the battle, that contest has been decided in favor of Alba.
Alba's three warriors demonstrate superior strength not only by prevailing, but by terrifying the enemy into dishonorably vacating the
battlefield. The sole surviving Roman is on the run and badly
wounded, pursued by three much healthier Albans:

> Il s'est fait admirer tant qu'ont duré ses frères;
> Mais comme il s'est vu seul contre trois adversaires,
> Près d'être enfermé d'eux, sa fuite l'a sauvé. (1003–05)

Although the death of Horace's brothers demonstrates the physical superiority of the Alban force, Horace triumphs ultimately by
relying on artifice. A clever tactical manoeuver on Horace's part allows him to effect a change of rules and intercept the victory from
the physically superior Albans. But the Albans lose the battle in turn
by falling into Horace's trap and re-engaging a battle they had technically won. Rather than allow the deserter to flee, the Albans follow
in pursuit. In the political context overdetermining this battle for ter-
ritorial control, cowardice is as debasing as feminine emotionality.
Horace relies on this traditional contempt for unmanliness when plot-

ting his winning strategy. Had the Curiace brothers let Horace continue his flight, his cowardice and their victory would have passed into legend. Instead, the lure of crushing totally their enemy lets them fall prey to Horace's theatrical ruse. Once divided, they are ultimately conquered. Their defeat, it bears repeating, results directly from their obsession with ideological conformity: the warrior's imperative to fight to the death. To have allowed Horace to flee unimpeded would have been an act without heroic precedent and it would have presented the spectators with an open-ended ambiguity rather than decisive tragic closure. Horace's faith in his adversaries' respect for the rules of tragic performance proves well-placed, and it allows him to emerge victorious.

The end of the battle, however, is more contrived than natural. The forced enactment of a pre-scripted scenario (Rome's manifest destiny as a result of its presumed privileged status) trumps the logical unfolding of events. The battle's outcome, however contrived, does fulfill the prophecy of Roman supremacy established from the outset. Consequently, Horace achieves a goal that was considered by many to be a pre-ordained conclusion.[17] Rome's ultimate triumph over its adversaries, a scenario scripted by the Gods themselves, justifies any and all means required for success. What matters is not the manner of victory, but the victory itself. This machiavellian attitude obliges Horace to improvise, to defy tradition in order to save it. The Curiace brothers assume Horace's flight to be a sign of surrender, an indication that he is incapable of continuing to fight. His flight is only a deceptive strategy, however, a ruse that not only taints his victory but brings dishonor to the warriors he duped and defeated. As if ashamed of his own gullibility, the last Curiace brother does not so much succumb to Horace's powerful strokes as self-immolate. His death results as much from personal surrender as physical inferiority:

> L'Albain percé de coups ne se traînait qu'à peine,
> Et, comme une victime aux marches de l'autel,
> Il semblait présenter sa gorge au coup mortel:

---

17. "La fondation possède, pour les Romains un caractère sacré," Apostolidès, 25.

Aussi le reçoit-il, peu s'en faut, sans défense,
Et son trépas de Rome établit la puissance. (1136–40)

    Amidst the general rejoicing over Horace's victory can be found one dissident voice refusing to praise Horace's manipulative triumph. Camille's disdain leaves her politically and socially isolated, an alienation already in evidence at the play's outset. Roman by birth, but betrothed to an Alban, Camille reveals ambiguous allegiances from the start. The intensity with which she bemoans her socio-political limbo foreshadows its potential for a catastrophic outcome (135–58). Because Curiace dies as her betrothed and not her husband, Camille remains fixed and marginalized within a transitional no-man's land.[18] No longer child, never to be wife, neither Roman nor Alban, neither subject nor victor, Camille is duty-bound to no specific family or country. She has, then, no example to emulate, no model to mimic, no protocol to respect. Whereas Sabine can take some comfort in pledging allegiance to her husband's patriotic causes, the disenfranchised Camille is no longer emotionally able to support Rome, and Curiace's death destroys her potential link to Alba. Camille's ambivalent status leaves her free to invent an entirely new script for herself, a situation of which she takes full advantage.

    When Horace bursts upon the scene demanding verbal compensation for his heroic slaughter of the Curiace brothers ("Et rends ce que tu dois à l'heur de ma victoire" [1255]), Camille refuses to accommodate his request. Instead, she launches a verbal assault against the state-sanctioned murder that took the life of her fiancé. Rather than express grateful accolades, she offers a blistering invective decrying Horace's brutal inhumanity and his decision to place politics on a higher plane than moral principle ("Cette gloire si chère à ta brutalité" [1294]). Horace tries unsuccessfully to force Camille to change her aberrant discourse, to persuade her to speak more like a Roman patriot, to praise the victor and cease to mourn the van-

---

18. Mitchell Greenberg's attention to Sabine's in-between space is particularly interesting: "She situates herself in a space that is neither a man's nor a woman's but is somewhere 'in-between.' It is this space 'in between' which is uninhabitable" (*Corneille, Classicism and the Ruses of Symmetry*, 68).

quished. Confronted with Camille's continuing refusal to echo Roman platitudes and to imitate the responses of others, Horace stabs his sister in the name of patriotic duty ("C'est trop, ma patience à la raison fait place" [1319]).

Much debate has centered around the motivational impetus prompting Horace's murder of his sister. While her acerbic repudiation of Roman values justifies his anger, even his contempt, her invective fails to account fully for the violence of his response. In support of this affirmation, one need only compare Camille's remarks to Sabine's similar denunciation in the aftermath of Camille's murder ("Mais enfin, je renonce à la vertu romaine, / Si, pour la posséder, je dois être inhumaine" [1367–68]). Although the tone and tenor of Sabine's comments are similarly vitriolic, Horace remains here curiously unmoved, much to Sabine's chagrin ("Que Camille est heureuse! elle a pu te déplaire" [1380]). On closer inspection, however, one discerns a clear difference between Sabine's and Camille's discursive manner, and it is perhaps this subtle distinction that explains Horace's murderous rage. Sabine attacks Rome in a discursive mode that represents her personal viewpoint, however offensive this view appears to Horace. Her negative remarks are based on an alternative perspective, on a hierarchy of values that places familial relationships on a higher plane than the interests of the state. She does not offer scenarios that are incompatible with historical and contemporary reality, however. Nothing she articulates alters the reality of Roman supremacy. Camille, too, begins her assault on Rome using a standard mode of representational discourse, but not for long. As her anger builds, her rhetorical manner moves from the mimetic plane, that is to say, from a discourse that translates her personal view of reality, to the fictional. Camille moves from the indicative to the subjunctive mode, from structures that repeat and recreate existing scenarios to a structure that creates and foretells scenarios without precedent.[19] In a frenzied hallucination, Camille depicts invincible Rome in catastrophic ruins, and envisions herself as the agent of this smoldering destruction:

19. Susan Tiefenbrun, 631, also focusses on Camille's use of the subjunctive.

Puissé-je de mes yeux y voir tomber ce foudre,
Voir ses maisons en cendre, et tes lauriers en poudre,
Voir le dernier Romain à son dernier soupir,
Moi seule en être cause, et mourir de plaisir! (1315–18).

Camille's fantasized depiction of a fallen Rome undermines the
ideological coherence underpinning Rome's self-perpetuating myth
of political pre-eminence. Camille's prophecy of a degraded Rome
suggests that the sacrifices committed in the name of destiny were
all for naught, that the historical imperative driving Rome's conquest
of Alba may have been in vain. Horace is not ready to accept such
heresies, however, and he takes violent action in order to prevent any
repetition of her treasonous discourse. Camille is murdered, then,
not just because she criticizes Rome or sympathizes with the enemy
(something Sabine does as well) but because she articulates an original and politically unsanctioned scenario. She does not imitate, she
envisions and innovates, a violation of the code of discursive mimicry that structures and controls Roman society. This linguistic transgression warrants the ultimate punishment, and Horace wastes no
time in obliging the state by silencing the discordant voice that dares
convey a contrary view of Roman supremacy.

Camille's punishment for articulating unorthodox views establishes a link between art and power that reflects a contemporary reality: the Academy's valorization of Ancient writers and the condemnation
of works in violation of theoretical mandates. Like writers aping Greek
and Roman models with mechanical exactitude, Horace respects the
principles of Roman law (slay the enemy) but in an arena where its
application is wholly inappropriate. He fails to alter his performance
to suit the changing environment and continues to play the soldier when
he should be acting the part of brother. Programmed for ideological
conformity, Horace fails to distinguish between heroism and butchery,
war and murder, political enmity and familial discord.[20] Ideologically
committed to the doctrine of imitation, he continues to slay the enemy
in an arena where violence is not sanctioned. Responding again to the

---

20. See my chapter on *Horace* ("The Sanctioning Power of Theatricality") in *Cornelian
Theater: The Metadramatic Dimension* (Summa: 1990), 43–51.

mimetic imperative that mandates death to those opposing Rome's political supremacy, Horace continues to function only in the role of Roman warrior. He is unable to distinguish between appropriate and inappropriate stages for the enactment of this role. Ultimately, his discursive posturing and compulsive mimicry render him wholly dysfunctional in a non-combative setting. He therefore fails to understand why his second act of heroism, the murder of Camille, engenders public contempt and disapproval, or why it is in fact so harshly judged.

Horace's murder of his sister is deemed so heinous that he can be saved from eternal ignominy only by royal edict. Tulle is one of the few to excuse Horace's behavior, and in so doing, he criticizes the unsophisticated citizens who are unable to appreciate Horace's heroic sacrifice ("Horace, ne crois pas que le peuple stupide / Soit le maître absolu d'un renom bien solide" [1711–12]). In defending Horace, Tulle calls once again upon the force of tradition: he justifies Horace's crime on the basis of mimetic precedent. The murder of Camille, he argues, loosely imitates the crime responsible for Rome's mythological genesis:

> Qu'elles se taisent donc; que Rome dissimule
> Ce que dès sa naissance elle vit en Romule,
> Elle peut bien souffrir en son libérateur
> Ce qu'elle a bien souffert en son premier auteur. (1755–58)

It can, therefore, he argues, be excused. In order to redeem Horace, Tulle places his actions in a context of repetition and familiarity:

> Et l'art et le pouvoir d'affermir des couronnes
> Sont des dons que le ciel fait à peu de personnes.
> De pareils serviteurs sont les forces des rois,
> Et de pareils aussi sont au-dessus des lois. (1751–54)

Arguably, Tulle's insistence on the value of precedent links this monarch more closely to Richelieu than Louis XIII.[21]

---

21. On the political motives behind Tulle's exculpation of Horace, see Apostolidès, 218–21 and Clarke, 193. Clarke also sees a link between Tulle and Richelieu: "For that reason above all it [the speech excusing Horace] has been cited as evidence that the play expresses the political convictions of a dramatist profoundly committed to Richelieu's policies" (193).

It is, I believe, significant that Tulle's exculpation fails to re-deem Horace's character in the eyes of the public. Despite Tulle's machiavellian arguments justifying Horace's actions, it is Camille who retains the spectator's sympathy. Her refusal to accept blindly the dictates of the state, her desire to forge new scripts for new situations, engage the audience in ways that Horace's blind commitment to precedent cannot. By demonstrating the awesome power of the creative word, she makes an eloquent argument for a poetics of innovation and for a repudiation of mimicry. The public reaction to Camille's death demonstrates convincingly the very message that *Le Cid*'s popularity implied. Theoretical principles may make dramatic spectacles more perfect in form, but in determining the true merits of dramatic spectacle, it is always the court of public opinion that has the final word. Richelieu, like Tulle, may have the authority to validate some scenarios over others, but in the long run it is the emotional investment of the audience that determines the aesthetic merit of theatrical spectacle.

CHAPTER 4

Illusions of Authority: Corneille's *Rodogune*

Despite his adherence to formal academic doctrine in *Horace,* Corneille's commitment to respecting the rules established by theoreticians remained tentative at best.[1] More than any other neo-classical writer, Corneille seemed torn between competing allegiances: respect for Richelieu's call for more regulated tragedies and fidelity to his own creative inspiration and baroque tendencies, these necessarily suppressed in deference to "academic" standards. Beginning with *Horace,* Corneille's tragedies become outwardly more conformist, more regulated, but they continue to betray revealing traces of a punishing self-discipline, even self-denial. Indeed, it seems at times as if the conflicts of the early tragedies reflect his own battle between the desire for self-expression and the need to respect the rules of neo-classical dramaturgy.[2] From *Le Cid* to *Polyeucte,* Corneille's plays are structured around the competing demands of self interest and self sacrifice. In these early tragedies, self sacrifice triumphs. Private ambitions are scrupulously sacrificed to familial (*Le Cid*), political (*Horace, Cinna*), or spiritual (*Polyeucte*) commitments that occupy a higher moral plane.

The reward for such sacrifice is public admiration. But "gloire" comes only at the expense of the hero's self interest, a situation that in some ways duplicates that of the creative artist himself. Like many of his early heroes, Corneille, eager to gain the approval of the *Académie,* was obliged to exchange creative abandon for the disciplined restraint imposed on writers by academicians. It is in this context that *Rodogune,* one of the author's favorite tragedies, takes on added significance. *Rodogune* marks a distinctive turning point in Corneille's dramatic evolution, one that led him away from the studied perfection of earlier masterworks and toward a more fluid inter-

1. For Corneille, practice always overrode theory, notes Louis Forestier in *Pierre Corneille: Trois discours sur le poème dramatique* (Paris: Société d'Enseignement Supérieur, 1963), 6.
2. In particular, readers may wish to consult M. J. Muratore, *Cornelian Theater: The Metadramatic Dimension* (Birmingham: Summa, 1990), 63–72.

pretation of dramatic theory.[3] Corneille's professed fondness for this tragedy is a matter of record. He was particularly pleased with its more innovative aspects: the steely determination of the heroine whose contained fury shades progressively into self-destructive rage; the bifurcated exposition; the shadowed sense of menace that hangs ominously over the ambiguous dénouement.[4] Though striking and unusual, perhaps, these features are in and of themselves insufficient to explain Corneille's attachment to a play that is by any conventional measure inferior to those preceding it. Most readers find the fragmented exposition frustratingly contrived, and although Cléopâtre's ruthless intensity elicits a certain admiration, her extraordinary character can scarcely account for the author's singular attachment to this play.[5] Surely something less evident, more nebulous, drew the author to this work, some compelling undertow beckoning from beneath the textual surface. We know from Corneille's own commentaries that the allure of *Rodogune* was linked closely to its unconventionality. It is therefore logical to assume that a deeper probe into the play's more uncharacteristic or irregular aspects might yield insights into precisely why this play struck such a responsive chord in the author's soul.

---

3. Gordon McGregor lends support to the argument that *Rodogune* marks a turning point in Corneille's theater in "*Rodogune, Nicomède* and the Status of History in Corneille," *Stanford French Review,* 11, 2 (1987), 133–156. His argument rests, however, on Corneille's changed perspective towards Rome: "What Corneille effects in *Rodogune* is no mere displacement of Rome from the center of dramatic interest to its fringes: Rome is banished, completely eliminated on every level at which it might be reasonably expected to figure" (140–41). According to McGregor, this obliteration of historical authority shows "the struggle between allegiance to authority and dramaturgical liberty that *Rodogune* so vividly represents" (141).
4. "No other texts more clearly underline his showman's love of innovation and the startling dramatic gambit: they have been interpreted as proof that he regarded his plays above all as machines for the production of theatrical emotion," notes Derek Watts in "A Further Look at *Rodogune,*" *Ouverture et Dialogue,* eds., Ulrich Doring, et.al. (Tübingen: Narr, 1998), 447. Georges Forestier, *Essai de génétique théâtrale: Corneille à l'oeuvre* (Paris: Klincksieck, 1966), 61–66, also comments on *Rodogune*'s more innovative aspects.
5. "On m'a souvent fait une question à la Cour, quel étoit celuy de mes Poëmes que j'estimois le plus, et j'ay trouvé tous ceux qui me l'ont faite si prévenus en faveur de Cinna, ou du Cid, que je n'ay jamais osé déclarer toute la tendresse que j'ay toûjours euë pour celuy–cy, à qui j'aurois volontiers donné mon suffrage, si je n'avois craint de manquer en quelque sorte au respect que je devois à ceux que je voyois pancher d'un autre costé," *Rodogune,* ed. Jacques Schérer (Paris: Droz, 1946), 12–13.

One feature that distinguishes *Rodogune* from earlier tragedies is the heroine's attitude toward the necessity of self denial. In contrast to Corneille's earlier masterworks, *Rodogune* does not portray a protagonist willing to sacrifice self interest to political duty. On the contrary, Cléopâtre is an unusually aggressive and selfish female whose savage ruthlessness is rivaled only by her unwavering commitment to achieve her goal. Cléopâtre admits boldly that she used her own sons as pawns in a power struggle with her second husband, Antiochus ("Il occupoit leur trosne, et craignoit leur presence, / Et cette juste crainte asseuroit ma puissance" [455–56]).[6] This egocentric ambition renders her something of a dramatic misfit in the Cornelian canon. Additionally, because the pursuit of power is traditionally the domain of male characters, Cléopâtre is presented to the viewer/reader as a political and sexual renegade as well.

The break Cléopâtre's ambition opens in the stable male order of things is reflected in the text's structural fragmentation and its incessant intrusions and frustrating delays. The exposition, of which Corneille was particularly proud, is interrupted twice, first by the arrival of one son, then the entrance of another. These early suspensions of the tragedy's exposition are but the first in a series of scenarios in *Rodogune* that are interrupted or halted outright. The marriage between Rodogune and Cléopâtre's elder son, a union intended to secure peace, is twice suspended, initially by Cléopâtre's demand that the sons kill Rodogune in order to earn the right to govern, and again, when Rodogune calls in turn for Cléopâtre's murder at the hand of a son. In fact, the much-anticipated ceremony never takes place at all. As Antiochus prepares to marry Rodogune, Timagène breaks in to report Séleucus' murder. Séleucus' attempt to identify his killer, like the wedding ceremony itself, is interrupted prior to completion. A second attempt to conclude the ceremony fails when Cléopâtre drinks from a cup she herself poisoned.

These intrusions appear to confirm structurally the ideological viewpoint that Cléopâtre's gender makes her unfit to occupy the cen-

---

6. All verse references are to Jacques Schérer's edition.

ter stage of power.[7] Despite her steely strength of will, she is unable to maintain theatrical dominance. Her defiant attempt to retain power in the face of legal and public opposition yields only disjunction and political fragmentation. Her failure to take and hold the dramatic center seems to bear out the popular prejudice that women are not meant to wield political power. Even the title of the tragedy deflects attention away from Cléopâtre, the central focus of the exposition, onto her inferior, but properly submissive rival, Rodogune.[8] For Cléopâtre, the dramatic force is frustratingly centrifugal, relentlessly displacing her from center stage to a secondary plane in her own drama. This marginality is graphically and decisively confirmed during the wedding ceremony where she is obliged to take her place on a lower seating plane than her son and her rival Rodogune.

Cléopâtre's inability to control the scenario seems to justify the cultural bias that allows women only a limited and marginal role in political theater. At key moments, just when Cléopâtre appears to be on the verge of securing her shaky authority, events conspire to negate her progress. Again, the fragmented exposition offers an excellent case in point. When Antiochus intrudes upon Laonice's récit during the opening moments of the tragedy, he does so at a moment of high triumph in her story. Cléopâtre has assumed power by proxy over her husband, the puppet king Antiochus. Moreover, he is about to avenge the murder of Cléopâtre's first husband. This triumphant moment in the narrative is abruptly halted by her sons' successive entrances. These scenic ruptures subversively undermine and cut short the exposition tracing Cléopâtre's triumphant rise to power. The sons' trespass onto Cléopâtre's narrative stage, in tandem with her titular exclusion, convey quickly to the audience an impression of her fundamental irrelevance. The males' abrupt encroachment of center stage in fact foreshadows what Laonice's continuing récit will soon reveal: Cléopâtre's impending erasure from the political arena. After the sons'

---

7. See also, Harriet Allentuch, "Reflections on Women in the Theatre of Corneille," *Kentucky Romance Quarterly* 21 (1974), 97–111, who discusses at length the patriarchal attitudes found in Corneille's plays.

8. The author agrees (". . . je confesse ingenuëment que ce Poëme devoit plustost porter le nom de Cleopatre, que de Rodogune" [Schérer, *Rodogune,* 7]), but his justification for not doing so (avoiding confusion with the Egyptian Cléopâtre) is not wholly convincing.

exit, Laonice resumes the exposition, but when she does, we quickly discover that Cléopâtre's narrated fortunes have turned. Her husband did not die after all, and, worse yet, is so angered by her remarriage that he intends to deprive Cléopâtre and her children of their royal birthright by marrying Rodogune.

While the sons' successive entrances serve to interrupt structurally and symbolically Cléopâtre's rise to power, their refusal to participate in their mother's plan to kill Rodogune serves to definitively and decisively trivialize Cléopâtre's role in the drama. Her promise to name as the elder he who kills Rodogune is opposed immediately by the sons she entrusts with executing the order. Undaunted, Cléopâtre merely adds their names to the list of obstacles impeding her forward progress. Events conspire again to block her path, however. Although she manages to eliminate one of the sons, Séleucus, he lives just long enough to articulate a cryptic message regarding the identity of his killer. This revelation, announced by Timagène in yet another alteration of Cléopâtre's carefully crafted scenario, momentarily suspends the attempted poisoning of her second son. Still refusing to accept defeat, Cléopâtre drinks from the poisoned cup herself in the hope of living long enough to witness the death of her enemies. Time runs out, and a dying Cléopâtre is forced finally to vacate definitively the theatrical space she fought so diligently to occupy.

Cléopâtre's failure to survive her enemies should not be interpreted as confirmation of the prejudice that men make better rulers than women. Though the laws forbid her from reigning independently, Cléopâtre demonstrates during her reign that neither traditions nor laws can predict or guarantee success or failure. She manages to triumph in spite of both historical practice and popular prejudices. The general assumption that women are biologically unfit to rule is revealed by Cléopâtre's political successes to be nothing other than a self-serving patriarchal fantasy. Comparatively speaking, Cléopâtre's talent for governing is far superior to the meager potential evidenced by her sons, both legally sanctioned to govern independently and both more interested in the courtship of Rodogune than leadership of the realm. Additionally, Cléopâtre reveals a superiority of resolve

and will that distinguishes her from those who claim to be her moral
superiors. Her relegation to the margins of power, it must be underscored, is the result of gender bias, not actual performance. To argue
that Cléopâtre is unfit to reign because power belongs by tradition to
males is to offer a long-standing custom, or rather, a historical prejudice, in place of truth. Cléopâtre has proven herself more than capable of defending her terrain:

> Et changeant à regret son amour en horreur,
> Elle abandonne tout à sa juste fureur.
> Elle mesme leur dresse une embûche au passage,
> Se mesle dans les coups, porte par tout sa rage,
> En pousse jusqu'au bout les furieux effets.
> Que vous diray-je enfin? les Parthes sont défaits,
> Le Roy meurt, et dit-on, par la main de la Reine. (257–63)

Even though Cléopâtre has demonstrated convincingly her capacity to govern effectively, the general public refuses to break with
tradition. Despite her political successes, even her supporters demand
she share her rule with a male, however impotent he might be:

> Le peuple épouvanté, qui déja dans son ame
> Ne suivoit qu'à regret les ordres d'une femme,
> Voulut forcer la Reine à choisir un époux.
> Que pouvoit-elle faire, et seule, et contre tous? (47–50)

Cléopâtre demonstrates little patience for such narrow-minded
traditionalism. She does appear to be as capable of leading a nation
as any man, and she therefore claims the right to govern independently. From the outset, she voices contempt for superstitions that
masquerade as political necessity, and prejudices that pass for divine
will. Unable to contain her disdain for her subjects who believe that
politics is the natural domain of males ("Toy qui connois ce Peuple,
et sçais qu'aux champs de Mars / Lâchement d'une femme il suit les
étendarts" [489–90]), she expresses derision for rituals that continue
to exist in defiance of logic. The sacrosanct right of the first-born to
inherit the throne, for example, is manipulated by Cléopâtre who
believes that merit, rather than chronology, should determine the se-

quence of royal succession. For the more practical minded Cléopâtre, birth order appears an inefficient means of determining royal legitimacy. Rather, the crown should pass to the son who proves himself most worthy of the title, that is to say, the son who acquiesces first to her demands. Consequently, Cléopâtre promises to name as the elder son he who agrees to destroy Rodogune:

> Si vous voulez régner, le Trosne est à ce prix.
> Entre deux fils que j'aime avec mesme tendresse
> Embrasser ma querelle, est le seul droit d'aînesse,
> La mort de Rodogune en nommera l'aisné. (642–45)

Cléopâtre's views are not shared by others, however. Her lust for power is regarded as a violation of precedent and a denatured character flaw. History demonstrates and Salic law requires that women surrender power to legitimate male heirs. With the political conflict under control, Cléopâtre is expected to subordinate her desire to govern to the needs of her sons ("A present que l'amour succéde à la colére, / Elle ne vous voit plus qu'avec les yeux de mére" [343–44]). Female subordination is, after all, the natural order of things, as Rodogune is quick to affirm:

> Plus la haute naissance approche des Couronnes,
> Plus cette grandeur mesme asservit nos personnes,
> Nous n'avons point de coeur pour aimer, ny haïr,
> Toutes nos passions ne sçavent qu'obéïr.
> Après avoir armé pour venger cét outrage,
> D'une paix mal conceuë on m'a faite le gage,
> Et moy, fermant les yeux sur ce noir attentat
> Je suivois mon destin, en victime d'Etat. (867–74)

This widespread belief in a woman's innate propensity for self sacrifice also explains Antiochus' unflinching optimism regarding his mother's attitude towards Rodogune. Convinced that Cléopâtre's hostility is but a temporary spasm caused by a series of personal and political crises, he believes that nature will ultimately override ambition ("Voicy la Reine. Amour, Nature, justes Dieux, / Faites-la-moy fléchir, ou mourir à ses yeux" [1257–58]). Now that the dangers to the rightful male heirs have passed and peace is at hand, Antiochus believes that his mother's kinder and gentler feminine side will re-assert itself. Even after his brother Séleucus underscores the self-serving strategy behind Cléopâtre's "silence obstiné" regarding her sons' birth order (". . . mais quel autre intérest / Nous fait tous deux aisnez, quand, et comme il vous plaist?" [1457–58]), Antiochus stub-bornly refuses to believe that his mother's aggression is permanent. Placing his faith in the "call of blood," he is confident he can per-suade his mother to respect natural law, to abide by the accepted rules of patriarchy, to recognize male privilege. Antiochus is con-vinced his mother's rebellious behavior constitutes but a temporary overreaction to events at hand. An appeal to Cléopâtre's maternal feelings, he reasons, will swiftly correct this irrational lapsus. He is certain that the "droits de la Nature" (687) will triumph ultimately:

> Je conserve pourtant encor un peu d'espoir,
> Elle est mére, et le sang a beaucoup de pouvoir,
> Et le sort l'eust-il faite encor plus inhumaine,
> Une larme d'un fils peut amollir sa haine. (725–28)
> . . . .
> Cependant allons voir si nous vaincrons l'orage,
> Et si contre l'effort d'un si puissant couroux
> La Nature, et l'Amour voudront parler pour nous. (1128–30)

The notion that Cléopâtre's desire for power is a violation of natural law derives from a widespread gender bias that prescribes specific roles and attitudes for women. Cléopâtre's reluctance to re-linquish power is regarded as aberrational for her gender, an assess-ment shared by Jacques Schérer who describes Cléopâtre as having "rien de féminin" (*Rodogune*, p. xx). The political fragmentation wrought by Cléopâtre's usurpation of masculine rights and privileges is cast as the logical consequence of trespassing against the laws of nature. As a wife and mother, Cléopâtre is obliged to conform to conventional expectations for these roles. In particular, the selfless desire to protect one's children, to safeguard their royal heritage, is regarded as an innate and irrepressible maternal instinct. So solidly entrenched is the myth of maternal self sacrifice that Laonice as-sumes this to be the motive behind Cléopâtre's earlier decision to abandon her sons when she believed their father was dead:

> La Reine, craignant tout de ces nouveaux orages,
> En sçeut mettre à l'abry ses plus précieux gages,
> Et pour n'exposer pas l'enfance de ses fils,
> Me les fit chez son frére enlever à Memphis. (35–38)
> . . . .
> Quelque promesse alors qu'il eut faite à la mére
> De remettre ses fils au trosne de leur pére,
> Il témoigna si peu de la vouloir tenir,
> Qu'elle n'osa jamais les faire revenir. (59–62)

Laonice believes also that it was filial protection that prompted Cléopâtre to murder Nicanor, an action which she therefore excuses. Female violence, we are led to believe, is justifiable when required to protect the rights of male offspring:

> Il vient deshériter ses fils par son retour,
> Et qu'un gros escadron de Parthes pleins de joye
> Conduit ces deux Amans, et court comme à la proye,
> La Reine au desespoir de n'en rien obtenir
> Se résout de se perdre, ou de le prévenir.
> Elle oublie un mary qui veut cesser de l'estre,
> Qui ne veut plus la voir qu'en implacable maistre,
> Et changeant à regret son amour en horreur,
> Elle abandonne tout à sa juste fureur. (250–58)

When it is determined that personal ambition rather than maternal sacrifice motivated Cléopâtre's behavior, the reaction is decidedly different:

> Et qu'ayant reconnu sa haine, et mon erreur,
> Le coeur gros de soûpirs, et fremissant d'horreur,
> Je romps une foy deuë aux secrets de ma Reine,
> Et vous viens découvrir mon erreur, et sa haine. (769–72)

What is significant about this reversal is that the same behavior in males is not condemned with equal fervor. Nicanor's disinheritance of his own sons raises little real protest from anyone. Cléopâtre's attempt to deprive her offspring of their political birthright, on the other hand, is deemed an act of denatured cruelty. The different verdicts are the result of a historical gender bias that exculpates the actions of men in pursuit of power while condemning the same actions in women. Whereas it is presumed natural to find males fighting aggressively for political control, women are expected to act as submissive accessories and to make whatever sacrifices are required to further the peace and prosperity of the patriarchal realm. As Rodogune points out, women are but disposable pawns in a game in which they have no real stake:[9]

> Comme sans leur avis les Rois disposent d'elles,
> Pour affermir leur trosne, ou finir leurs querelles,
> Le destin des Etats est arbitre du leur,
> Et l'ordre des Traitez régle tout dans leur coeur. (931–34)

Cléopâtre's conduct is deemed so reprehensible in part because it has no exemplary historical model. Cléopâtre is deemed an illegitimate ruler because of discriminatory practices rooted in the past and continuing into the present. In *Rodogune,* acceptable behaviors are those that are sanctioned by historical precedent. Actions are valorized only if they replicate a historical example. Because Cléopâtre's behavior has no legitimate precedent, it therefore has no legal or moral standing. Her alienated status demonstrates the role precedent plays in determining worth.

In a world so committed to replicating historical examples, Cléopâtre's failure to inspire imitation solidifies her defeat. Her attempts to change conventional attitudes, to convince her subjects that the precedents determining her fate are arbitrary and hence not necessarily binding, have no effect. She persuades no one to alter his/her perspective. Observes Doreena Ann Stamato, "Cléopâtre reste une femme dans un monde masculin."[10] Her options are to conform to male expectations, or face alienation and expulsion. Despite her plea

---

9. In the view of Derek Watts, the principal difference between Cléopâtre and Rodogune is that Cléopâtre "sees the essence of power as limitless, irresponsible freedom" whereas Rodogune equates power with rank, authority and obligation (456).
10. "Le Renversement symétrique des rôles masculins et féminins dans les pièces *Rodogune et Horace*," *Papers on French Seventeenth-Century Literature* 16, 31 (1989), 529–40.

that others justify her cause by making it their own ("Ce n'est qu'en m'imitant que l'on me justifie" [668]), she persuades no one to reject conformity or balk tradition. She remains stranded on the eccentric fringes of a static society. In order to triumph, Cléopâtre would have to convince others to ignore precedent, to pattern their behavior on hers, and she fails in almost every attempt to do so. The sons, following the example set by their father, fall in love with Rodogune ("C'est cette Rodogune, ou l'un et l'autre frére / Trouve encor les appas qu'avoit trouvez leur pére" [235–36]). Like their father, they are more committed to pleasing Rodogune than Cléopâtre. Even Laonice follows Nicanor's lead and elects to betray Cléopâtre in order to better serve Rodogune:

> Alors sans moy, mon frére, elle les eust soufferts,
> La Reine à la gesner prenant mille delices
> Ne commettoit qu'à moy l'ordre de ses supplices;
> Mais quoy que m'ordonnast cette ame toute en feu,
> Je promettois beaucoup et j'éxecutois peu. (266–70)

Cléopâtre inspires but one momentary act of mimicry. When Rodogune learns that Cléopâtre intends to reward the son who kills her, she pledges to equal Cléopâtre in cruelty. In a behavioral turn-about, Rodogune imitates Cléopâtre and promises to marry the son who kills his mother. For one revolutionary moment, the two women are linked by their gendered nonconformity, a resemblance that Séleucus is quick to condemn ("Une ame si crüelle, / Méritoit nostre mére, et devoit naistre d'elle" [1051–52]).[11] Though short-lived, Rogodune's imitation of Cléopâtre demonstrates convincingly the potential threat that Cléopâtre's quest for gendered equality poses to the political and social orders.[12] Once the sanctity of hallowed traditions is breached, further fissures are inevitable.

---

11. Cléopâtre and Rodogune become virtually indistinguishable, notes G. Mcgregor, 148.
12. See Mitchell Greenberg, *Corneille, Classicism and the Ruses of Symmetry* (Cambridge: Cambridge University Press, 1986), 149: "Male hierarchy has been usurped and in the place of the Father/King now stands the frightening image of a deranged queen. *Nicomède* and *Rodogune* play out the hidden fears of Patriarchy by figuring the return of what the Father and his Law had tried so hard to repress: the devouring, chaotic figure of omnipotent femininity."

The sons quickly halt the threat of anarchy by relying once again on conventional gender roles and attitudes. In order to placate an angry Rodogune, they avail themselves of one of the most manipulative and successful male strategies to keep women in their rightful place. They concede women a superior role in matters of the heart in order to safeguard the more meaningful political arena for themselves. Claiming to be a victim of passion, Antiochus easily persuades Rodogune to repudiate her ultimatum in exchange for his affection. With the aid of metaphors and images borrowed from the courtly love tradition, Antiochus convinces Rodogune to resume the traditional posture of obedient princess:

> Ce coeur qu'un saint amour rangea sous vostre empire,
> Ce coeur pour qui le vostre à tous momens soûpire,
> Ce coeur en vous aimant indignement percé
> Reprend, pour vous aimer, le sang qu'il a versé,
> Il le reprend en nous, il revit, il vous aime,
> Et montre, en vous aimant, qu'il est encor le mesme. (1159–64)

Rodogune's surrender means that Cléopâtre can claim no definitive converts within the internal world of her tragedy. She dies without persuading anyone that biology is not destiny. She does manage to score one significant victory, however. Her suicide effectively halts the ritual ceremony intended to perpetuate the status quo she so resolutely contested. In the end, Cléopâtre proves strong enough to halt the marriage of her son to Rodogune, a union that would have confirmed the legitimacy of patriarchal principles.[13] More significantly perhaps, Cléopâtre's dying curse suggests that the quest to spawn a new generation of rebellious royals may yet be realized. In other words, the tragedy's final disintegration suggests that Cléopâtre's subversive influence may yet survive her death. ("Et pour vous souhaiter tous les malheurs ensemble, / Puisse naistre de vous un fils qui me ressemble" [1823–24]).

---

13. Here I disagree with both McGregor (118) who sees the end as a victory for history, and with Marie-Odile Sweetser, "Les Femmes et le pouvoir dans le théâtre cornlélien" *Pierre Corneille*, eds. Alain Niderst and Georges Couton (Paris: Presses Universitaires de France, 1985), 614, who sees the end as a victory for Rodogune.

Rodogune appears initially to be moving resolutely towards a conventional ending. There is the promise of a secure and lasting peace, of an orderly royal succession, of requited love, of conflict resolution. At the tragedy's close, all these expectations are thwarted. The unconsummated marriage, the unfulfilled promise of peace, and the ambiguous denouement demonstrate convincingly that if Cléopâtre did not quite triumph in her quest to destroy tradition, she managed nevertheless to impede its progress. Cléopâtre's victory is in the disorder she leaves behind. We move from the promise of celebration to the sorrow of burial rites:

> Et vous, allez au Temple
> Y changer l'allegresse en un dueil sans pareil,
> La pompe Nuptiale en funébre appareil. (1840–42)

Corneille's favorite tragedy ends not in triumphant union but in scenic collapse. Cléopâtre leaves the stage unrepentant and unbowed, an exit that suggests a victory for innovation and a defeat for convention.[14]

What Corneille seemed to admire most about *Rodogune* was its unconventionality. *Rodogune's* distinctiveness from previous tragedies is exemplified not only by its fragmented structure and lack of closure, traits than can be found in earlier plays, but in the attitude of the heroine as well. Unlike previous Cornelian heroes (but similar to Médée), Cléopâtre respects only a duty to self, a fidelity that obliges her to remain faithful first and foremost to the internal voice within. The dramatic representation of this intense commitment to one's personal sense of "art" is perhaps what Corneille found so compelling in *Rodogune*. Cléopâtre's proud defiance stands in stark contrast to the weak-willed attitude of her sons, "legitimate" successors sanctioned to reign independently. In fact, one of the sons, Séleucus, is so traumatized by political pressure that he withdraws from the fray:

> J'en ferois comme vous, si mon esprit troublé
> Ne secoüoit le joug dont il est accablé.

14. See McGregor, 148: "And so, Rodogune's last scene confirms Cléopâtre's victory, not over Rodogune, but through Rodogune."

Dans mon ambition, dans l'ardeur de ma flame,
Je voy ce qu'est un Trosne, et ce qu'est une femme,
Et jugeant par leur prix de leur possession,
J'éteins enfin ma flame, et mon ambition. (1081–86)

By bestowing heroic stature upon his rebellious heroine,
Corneille establishes a possible correlation between Salic and dramatic laws, both rooted in the distant past and both based on theoretical opinions rather than factual evidence. In *Rodogune,* the
opposition between the world of the fathers who dominate by virtue
of their unearned entitlement, and a world of involuntary female subjugation reflects a contemporary debate that pitted Ancients against
Moderns in the quest for supremacy. Cléopâtre's quest to wrench
political power from males proclaiming her ineligibility to wield it
can be read as a metadramatic condemnation of the mimetic imperative established by Richelieu and the Academy. Like patriarchal privilege, mimesis is based on the presumption that the masters of the
past are destined to remain unequivocally superior to contemporary
writers by simple virtue of historical chronology (the accident of birth)
or the binding verdict of a politicized Academy. Although Corneille
did his best to remain on the Academy's side of the aesthetic fault
line, his writings often reveal a commitment to innovation rather than
ideological conformity, a tendency to foil, rather than confirm, audience expectations.

Corneille clearly admired both Cléopâtre's exuberance and her
continuous struggle to break free of the stranglehold of convention.
Cléopâtre's flamboyant exit, her lack of regrets ("Je maudirois les
Dieux s'ils me rendoient le jour," [1826]), and her uncompromising
spirit ("Sauve-moy de l'affront de tomber à leurs pieds" [1830]) underscore her commitment to recreate and redefine the performing
self, to escape the social and political limits imposed upon her. Fittingly, the drama that contains her seems ever on the verge of burst-
ing through its own formal structures, of falling outside prescribed
neo-classical parameters. Conventional dramaturgy is simply ill-suited
to convey the excesses of a Cléopâtre. In *Rodogune,* form cannot
quite contain its extraordinary heroine, creating an uneasy tension
that particularizes this tragedy. The strain of confinement leads to

Cléopâtre's final decision to destroy both the self and the political structures designed to keep her in check.

The lessons of both *Le Cid* and *Rodogune* are in this sense identical. Cléopâtre's political disenfranchisement recalls Corneille's academic spanking in the wake of *Le Cid,* a play that pleased the public, but not the theorists in power. Just as *Le Cid* demonstrates that a tragedy can please even in the absence of academic regularity, so does Cléopâtre demonstrate that gender has no bearing on effective governing. Both *Le Cid* and Cléopâtre succeed in the absence of formal sanction or historical resemblance. Conformity to theory and practice, after all, cannot guarantee fortune in either the realm of politics or theater. To the degree that spectators are drawn to Cléopâtre, and to the degree that her fitness for governance is determined by precedent rather than actual practice, the necessity of respecting conventions is severely compromised. Cléopâtre's ability to engage the audience demonstrates at least two dramaturgical truths that remain uncontrovertible: in the end, it is the emotional power of the performance that inspires the viewer, and the verdict of the audience is always final.

CHAPTER 5

Authority as Subtext: The *Bérénice* Debate

Corneille's reluctance to subordinate his art to theoretical mandates is often compared to the more scrupulous compliance of his
contemporary rival, Racine.[1] Their two versions of the *Bérénice* tragedy illustrate quite cogently their respective attitudes towards theory.
Although Racine's and Corneille's competing versions of the love
story between Titus and Bérénice are often regarded as "a-typical"
creative efforts, I believe the tragedies actually bear out each author's
conventional position towards textual regulation.[2] It is true that
Corneille's *Tite et Bérénice,* with its focus on the dysfunctionality of
the impassioned hero, seems uncharacteristically Racinian, whereas
Racine's characters betray in turn a familiar Cornelian stoicism in
choosing to sacrifice their love for the good of the state.[3] Despite
these anomalistic and surfacial observations, however, the plays offer metatextual evidence that serves to confirm each author's conventional attitude and theoretical viewpoint. As we have seen in
previous chapters, Corneille's resistance to adhering strictly to academic doctrine is betrayed in a number of thematic and structural
elements found in his early plays. He continues to reveal his uneasi-
ness with imposed aesthetic regulations in his version of *Tite et
Bérénice,* a tragedy wherein regulatory compliance is cast as an un-
workable response to the situation at hand. Racine demonstrates a
far more compliant view of academic regulation, and he uses neo-
classical dramatic theory to decided poetic advantage. It is perhaps

---

1. It is inaccurate, notes Georges Forestier, *Essai de génétique théâtrale: Corneille à
l'oeuvre* (Paris: Klincksieck, 1996), 191, to portray Corneille as an aesthetic rebel. Corneille
consistently argues that he did comply with Aristotelian theoretical principles. It must be
noted, however, that this compliance reflected his personal interpretation of the rules
underpinning dramatic theory, an interpretation which often countered that of the authorities.
2. Lucien Goldmann identifies Racine's *Bérénice* as the most "cornélienne" of his plays
in *Le Dieu caché* (Paris: Gallimard, 1959), 377.
3. Not everyone concurs with this assessment of course. Of particular interest is the view
of Gérard Defaux in "Titus ou le héros tremblant," *French Forum* 10, 3 (1985), 273. Whereas
he does concede that Titus has Cornelian impulses, he argues that Racine's play is designed
specifically to counter Corneille's entire theoretical perspective and is in essence "une
déconstruction radicale et systématique de ce que nous sommes convenus d'appeler
l'héroïsme cornélien."

not surprising, therefore, to discover that his version of *Bérénice,* in
contradistinction to Corneille's, portrays an inevitable and necessary
correlation between conformity to prescribed laws and spectator satisfaction.[4]

Both versions of *Bérénice* center around a wedding ceremony
that constitutes the focal event of each respective tragedy. Corneille's
tragedy partners his hero not with a fiancée barred by law from serving as queen (the premise of Racine's version), but with a politically
legitimate bride-to-be, Domitie. In *Tite et Bérénice,* the wedding is
cast as a social and familial imperative, an event that is regarded by
both partners as a contractual obligation resulting from a pre-arranged
agreement of their parents ("Mais ce qui consolait ce juste et long
ennui, / C'est que Vespasian me regardait pour lui" [137–38]; "C'est
le choix de mon père; et je connais trop bien / Qu'à choisir en César
ce doit être le mien" [389–90]).[5] Bérénice, Tite's former lover, has
already departed, and the only remaining obstacle appears to be that
nobody is particularly eager for the ceremony to take place.[6] Although
Tite has no fundamental objection to marrying Domitie, he reveals
no enthusiasm for doing so either:

> En vain de mon hymen Rome presse la pompe:
> J'y veux de la lenteur, j'aime qu'on l'interrompe,
> Et n'ose résister aux dangereux souhaits
> De préparer toujours et n'achever jamais. (411–14)

Domitie, like Tite, also appears apprehensive, even though she
has perhaps the most to gain from the union:

> Et plus nous approchons de ce grand hyménée,
> Plus en dépit de moi je m'en trouve gênée:

4. The importance of theory in the construction of Racine's play is insightfully highlighted
by Defaux, 274–75.
5. All verse references are to Pierre Corneille, *Théâtre complet,* ed. Maurice Rat (Paris:
Garnier Frères, 1960).
6. Georges Forestier takes note of Corneille's historical accuracy in comparison to the
more impressionistic rendering by Racine in his article "Où finit *Bérénice* commence *Tite
et Bérénice,*" *Onze études sur la vieillesse de Corneille dédiées à la mémoire de Georges
Couton,* eds. Madeleine Bertaud and Alain Niderst (Boulogne: ADIREL, 1994), 53–75.

Il fait toute ma gloire; il fait tous mes désirs:
Ne devrait-il pas faire aussi tous mes plaisirs? (3–6)

The primary reason for this lack of enthusiasm has its roots in events of the past, in conflicts formerly acute, but currently resolved, at least in theory, if not in practice. Tite was in love with Bérénice, whom he exiled prior to becoming emperor:

Avant qu'il vous aimât, il aimait Bérénice;
Et s'il n'en put alors faire une impératrice,
A présent il est maître; et son père au tombeau
Ne peut plus le forcer d'éteindre un feu si beau. (19–22).

Domitie, too, loved elsewhere. Before her betrothal to Tite, Domitie had a relationship with Tite's brother, Domitian. It will be noted, however, that the transfer of affection from Domitian to Tite appears to have been achieved easily enough. Although Domitie readily admits to being more physically attracted to Tite's brother than to Tite, she concedes that her greatest passion is gaining the prestige and power that marriage to the emperor ensures. Consequently, when Tite first turned an amorous eye towards her, she had little difficulty suppressing her physical attraction for Domitian in order to fulfill her political ambitions:

Je ne veux point, seigneur, vous le dissimuler,
Mon coeur va tout à vous quand je le laisse aller:
Mais sans dissimuler j'ose aussi vous le dire,
Ce n'est pas mon dessein qu'il m'en coûte l'empire. (217–20)

She continues to insist, however, that her passion for Domitian proves impossible to eradicate totally, and this serves ostensibly to restrain her exuberance as the wedding day approaches ("Si l'amour quelquefois souffre qu'on le contraigne, / Il souffre rarement qu'une autre ardeur l'éteigne" [63–64]).

Her feelings for Domitian are not the only obstacle to her unqualified happiness, however. She is also distressed by Tite's rather measured emotional response to the prospect of marrying her, and it is this complaint that opens Corneille's play. The spectator is con-

fronted immediately with the image of a distraught Domitie bemoaning her "unhappy," albeit arduously quested, fate. Although she admits freely that she does not love the man she is destined to wed, she
decries Tite's lack of impassioned intensity for her ("J'ambitionne et
crains l'hymen d'un empereur / Dont j'ai lieu de douter si j'aurai
tout le coeur" [25–26]). The fear that Tite's deeds and desires are not
in consonance dampens her enthusiasm for the wedding and is responsible for creating feelings of insecurity:

> Son feu de sa raison est l'effet et l'étude;
> Il s'en fait un plaisir bien moins qu'un embarras,
> Et s'efforce à m'aimer; mais il ne m'aime pas. (36–38)

Although it is clear that Tite and Bérénice are reluctant to marry
one another, the reasons for their hesitancy are not that apparent. The
decision to exile Bérénice, voluntarily made, predates the play's exposition. Tite is not reconsidering its wisdom. Therefore, his reluctance to marry Domitie cannot be convincingly attributed to his
attachment to the now absent Bérénice. Domitie's distress is even
less comprehensible. She is clearly more consumed by political ambition than passion for Domitian. The rhetorical reluctance of the
protagonists, therefore, appears more than a little contrived. In fact,
it seems as if Tite and Domitie are using the upcoming marriage as a
pretext to generate a series of purely rhetorical conflicts. Domitie,
for example, struggles to convey a conflicted attitude by hiding behind the façade of dutiful submission, a traditional Cornelian value
("L'effort que je me fais me tue autant que vous; / Mais enfin
l'empereur veut être mon époux" [201–02]). Her formulaic angst
convinces no one, however, least of all, the intended audience,
Domitan ("Non, votre ambition ne se peut démentir" [210]). Indeed,
Domitie is forced ultimately to admit that she finds power more compelling than physical passion, revealing her conflict to be more superficial than substantive ("La passion du trône est seule toujours
belle, / Seule à qui l'âme doive une ardeur immortelle" [223–24]).
   Hypocrisy is a character flaw revealed by most of the characters
in *Tite et Bérénice*. The tragedy is most notable perhaps for the pre-
ponderance of characters who can be caught in the act of insincere

role-playing. Domitie hides her ambition behind the convenient mask of dutiful submission. Domitian feigns indifference for Domitie ("Et comme aux lois d'un père il fallait obéir, / Je feignais d'oublier" [477–78]) and then he claims later to be in love with Bérénice ("Je l'aime, et l'aimerai si votre âme y renonce" [1399]). Tite attempts, but is unable, to convey a convincing posture of heroic self denial. Although he would have us believe that a lingering attachment to Bérénice is what contributes to his current pre-marital lethargy, his argument loses persuasiveness upon his admission that he is not impervious to Domitie's considerable charms. This affirmation diminishes significantly the self sacrificial nature of his gesture, and renders his protests insincere. Emotionally vacant, with no real sense of commitment to either love or duty, Tite bemoans the loss of his one true love while simultaneously making plans to marry a woman he admittedly finds both charming and attractive. In fact, Tite's sacrifice of Bérénice appears no more agonizing to him than Domitie's discarding of Domitian. Tite surrenders a passion already on the wane to a blossoming romance with Domitie; Domitie sacrifices a lukewarm physical passion to her greater lust for power. In short, just as Domitie's ambition compensates for the loss of Domitian, Tite's growing affection for Domitie enables him to better endure the loss of Bérénice:

> Non: malgré les attraits de sa belle rivale,
> Malgré les voeux flottants de mon âme inégale,
> Je veux l'aimer, je l'aime; et sa seule beauté
> Pouvait me consoler de ce que j'ai quitté.
> Elle seule en ses yeux porte de quoi contraindre
> Mes feux à s'assoupir, s'ils ne peuvent s'éteindre,
> De quoi flatter mon âme, et forcer mes douleurs
> A souhaiter du moins de n'aimer plus ailleurs. (439–46)

Upon her unexpected return, even the newly arrived Bérénice quickly perceives that Tite's "duty" is not exactly contrary to his desires:

> Il fait en liberté ce qu'il faisait contraint.
> Cet ordre de sortir, si prompt et si sévère,

N'a plus pour s'excuser l'autorité d'un père;
Il est libre, il est maître, il veut tout ce qu'il fait. (890–93)
. . . .
Mais Domitie est belle, elle a tout l'avantage
Qu'ajoute un vrai mérite à l'éclat du visage. (963–64)

The characters' hypocritical posturing can be traced to one fundamental cause. They are not fundamentally committed to the principles they are ostensibly defending. Unlike those earlier Cornelian figures who were genuinely torn by competing duties to which they are equally drawn, the characters in *Tite et Bérénice* seem to be aping passions they do not feel. Rather, they labor to create the impression of being internally conflicted, when in fact, they are not. Domitie's attachment to Domitie and her feelings for Tite appear equally unauthentic. Her affirmation of an emotional conflict is intended to camouflage her more material (and less honorable) desire for status. The duty that so moved Rodrigue and Chimène is revealed in both Domitie and Tite to be only a rhetorical accessory. Tite claims to be respecting his duty as emperor:

Je m'impose à mon tour les lois qu'il m'imposait,
Et me dis après lui tout ce qu'il me disait.
J'ai des yeux d'empereur, et n'ai plus ceux de Tite. (493–95)

However, he seems to have no real commitment to his post. He even ponders abdication in order to spend the rest of his life in tranquil exile with Bérénice ("Pour aller de mes feux vous demander le fruit, / Je quitterais l'empire et tout ce qui leur nuit" [1641–42]). In point of fact, he seems to derive little satisfaction from his role as emperor:

Cette toute-puissance est bien imaginaire,
Qui s'asservit soi-même à la peur de déplaire,
Qui laisse au goût public régler tous ses projets,
Et prend le plus haut rang pour craindre ses sujets. (1455–58)

Because heroism in the absence of conflict is impossible, the characters in *Bérénice* seem intent on inventing conflicts, even where none exist. Histrionic rhetoric is here made to stand in for heroic sacrifice. The reliance on rhetoric to achieve heroic stature contributes to an overall impression of insincerity as characters labor to provide evidence of self abnegation in the absence of genuine deprivation. This masquerade consumes most of their effort, and obliges them to avail themselves of a vast repertoire of histrionic postures. Domitie in particular enacts a number of staged attitudes that serve to render her not only inconsistent, but downright irksome. Depending on the emotion she is endeavoring to reveal, she moves from playing the role of insecure and vulnerable bride-to-be (". . . j'ai leu de douter si j'aurai tout le coeur" [26]), to that of dutiful daughter ("Pour remplir tous nos voeux nous n'attendions qu'un père" [107]), calculating upstart ("La passion du trône est seule toujours belle" [223]), and avenging fury (". . . je suis à qui me venge" [1204]). Domitian plays the role of suffering suitor no better. At one point, he feigns interest in Bérénice, a childish ploy that fools no one ("Quoi! madame, il vous aime? / Non; mais il me le dit, madame." [767–68]). His acting deficiencies are brought to the forefront by Domitie who is particularly critical of his performance. In a blistering attack, she faults him for failing to portray adequately the role of courtly lover. The truly committed suitor, she argues, would proclaim more emphatically his readiness to sacrifice personal happiness for the greater glory of his beloved:

> Pour peu que vous m'aimiez, aimez mes avantages:
> Il n'est point d'autre amour digne des grands courages. (259–60)
> . . . .
> Vous le sauriez, ingrat, si vous saviez aimer. (782)
> . . . .
> Si vous vouliez passer pour véritable amant,
> Il fallait espérer jusqu'au dernier moment. (793–94)

Tite also struggles to project a convincing image of the tragic hero. His attempt to present himself as a martyr to political necessity is undermined significantly by his voluntary decision to send Bérénice away, and his rather affectionate leanings towards Domitie. Domitie reviews Tite's performance as critically as she does Domitian's, enraged by what she interprets as an inability to commit himself emotionally to her. She derides Tite's inability to provide a more convincing portrait of the eager bridegroom ("Souvent même, au milieu des offres de sa foi, / Il semble tout à coup qu'il n'est pas avec moi" [33–34]), and she finds his behavior in the wake of Bérénice's arrival to be particularly inappropriate and insulting:

> Il m'en aurait donné des sûretés nouvelles,
> Il m'en aurait laissé quelques marques fidèles:
> S'il me voulait cacher le trouble où je le voi,
> La plus mauvaise excuse était bonne pour moi.
> Mais, pour toute réponse, il se tait, il me quitte:
> Et tu ne peux souffrir que mon coeur s'en irrite! (671–76)

What is significant in all these histrionic performances is how Bérénice's return succeeds in exposing their lack of sincerity. Her unexpected arrival forces masks to shift, poses to collapse. The threat of a renewed rival for Tite's affection prompts Domitie's ambition to be placed more strikingly and unmistakably in evidence as she pleads shamelessly for the opportunity to become the emperor's wife. Domitian's love for Domitie is also more explicitly revealed. Tite's passion for Bérénice is quickly rekindled, and this in turn renders his reluctance to marry Domitie quite authentic, and hence, more credible.[7] Bérénice's return provides Tite finally with a palpable and concrete internal conflict. He is now visibly torn between the competing demands of passion and duty, an internal conflict worthy of heroic stature.

Bérénice's presence is not limited to authenticating the behaviors of the other characters, however. Her arrival allows the author to metatextually affirm what is often seen as the defining characteristic of Cornelian theater: a hostility to complying with imposed regulations. When an overwhelmed Tite proclaims his readiness to surrender to passion and abdicate, he is acting in support of external regulations:

---

7. Georges Forestier, *Essai de génétique*, 69, argues that Bérénice was in fact never off the minds of the principal characters: "Absente et (déjà) présente tout à la fois, aussi bien dans les esprits de ceux qui la croient loin que dans les faits, tel est le statut de Bérénice avant son entrée en scène."

Eh bien! madame, il faut renoncer à ce titre
Qui de toute la terre en vain me fait l'arbitre.
Allons dans vos États m'en donner un plus doux;
Ma gloire la plus haute est celle d'être à vous. (1027–30)

Bérénice advises against such a course of action, however. In explaining her resistance, she focuses on the need to remain free from the tyranny of law ("la tyrannique loi" [929]). To have only the power to comply with directives, she argues, is to have no real power; to be allowed only to obey is to be indistinguishable from being enslaved. Bérénice believes her status gives her the right to determine her own fate and the fate of subordinates, including Domitie:

Qu'en dépit des Romains, leur digne souverain,
S'il prend une moitié, la prenne de ma main;
Et pour tout dire enfin, je veux que Bérénice
Ait une créature en leur impératrice. (1129–32)

She counsels Tite to demand no less. Tite's primary duty is neither to his father, nor to her, but to his own vision of Rome's destiny ("Quoi! Rome ne veut pas quand vous avez voulu?" [989]). He must therefore place his trust not in the wisdom of precedent or paternal commitments, but in his personal assessment of what is right and wrong. As emperor, he cannot shift the burden of responsibility to others; he alone can determine the course of action to follow:

Que faites-vous, seigneur, du pouvoir absolu?
N'êtes-vous dans ce trône, où tant de monde aspire,
Que pour assujettir l'empereur à l'empire? (990–92).

Bérénice urges Tite to emancipate himself from the prison of unexamined compliance, and to begin by making an independent decision on her fate:

S'il faut partir demain, je ne veux qu'une grâce;
Que ce soit vous, seigneur, qui le veuilliez pour moi,
Et non votre sénat qui m'en fasse la loi. (1648–50)

Inspired by Bérénice's strength of will, Tite decides to take control of his destiny. In a final gesture of self-mastery, he claims the right to determine the laws by which he must live ("Je veux qu'il obéisse aux lois que je prends d'elle, / Qu'il laisse à notre amour régler notre intérêt" [1664–65]). His self-affirmation, it will be noted, comes only after the senate has already decided on whether or not Tite and Bérénice may marry. In a surprising ruling, the senate, without much consideration for the consequences of its decision, agrees to suspend its long-standing prohibition against marriage between Roman emperors and foreign queens:

> D'une commune voix Rome adopte la reine;
> Et le peuple à grands cris montre sa passion
> De voir un plein effet de cette adoption. (1672–74)

The senate having sanctioned the marriage, it would appear that a happy ending is in store. But the principles which Bérénice so eloquently embraced remain valid, even when they are in conflict with her self interest. Despite the favorable ruling, Bérénice again urges Tite to refuse to comply, and again she cites the need for him to establish the laws of his own governance. The senate has made its ruling from its own subjective and skewed vantage point. It cannot have taken the full impact of its ruling into consideration. It is precisely this lack of vision that Bérénice cites in her opposition to the ruling. The senate's decision is too hasty ("Qui semble un peu bien prompt pour n'être point suspect" [1682]), too subjective ("Rendons lui, vous et moi, cette reconnaissance / D'en avoir pour vous plaire affaibli la puissance" [1699–1700]), and too shortsighted ("D'autres sur votre exemple épouseraient des reines / Qui n'auraient pas, seigneur, des âmes si romaines" [1703–04]) to be allowed to stand. It is therefore up to Tite to correct the flawed nature of the senate's decision, to place the empire's needs on a higher plane than those of the emperor ("Sauvons-lui, vous et moi, la gloire de ses lois" [1698]). Just as Bérénice opposes the mandate forbidding her from marrying the emperor, so does she refuse to comply with the order that she marry him in defiance of precedent. Upon reasoned reflection, Bérénice finds the legal sanction against her marriage to Tite to be politically well-grounded, and she urges continued respect for a precedent that remains valid, even essential, for Rome's continued prosperity and freedom. Although it is in Tite's and her own short term interest to accept the decision, it is Tite's obligation to decide independently on matters critical to Rome's survival. He must, in other words, consider the long-term, public consequences of a law that offers immediate private satisfaction. He therefore must oppose the ruling offered by the senate in order to respect the higher duty of political self mastery.

Bérénice's counsel to reject the senate's decision is not a totally self abnegating gesture. It is linked to a desire to protect that very Cornelian value of reputation or *gloire*. By demonstrating superiority to the laws imposed upon them, both Tite and Bérénice can move from the mortal to the legendary plane. Privileging legacy over legality, Bérénice willingly exchanges private and temporary gratification for the prospect of eternal public admiration:

> On nous aime; faisons qu'on nous aime à jamais. (1702)
> . . . .
> Du levant au couchant, du More jusqu'au Scythe,
> Les peuples vanteront et Bérénice et Tite;
> Et l'histoire à l'envi forcera l'avenir
> D'en garder à jamais l'illustre souvenir. (1755–58)

Just as fidelity to precedent cannot guarantee eternal justice ("Aux zèles indiscrets tout paraît légitime, / Et la fausse vertu se fait honneur du crime" [1695–96]); compliance with political mandates cannot ensure public approval:

> D'autres sur votre exemple épouseraient des reines
> Qui n'auraient pas, seigneur, des âmes si romaines,
> Et lui feraient peut-être avec trop de raison,
> Haïr votre mémoire et détester mon nom. (1703–06)

Even the best-intentioned laws can prove unjust over time. Regulations revered as sacrosanct in one age are often viewed as acts of folly in another. Metatextually speaking then, Corneille's *Tite et Bérénice* stands in bold opposition to what Richelieu maintained, and Racine practiced. Despite the Academy's attempt to create a fool-proof blueprint for aesthetic perfection, in the end it is always the artist who must determine the appropriateness of his own aesthetic convictions. Rules and mandates cannot override the judgment of the writer who controls and creates the aesthetic artefact, because ultimately it is he who bears sole responsibility for its fate.

Corneille's independent view is of course in stark contrast to that of Racine, whose unqualified respect for academic discipline not only ensured Academic favor, but earned him a place of unchallenged renown in literary history. Unlike Corneille, Racine had little difficulty constructing plays that respected the demands of neo-classical dramaturgy to the letter. Not surprisingly, his plays betray no metatextual resentment towards the academic imperatives that contributed to his success. Significantly, Racine's version of *Bérénice* begins by casting respect for authority as a sacred, indeed, an inviolable tenet. In a shocking and unanticipated revelation, Antiochus informs Paulin that he is about to break a five year silence imposed on him by Bérénice, the woman he loves. Barred from making reference to his feelings as the price of friendship, Antiochus has remained faithful to his pledge for five long years. He can remain silent no longer, however, and as the play opens, he prepares to risk all in order to proclaim his undying love for her in defiance of her orders:

> Pourrai-je, sans trembler, lui dire: "Je vous aime?"
> Mais quoi? déjà je tremble, et mon coeur agité
> Craint autant ce moment que je l'ai souhaité.
> Bérénice autrefois m'ôta toute espérance;
> Elle m'imposa même un éternel silence. (20–24)[8]

Fittingly, Antiochus' transgression is harshly rebuked, an early and decisive indication that respect for authority is expected to take precedence over even the most loyal of long-term friendships:

> Seigneur, je n'ai pas cru que dans une journée
> Qui doit avec César unir ma destinée,

---

8. References are to Racine, *Oeuvres* (Paris: Hachette, Les Grands Ecrivains de la France, 1929).

Il fût quelque mortel qui pût impunément
Se venir à mes yeux déclarer mon amant. (259–62)

Indeed, Antiochus' transgression appears all the more serious in light of its twin violations of friendship and royal protocol. Not only is Titus his political superior, but Antiochus is Titus' trusted confidant and loyal friend as well. Bérénice is quick to remind Antiochus of these bonds in order to underscore the multi-layered nature of his failing ("Titus vous chérissoit, vous admiriez Titus" [270]).

Bérénice's admonishments are not unanticipated. Antiochus is only too aware of his culpability, an awareness that explains his obsessive preoccupation with secrecy and privacy. He had hoped, however, that a private audience would enable him to better persuade Bérénice of his affection for her, allow him to perform more effectively, as it were, with only her in witness. Before speaking to Bérénice, he takes care to ensure that his words will be uttered in the absence of disapproving onlookers:

Va chez elle: dis-lui qu'importun à regret
J'ose lui demander un entretien secret. (9–10)
. . . .
Ainsi donc sans témoins je ne lui puis parler? (62)
. . . .
Vous la verrez, Seigneur: Bérénice est instruite
Que vous voulez ici la voir seule et sans suite.
La Reine d'un regard a daigné m'avertir
Qu'à votre empressement elle alloit consentir;
Et sans doute elle attend le moment favorable
Pour disparoître aux yeux d'une cour qui l'accable. (63–68)

With Bérénice's undivided attention, and on a stage unencumbered with traces of his rival's pomp and circumstance, he hopes to minimize the offensiveness of his egregious violation of political protocol. Moreover, he hopes that Bérénice will be more tolerant of his transgression in the absence of a scrutinizing public. In the hope that he will at the very least provoke Bérénice's pity ("Au lieu de s'offenser, elle pourra me plaindre" [47]),[9] Antiochus crafts an eloquent state-

9. I disagree here with Gérard Defaux, "Titus ou le héros tremblant," 290–91, who argues that Antiochus' expression of affection is wholly gratuitous.

ment designed to melt her resistance and weaken her resolve. His eloquence fails to diminish the impropriety of his action, however. Even in private, Bérénice considers Antiochus' avowal to be patently offensive. Outraged at his blatant disrespect for hierarchical imperatives ("J'oublie en sa faveur un discours qui m'outrage" [264]), Bérénice condemns unequivocally his indiscretion.

If Antiochus' expression of love for Bérénice violates established political protocols, Bérénice's love for the emperor represents a transgression of its own. It violates cultural prejudices and political law. Ultimately, the reaction of the public to the possible marriage between Bérénice and the new emperor generates the same disapproval as Antiochus' confession of love to Bérénice. Initially, public reaction to the relationship between Bérénice and Titus seems overwhelmingly positive. In fact, as the play opens, Bérénice has difficulty extricating herself from the crowd in order to honor Antiochus' request for a private meeting:

> Seigneur, j'ai vu la Reine;
> Mais pour me faire voir, je n'ai percé qu'à peine
> Les flots toujours nouveaux d'un peuple adorateur
> Qu'attire sur ses pas sa prochaine grandeur. (51–54)

Public approval is vital to the future of Titus' and Bérénice's relationship because under current Roman law, marriage between the Roman emperor and a foreign queen is forbidden.

Despite these early signs of public support for Bérénice, however, there are worrisome signals indicating her public support is fading, that the façade of popular affection is crumbling. Bérénice herself is well aware that the outpouring of public support is less than sincere:

> Enfin je me dérobe à la joie importune
> De tant d'amis nouveaux que me fait la fortune;
> Je fuis de leurs respects l'inutile longueur,
> Pour chercher un ami qui me parle du coeur. (135–38)

Her fears are quickly confirmed. Appearances are in fact quite deceiving. As it turns out, the approval Bérénice currently enjoys is linked to an earlier time, a time before Titus wore the crown of Roman emperor. The affection now in evidence is simply the residual tolerance of their former relationship, a relationship that developed when Titus was without political responsibilities ("J'aimois, je soupirois dans une paix profonde: / Un autre étoit chargé de l'empire du monde" [455–56]), a time when Bérénice had no legitimate stake in Rome's political destiny. Now that Titus is emperor, the spectacle of Bérénice and Titus in wedded bliss is seen from an entirely different perspective. In an ironic turn of events, then, Bérénice discovers that her relationship to Titus violates protocols as much as Antiochus' expression of love to her. Although both scenarios may be in and of themselves inoffensive, they are contextually inappropriate. Current regulations and cultural practices forbid both scenarios, and both are therefore condemned by those who are obliged to witness them.

While Vespasian lived and reigned, Titus was just another spectator to his father's drama. With no weighty responsibilities encumbering him, Titus could court Bérénice without fear of public disapproval or political reprisals. Upon the death of Vespasien, however, a more intent and scrutinizing public gaze falls on Titus, the new emperor. Titus no longer has the luxury of being an idle, ill-informed spectator to his father's stage of power. He is now called upon to perform on that very stage, a change of role that brings with it a different set of behavioral expectations. Titus is now accountable to Rome, not to Bérénice. The death of Vespasien transforms Titus from public citizen to public servant, from individual to icon, from spectator to spectacle. In order to ensure that his reign please his subjects, Titus must scrupulously respect those laws he is called upon to enforce. In other words, he must now perform to the satisfaction of Roman citizens, not Bérénice:

> Dès que ma triste main eut fermé sa paupière,
> De mon aimable erreur je fus désabusé:
> Je sentis le fardeau qui m'étoit imposé;
> Je connus que bientôt, loin d'être à ce que j'aime,
> Il falloit, cher Paulin, renoncer à moi-même;
> Et que le choix des Dieux, contraire à mes amours,
> Livroit à l'univers le reste de mes jours. (460–66)

Now emperor, Titus emerges from the margins of politics to live a life center-staged for all to witness and critique. His new role obliges him to rethink the cast of characters around him, in particular, the role of Bérénice. Paulin's report to Titus regarding the public's attitude towards the queen confirms a long-standing Roman prejudice: antipathy for any foreigner who would govern Rome's empire. Public opinion and Roman law here seamlessly coincide. In the eyes of Titus' constituents, Bérénice is regarded as an unsuitable partner for the new Roman emperor:

> N'en doutez point, Seigneur: soit raison, soit caprice,
> Rome ne l'attend point pour son impératrice.
> On sait qu'elle est charmante; et de si belles mains
> Semblent vous demander l'empire des humains.
> Elle a même, dit-on, le coeur d'une Romaine;
> Elle a mille vertus. Mais, Seigneur, elle est reine.
> Rome, par une loi qui ne se peut changer,
> N'admet avec son sang aucun sang étranger,
> Et ne reconnoît point les fruit illégitimes
> Qui naissent d'un hymen contraire à ses maximes. (371–80)

Confronted with this information, the newly-crowned emperor Titus has little choice but to remain faithful to the role in which destiny has cast him. No longer free to indulge personal fantasies that risk offending cultural sensitivities, he embraces his role as Rome's leader, and renounces his plans to marry Bérénice, a foreign queen ("Mais il ne s'agit plus de vivre, il faut régner" [1102]). Although his unlimited power enables him to change the law that forbids the union, he is powerless to diminish the public resentment such a self centered gesture would entail. Were he to bring to the stage of Roman power a foreign queen, he would lose inevitably the support of his ever-watchful, ever-critical constituents:

> Rome observe aujourd'hui ma conduite nouvelle.
> Quelle honte pour moi, quel présage pour elle,
> Si dès le premier pas, renversant tous ses droits,
> Je fondois mon bonheur sur le débris des lois! (467–70)

Like Antiochus, Bérénice is now a marginal spectator in Titus'
political drama. Titus has in fact already scripted the obligatory exit
of both Antiochus and Bérénice ("Prince, il faut avec vous qu'elle
parte demain" [718]). This coupling of the two political "spectators"
is a clear indication of Bérénice's fall from grace and constitutes an
unmistakable loss of stature and influence. Antiochus' irrelevant status is what contributes to his overall lack of influence throughout the
drama. He is viewed by both Bérénice and Titus as primarily a passive spectator rather than a significant contributor. Bérénice limits
Antiochus' function to that of witness to the more vital story of her
personal life:

> Je n'attendois que vous pour témoin de ma joie. (268)
> . . . .
> Depuis trois ans dans Rome elle arrête vos [Antiochus'] pas;
> Et lorsque cette reine, assurant sa conquête,
> Vous attend pour témoin de cette illustre fête,
> Quand l'amoureux Titus, devenant son époux,
> Lui prépare un éclat qui rejaillit sur vous . . . (82–86)

Antiochus has grown accustomed to his secondary status as awed
spectator in witness of Titus' heroic adventures. He acknowledges,
with some bitterness, his place in the cold shadow of his more daz-
zling rival:

> Je fuis Titus; je fuis ce nom qui m'inquiète,
> Ce nom qu'à tous moments votre bouche répète.
> Que vous dirai-je enfin? Je fuis des yeux distraits,
> Qui me voyant toujours, ne me voyoient jamais. (275–78)

Although the role of spectator is rather new for Bérénice, it is a
position she assumed almost immediately upon Titus' coronation.
Prior to the death of his father, it was Titus who was assigned the role
of "spectator" in the relationship. Titus stood silently in awe while
Bérénice guided his adrift adolescence toward principled maturity
("Je me suis fait un plaisir nécessaire / De la voir chaque jour, de
l'aimer, de lui plaire" [423–24]). The situation has now reversed itself and it is Bérénice who casts an enraptured gaze upon Titus. This

change of perspective confirms the inevitability of her textual reassignment and solidifies her transformation from spectacle to spectator:[10]

> De cette nuit, Phénice, as-tu vu la splendeur?
> Tes yeux ne sont-ils pas tous pleins de sa grandeur?
> Ces flambeaux, ce bûcher, cette nuit enflammée,
> Ces aigles, ces faisceaux, ce peuple, cette armée,
> Cette foule de rois, ces consuls, ce sénat,
> Qui tous de mon amant empruntoient leur éclat;
> Cette pourpre, cet or, que rehaussoit sa gloire,
> Et ces lauriers encor témoins de sa victoire;
> Tous ces yeux qu'on voyoit venir de toutes parts
> Confondre sur lui seul leurs avides regards;
> Ce port majestueux, cette douce présence.
> Ciel! avec quel respect et quelle complaisance
> Tous les coeurs en secret l'assuroient de leur foi! (301–13)

Bérénice's abrupt excision from Titus' drama is hardly a welcome turn of events, and she responds with anticipated resentment. Initially, she does not share Titus' respect for the laws opposing their marriage. As she accurately points out, Titus, as emperor, has the power to suspend current laws and marry anyone he chooses:

> Quoi? pour d'injustes lois que vous pouvez changer,
> En d'éternels chagrins vous-même vous plonger?
> Rome a ses droits, Seigneur: n'avez-vous pas les vôtres?
> Ses intérets sont-ils plus sacrés que les nôtres? (1149–52)

What Bérénice fails at first to comprehend, however, is that Titus' commitment has changed. His duty is now to Rome, not Bérénice. He is no longer functioning in a private, but in the political arena wherein his behavior is more precisely regulated. His new role requires him to pay closer attention to established conventions and precedents. The unorthodox relationship between Titus and Bérénice was valid for another time and another stage. Titus now must per-

---

10. For more on the "gaze" see J. A. Dainard, "The Power of the Spoken Word in *Bérénice*," *Romanic Review* 67 (1976), 157–171.

form before a much wider and more critical audience, and in an arena where different rules apply. Were Titus and Bérénice to defy Roman law and marry, the union would be in constant jeopardy from angry Romans who might retaliate with violence ("Faudra-t-il par le sang justifier mon choix?" [1141]). More importantly, such reckless action would surely invite the contempt of future generations and forever sully his glorious reputation:

> S'ils se taisent, Madame, et me vendent leurs lois,
> A quoi m'exposez-vous? Par quelle complaisance
> Faudra-t-il quelque jour payer leur patience? (1142–44)

Clearly, the relationship between Titus and Bérénice can function now only at the level of historical legend, as a memorable narrative extolling the virtues of political self sacrifice:

> Que la gloire du moins soutienne nos douleurs,
> Et que tout l'univers reconnoisse sans peine
> Les pleurs d'un empereur et les pleurs d'une reine. (1058–60)

In order to preserve the relationship as exemplary narrative, Titus casts Bérénice's exile and the renunciation of passion as aesthetic events. Theirs will be an exemplary love story for the ages to contemplate and admire. In order to solemnize the transformation of life into legend, he calls upon traditional witness, Antiochus, to stand in for the allegorical audience selected to appreciate this heroic gesture of self sacrifice:

> Venez, Prince, venez, je vous ai fait chercher.
> Soyez ici témoin de toute ma foiblesse;
> Voyez si c'est aimer avec peu de tendresse:
> Jugez-nous. (1426–29)

Antiochus, a metaphor here for future generations that will critically assess the tragic love story of Titus and Bérénice, is asked not only to witness, but to evaluate Titus' performance. The separation between the lovers, then, is portrayed as an exemplary love story for future generations to admire. As legend, the relationship between these lovers will transcend temporal and physical limits. Through narrativized repetition, Titus and Bérénice will remain forever linked. Their physical separation will be overshadowed by the legacy that succeeds it and compensates to some degree for the suffering endured. They will in other words sublimate their desires to satisfy the demands of art.

When Bérénice realizes finally that the only sure way to remain linked to Titus is through the medium of historical narrative, her resistance fades. Bérénice accepts finally the necessity of subservience to law and the inevitability of exile in exchange for the promise of a more durable union through the permanence of art.[11] Whereas she earlier shunned the formality of protocol between herself and Titus ("Ah! Titus, car enfin l'amour fuit la contrainte / De tous ces noms que suit le respect et la crainte" [571–72]), she now accepts her newly acquired inferior status and recognizes Titus as her "Seigneur":

> Je vivrai, je suivrai vos ordres absolus.
> Adieu, Seigneur, régnez: je ne vous verrai plus. (1493–94)

In the end, Bérénice is obliged to accept the same rules of protocol breached by Antiochus in the opening scenes of the tragedy. In deference to Titus' rank and to political necessity, she submits to the rule of law because only in so doing can she ensure a legitimate link to Titus.[12] The relationship between Titus and Bérénice can endure only if transposed from the political stage to a "plus noble théâtre" (356), that is to say, if it is transferred to the aesthetic realm. Bérénice accepts finally to exit the unstable world of political reality in order

---

11. "La pièce s'enfonce au plus profond de la convention théâtrale," notes Laurence Mall in "Dire le départ, ou comment faire quelque chose de rien: Etude sur *Bérénice*," *Neophilologus* 75 (1991), 41. "Car le défi est là: dire le départ, parler la mort, où n'atteindre à l'existence scénique—langagière—que peut annoncer un éternel silence sans cesse imminent."

12. William J. Cloonan offers an interesting metatextual perspective in his article "Love and Gloire in *Bérénice:* A Freudian Perspective," *Kentucky Romance Quarterly* 22 (1975), 517–25. Here he argues that it is the need for structure that forces the characters to accept Roman law and thereby resist disintegration. Although Cloonan is referring to historical order, I believe the same argument can be made for aesthetic order. In other words, only by complying with established aesthetic principles can a tragedy remain properly "structured" and coherent.

to enter the realm of aesthetic permanence:[13]

> Je l'aime, je le fuis; Titus m'aime, il me quitte.
> Portez loin de mes yeux vos soupirs et vos fers.
> Adieu: servons tous trois d'exemple à l'univers
> De l'amour la plus tendre et la plus malheureuse
> Dont il puisse garder l'histoire douloureuse. (1500–04)

In Corneille's and Racine's version of the Bérénice story, it is the departure of the heroine that conveys the final, and in this case, antithetical, metatextual message. In Corneille's version, Bérénice elects to leave in order to affirm the supremacy of ideological independence. In Racine's version, the opposite point is made. Here, the correlation between law and popular opinion establishes the necessity of conforming to both. The transmutation of politics into art effectively links the principles of statecraft with those of stagecraft, metatextually echoing one of Racine's most cherished aesthetic principles: a performance in violation of established rules and protocols is certain to displease the audience.[14] For Racine, aesthetic success depends upon artistic self-discipline, on the writer's voluntary compliance with laws designed to ensure public approbation. Those artists who insist on transgressing established literary codes do so at the peril of their future reputation. Their rebellion will one day prove as reckless as emperor-to-be Titus' belief that public opinion would sanction indefinitely his youthful indiscretions.

What is most intriguing in these dueling tragedies is that both end with a metatextual call for aesthetic approval. Corneille's pro-

---

13. For Dainard, 171, this final silence serves to metatextualize both death and tragedy.
14. Interesting metatextual parallels are also discussed in Harriet Stone's "Les Voiles du pouvoir," *Ordre et contestation au temps des Classiques*, I, eds. Roger Duchêne and Pierre Ronzeaud (Paris: Biblio 17, 1992), 225–33, and Mitchell Greenberg, "Racine's *Bérénice:* Orientalism and the Allegory of Absolutism," *Esprit Créateur* 32 (1992), 75–86. Greenberg's article is expanded in *Canonical States, Canonical Stages: Oeidipus, Othering and Seventeenth-century Drama* (Minneapolis: University of Minnesota Press, 1994) where he establishes a link between theatrical pleasure and political subjugation: "By one and the same stroke Racine not only redefines the locus of theatrical tragedy, and thus of theatrical pleasure, he politically prefigures (the inextricable interrelation between the space of theatrical pleasure, and the locus of political subjugation, their commingling) the future of the absolutist state" (136).

tagonists equate heroism with their daring challenge to authority and their questioning of the validity of prejudice that passes for law. Racine's characters, on the other hand, anticipate praise for sacrificing personal preference to established codes of conduct. While it may be tempting to argue that Racine's aesthetic perfection appears to justify his respect for rules and theoretical mandates, it is equally difficult to fault Corneille for opposing the calcification of dramatic theory, and questioning the blind acceptance of theoretical mandates inherited from the distant past. Eventually, even Racine will begin to question authority as well. Although many of Racine's tragedies lend metatextual support for compliance with the rules and unwavering faith in the wisdom of the Fathers who established them, Racine's submissive position will slowly, but surely, evolve and culminate in his own metatextual repudiation of authority in *Athalie.*

CHAPTER 6

Hermione's Suicide and the Surrender to History

According to the theorists of the time, the well made tragedy was one that imitated successful models of the past; innovation was tolerated only within strict and prescribed limits. This respect for aesthetic precedents can be detected in nearly every Racinian tragedy, a sign of support for aesthetic theory that distinguishes his dramas from those of his more experimental rival, Pierre Corneille. As we noted in the preceding chapter, Racine's *Bérénice* conveys an orthodox view that is borne out by many if not most of his other tragedies.[1] In this chapter, I focus more specifically on how *Andromaque* provides an example of Racine's early allegiance to the mimetic imperative. Indeed, so concerned was Racine with faithful imitation that he felt obliged to justify the minor creative liberties he took with his third tragedy, *Andromaque*.[2] His commitment to imitation is manifested in part by the circular nature of this tragedy. In *Andromaque*, the denouement returns us to the very conflict that the marriage between Pyrrhus and Hermione was intended to resolve. Consequently, as the tragedy ends, we are confronted not with the promise of future prosperity, but with a repeat of history. The spectators are left with the image of a widowed Andromaque leading the charge against the Greeks who just claimed victory over Troy. The repetition (imitation) of history, then, triumphs over Hermione's concerted efforts to move the tragedy forward, beyond the defining and pivotal historical moment of the Trojan war.[3]

---

1. In an earlier article, "The Pleasures of Re-Enactment in *Andromaque*," *Dalhousie French Studies* 24 (1993), 57–70, I argue that Racine's compulsion to bring events back to their point of origin, that is to say, the overriding static and circular nature of Racinian tragedy, constitutes a metatextual affirmation of his surrender to theoretical imperatives, specifically, the mandate to imitate Greek and Roman models of literary perfection.

2. "Je ne crois pas que j'eusse besoin de cet exemple d'Euripide pour justifier le peu de liberté que j'ai prise. Car il y a bien de la différence entre détruire le principal fondement d'une fable, et en altérer quelques incidents, qui changent presque de face dans toutes les mains qui les traitent." (*Seconde préface*, 39). References are to Racine, *Oeuvres* (Paris: Les Grands Ecrivains de la France, 1929).

3. Roland Racevskis' article, "Generational Transition in *Andromaque*" in *Les épreuves du labyrinthe: Essais de poétique et d'herméneutique raciniennes*, ed. Richard-Laurent Barnett, special number of *Dalhousie French Studies* 49 (Winter, 1999), 63–72, uncovers a variety of interesting perspectives on the characters' relationship to past and present, some diametrically opposed to my own.

The inevitable repetition of history is foreshadowed from the outset. Despite Pylade's optimistic references to winds of change, despite Hermione's determined effort to move events beyond the gridlock of history and to propel the scenario forward, the tug of history proves too overpowering to overcome. From the opening scenes, Andromaque's dominance remains unchallenged, belying her prisoner status and thwarting rival Hermione's attempt to take her rightful place on center stage. Frustrated by her marginal status in a sequence of events she intended to control rather than witness from the margins, Hermione stages a number of scenarios designed to reclaim the spotlight. She is unsuccessful, however, and in the end, she commits suicide on the stage set for Pyrrhus' and Andromaque's wedding. Although the motive behind Hermione's action is not all that readily apparent, the very public nature of her self-immolation suggests that neither private grief nor self-recrimination constitutes her primary impulse. The histrionic nature of her suicide dulls its ostensible moral sheen, and transforms its ethical implications into aesthetic ones. In this analysis, I argue that Hermione's suicide constitutes a desperate attempt to write herself into the primary and overriding narrative of the Trojan war. In this pivotal event, Hélène, Pyrrhus and Andromaque played significant roles. Hermione, on the other hand, was wholly excluded. In order to affiliate herself with the predominant legend, Hermione is willing to sacrifice her life in order to forge some link, however tentative, to those celebrated figures of the past. By the violent grafting of her corporal remains onto the staged representation of history in infinite replay, Hermione surrenders to the supremacy of historical imitation.

Self-inflicted death was one of the few forms of violence not barred from the neo-classical stage. Indeed, suicide was deemed more honorable than either debasing captivity, or death by an unworthy adversary. Racine's tragedies contain a number of suicides that can be generally depicted as acts of renunciation. That is to say, the suicide is motivated by an earnest desire to repudiate the world as it is represented on stage. Hermione's suicide, however, does not fit this category. It does not constitute a gesture of true renunciation or a desire to relinquish definitively the theatrical space, but reveals instead a desire to impose herself upon it. Hermione's suicide is not a means of escape, but a means to occupy the theatrical center from where she was displaced by rival Andromaque. Suicide is in fact the only means available to occupy finally the stage with Pyrrhus. It provides her legitimate access to an arena from where she would be otherwise excluded.

For many readers and viewers, however, Hermione's death appears most notable for its total irrelevance. Indeed, it seems to put in relief the very reality that she struggles throughout the tragedy to deny and conceal: her debasing lack of influence. Scorned by the fiancé to whom she is lawfully betrothed, she labors unsuccessfully to rekindle Pyrrhus' passion. Unmoved by her efforts, he stridently takes full responsibility for what he admits is a deliberate breach of contract ("J'épouse une Troyenne. Oui, Madame, et j'avoue / Que je vous ai promis la foi que je lui voue" [1281–82]).[4] He admits to having shamefully courted her rival Andromaque, his prisoner and widow of Hector, an enemy of the state. Pyrrhus' confession only underscores how it is Andromaque, rather than Hermione, who is in full control of the scenario. Hermione can only wait passively while Andromaque decides whether to accept or reject Pyrrhus' amorous overtures, and while Pyrrhus decides whether or not to honor his commitment to Hermione ("Hermione elle-même a vu plus de cent fois / Cet amant irrité revenir sous ses lois" [115–116]).

Hermione's lack of influence over Pyrrhus is not an isolated event. She proves equally unable to command the heart of Oreste. Despite the latter's verbal assurances of undying affection for her ("J'aime: je viens chercher Hermione en ces lieux, / La fléchir, l'enlever, ou mourir à ses yeux" [99–100]), Oreste, unlike Pyrrhus, is reluctant to sacrifice principle to passion. When Pyrrhus' betrayal of Hermione is no longer in doubt, Hermione orders Oreste to avenge her. Once again, however, she is obliged to confront the impotence of her seductive powers. Although Oreste agrees, reluctantly and begrudgingly, to avenge Hermione's honor by killing Pyrrhus, he fails in the end to fulfill his promise. Hermione's fantasies of revenge are

---

4. All references are to Racine, *Oeuvres* (Paris: Les Grands Ecrivains de la France), 1929.

deflected by political realities. Oreste does manage to position his
men in the temple wherein Pyrrhus and Andromaque are to be united
in marriage, but he neither delivers the death blow, nor informs Pyrrhus
that he dies on Hermione's orders. More importantly, perhaps, his
men do not act in time to prevent Pyrrhus' marriage to Andromaque.
The marriage that Hermione so ardently hoped to prevent takes place
after all. In fact, it is the articulation of the marriage vows that provokes Oreste's men to action. Incensed at the spectacle of Pyrrhus
pledging protective allegiance to Andromaque and her son, the Greek
forces slay Pyrrhus as an enemy of the state. Worse yet, Oreste strikes
no blows of any kind on Hermione's behalf ("Et je n'ai pu trouver de
place pour frapper" [1516]), and Pyrrhus dies without knowing
Hermione willed it so. In fact, she could not be further from Pyrrhus'
thoughts ("Madame, il ne voit rien. Son salut et sa gloire / Semblent
être avec vous sortis de sa mémoire" [1449–50]). Pyrrhus dies as
Andromaque's lawfully wedded husband, and he dies at the hands of
political enemies rather than Hermione's avenging lover, Oreste:

> A ces mots, qui du peuple attiroient le suffrage,
> Nos Grecs n'ont répondu que par un cri de rage;
> L'infidèle s'est vu partout envelopper,
> Et je n'ai pu trouver de place pour frapper. (1513–16)

Herimone's lack of influence contrasts sharply with that of
Andromaque whose hold over Pyrrhus is as effortless as it is unwelcome. It will be noted, however, that the heroines differ not only in
the effect they have on Pyrrhus, but in their respective attitudes towards the past. Hermione does not feel morally bound to remain faithful to tradition, to revere historical precedents.[5] Andromaque, on the
other hand, defines herself exclusively by her past commitments.
Andromaque's fidelity to Hector cannot be deterred, not even in death;
Hermione, on the other hand, is unable to commit to a single course

---

5. For Racine, the need to focus on Andromaque's essential fidelity justifies the liberties
taken with some of the dramatic events: "J'ai cru en cela me conformer à l'idée que nous
avons maintenant de cette princesse. La plupart de ceux qui ont entendu parler
d'Andromaque, ne la connoissent guère que pour la veuve d'Hector et pour la mère
d'Astyanax. On ne croit point qu'elle doive aimer ni un autre mari, ni un autre fils" (*Seconde
préface,* 38).

of action or attitude. She was quick to scorn Oreste in favor of Pyrrhus when her father arranged her betrothal to the latter. Confronted with Pyrrhus' preference for Andromaque, she feigns renewed affection for the rejected Oreste ("Enfin qui vous a dit que malgré mon devoir / Je n'ai pas quelquefois souhaité de vous voir?" [527–28]). Her enmity towards Pyrrhus proves no more durable than her affection for Oreste, however. Hermione's volatile inconstancy annoys even her confidante ("Quoi! vous en attendez quelque injure nouvelle?" [422]). Hermione's inability to commit to a sustained point of view even causes Pyrrhus to question the depth of her affection for him. Although she is by all accounts passionately attached to Pyrrhus, he believes that her commitment is motivated more by duty rather than inclination:

> Un autre vous diroit que dans les champs troyens
> Nos deux pères sans nous formèrent ces liens,
> Et que sans consulter ni mon choix ni le vôtre,
> Nous fûmes sans amour engagés l'un à l'autre. (1283–86)
> . . . .
> J'ai craint de vous trahir, peut-être je vous sers.
> Nos coeurs n'étoient point faits dépendants l'un de l'autre;
> Je suivois mon devoir, et vous cédiez au vôtre. (1352–54)

Like Pyrrhus, Oreste has difficulty believing that Hermione's current display of affection for him is genuine. Even though he desperately wants to be deceived by the woman he loves, he pierces effortlessly the porous veil of illusion that is intended to pass for authenticity:

> Et vous le haïssez? Avouez-le, Madame,
> L'amour n'est pas un feu qu'on renferme en une âme:
> Tout nous trahit, la voix, le silence, les yeux. (573–75)

Hermione's inconsistency derives from her preference for living in the ever changing present rather than clinging to the fossilized past. As conditions change, she reveals a readiness to reinvent herself. Rather than remain faithful to commitments made in the past, she prefers to concentrate on manipulating present circumstances to realize her goals. When Oreste suggests that he and Hermione stage a historical re-enactment ("Prenons, en signalant mon bras et votre nom, / Vous, la place d'Hélène, et moi, d'Agamemnon" [1159–60]), Hermione is patently unmoved by the invitation to participate in any historical replay. She remains interested only in forging a new life and future with Pyrrhus. For Hermione, the past represents nothing other than an impediment to forward progress. Her disregard for history reveals itself explicitly when she refuses to acknowledge her moral obligation to repay Andromaque for the latter's assistance to Hermione's mother Hélène during the Trojan war:

> Je conçois vos douleurs. Mais un devoir austere,
> Quand mon père a parlé, m'ordonne de me taire.
> C'est lui qui de Pyrrhus fait agir le courroux.
> S'il faut fléchir Pyrrhus, qui le peut mieux que vous?
> Vos yeux assez longemps ont régné sur son âme.
> Faites-le prononcer: j'y souscrirai, Madame. (881–86)

The notion that past favors require reciprocity is for Hermione wholly incomprehensible. When Andromaque reminds Hermione of her prior assistance to Hélène, Hermione refuses to reciprocate and try to persuade Pyrrhus to spare Astyanax' life.

This textual linking of Andromaque and Hélène serves to bond these ostensible adversaries while further alienating Hermione from both. Andromaque and Hélène are known for their seductive prowess. Andromaque's erotic hold over Pyrrhus leads him to commit political treason; Hélène's influential role in launching the war just ended haunts the general discourse. Hermione's erotic inferiority to both women is rendered even more painfully apparent by contrast. The beauty of Hélène sufficed to launch a legendary conflict; Hermione, on the other hand, is unable to inflame the heart of the man to whom she is legitimately betrothed. Worse yet, she cannot even persuade her former lover to avenge her sullied reputation. Finally, she fails even to persuade Pyrrhus to honor her more modest request that he merely postpone the wedding ("Différez-le d'un jour; demain vous serez maître" [1374]). Pyrrhus refuses to spare her the public humiliation of witnessing his marriage to another by postponing the ceremony even by one day.

The seductive failures of Hermione relative to the successes of her mother serve to differentiate her from her dramatic counterparts, from characters whose link to history is established by their resemblance to ancestral sources. Hermione's link to Hélène is only genealogical. She is "la fille d'Hélène" (245, 342), but she has none of her legendary attributes. She can rival her mother neither in influence nor beauty, and appears destined to remain ever in her shadow. Painfully aware of her own deficiencies, Hermione bemoans her erotic shortcomings:

> Quoi? sans qu'elle employât une seule prière,
> Ma mère en sa faveur arma la Grèce entière?
> Ses yeux pour leur querelle, en dix ans de combats,
> Virent périr vingt rois qu'ils ne connoissoient pas?
> Et moi, je ne prétends que la mort d'un parjure,
> Et je charge un amant du soin de mon injure. (1477–82)

Hermione's fellow characters, on the other hand, link current identity and historical genealogy. The filtering of contemporary reality through a historical prism is accomplished partly through the technique of referring to characters on the basis of lineage rather than name, a poetic strategy that situates them solidly in their historical context.[6] Pyrrhus is proud to be nominally and behaviorally linked to Achille:

> C'est Pyrrhus, c'est le fils et le rival d'Achille,
> Que la gloire à la fin ramène sous ses lois,
> Qui triomphe de Troie une seconde fois. (630–32)

Achille's heroic record inspires Pyrrhus to emulate his father's achievements, to bear heroically and proudly the burdens of his heroic legacy. Andromaque, too, derives her sense of identity from the husband she survives (108, 662, 860), so much so that she prefers

6. The use of familial sources to identify characters has been extensively documented. See, for example, Jeanne Le Hir, "Puissance et prestige du passé dans *Andromaque* de Racine," *Etudes Classiques* 33 (1965), 401; Roland Racevskis, "Generational Transition in *Andromaque*," 64; and Jean-Claude Vuillemin, "Troie/Buthrote: Problématique de l'orgine dans *Andromaque*," *Australian Journal of French Studies* 27 (1990), 11.

death to the notion of altering that fixed identity in any way. All the participants of the war just past seem captivated by its tragic grandeur and link their current identity to an event that has presumably ended. Because of the vital role Hector played in the conflict, even his prisoner-child strikes fear in the hearts of the victorious Greeks. Astyanax assumes this mythic stature solely by virtue of his ancestry. It is the identity of his father that transforms an innocent infant into "l'ennemi de la Grèce" (70). In the eyes of the Greeks, Astyanax is perceived not as a harmless child but as the re-incarnation of his father, Hector.[7] As long as this duplicate Hector survives, the conflict cannot be considered resolved ("Peut-être dans nos ports nous le verrons descendre, / Tel qu'on a vu son père embraser nos vaisseaux" [162–63]).

These ancestral references fuel the impression that the past is more privileged than the future. This reverence for the past seems not merely to obsess the characters, but to beckon them to relive it. Reconnecting with the past, it will be noted, provides a sense of comfort and security. Oreste and Pylade, for example, view their reunion after a long separation as a harbinger of better things to come ("Oui, puisque je retrouve un ami si fidèle, / Ma fortune va prendre une face nouvelle" (1–2). Pylade is pleased to discover that Oreste appears to have conquered his recently acquired "demons" and reverted to the Oreste of old, both politically and emotionally:

> Mais je vous vois, Seigneur; et si jose le dire,
> Un destin plus heureux vous conduit en Épire:
> Le pompeux appareil qui suit ici vos pas
> Nest point d'un malheureux qui cherche le trépas. (21–24)

Oreste has in fact reverted wholly to type. His love for Hermione, a love Pylade assumed was extinguished ("Vous l'abhorriez; enfin vous ne m'en parliez plus. / Vous me trompiez, Seigneur" [36–37]), is revealed to be as intense as ever ("J'aime: je viens chercher

---

7. Notes Ray Bach, in "Fatal Identity: Parents and Children in Racine's *Andromaque*," *Stanford French Review* 16 (1992), 14: "... for his mother, Astyanax is not *like* his father, he *is* his father."

Hermione en ces lieux, / La fléchir, l'enlever, ou mourir à ses yeux" [99–100]). In fact, even Oreste's current mission in Épire is linked directly to past events. He is unable to sacrifice either his former political status or his attachment to Hermione. It is his irrational passion for the "inhumaine" who spurned his affection that explains Oreste's return. If Pyrrhus refuses to relinquish the boy, Hermione, he believes, will be his. Oreste can no more deny his affection for Hermione than deny destiny itself. His love for Hermione is his defining characteristic, his *raison d'être,* past, present, and future:

> Tel est de mon amour l'aveuglement funeste.
> Vous le savez, Madame; et le destin d'Oreste
> Est de venir sans cesse adorer vos attraits,
> Et de jurer toujours qu'il n'y viendra jamais. (481–84)

Oreste, like Pyrrhus, Andromaque, and Astyanax, sees himself as the immutable product of his ancestry. He is, notes Pyrrhus, the very image of his father Agememnon ("Vous y représentez tous les Grecs et son père, / Puisqu'en vous Ménélas voit revivre son frère" [621–22]), a resemblance that Oreste invokes again in a failed attempt to persuade Hermione to re-enact their parent's historical roles:

> Hé bien! allons, Madame:
> Mettons encore un coup toute la Grèce en flamme;
> Prenons, en signalant mon bras et vorte nom,
> Vous, la place d'Hélène, et moi, d'Agamemnon.
> De Troie en ce pays réveillons les misères;
> Et qu'on parle de nous, ainsi que de nos pères. (1157–62)

Oreste is neither willing nor able to move beyond his past, his passion for Hermione. When Pyrrhus suddenly agrees to deliver Astyanax to Oreste and marry Hermione as duty requires, a distraught Oreste threatens to kidnap her. He intends to conjoin their lives by force in the absence of her voluntary consent ("Il faut que je l'enlève, ou bien que je périsse. / Le dessein en est pris, je le veux achever" [714–715]).

Oreste's reverence for the past explains why his one anti-historical act, the plot to assassinate Pyrrhus, hurtles him into madness and despair.[8] Oreste's respect for Pyrrhus is linked to his reverence for the past in general ("Il respecte en Pyrrhus Achille, et Pyrrhus même" [1466]) and to his own ancestral link to their shared history. He is hesitant to commit a dishonorable act that would jeopardize his ancestral legacy, his *générosité:*

> Quoi? pour réponse aux Grecs porterai-je sa tête?
> Et n'ai-je pris sur moi le soin de tout l'État
> Que pour m'en acquitter par un assassinat? (1182–84)

Oreste's promise to assassinate Pyrrhus represents a fundamental break with every value and principle in which he believes, with every link to precedent, save that of his passion for Hermione. In the end, Oreste yields reluctantly to his passion but in so doing, he becomes alien to himself. By turning against past allegiances, he destroys his current identity. Hermione compounds his distress by denouncing the crime he intended to commit on her behalf and in her name. Exiled from the historical past he so revered, and cut off from the future he anticipated and for which he sacrificed his identity, Oreste loses all sense of chronological perspective. Confusing past with present ("Mais que vois-je? A mes yeux Hermione l'embrasse?" [1633]), illusion with reality, he falls into mental collapse.

Like Oreste, Pyrrhus, too, is reluctant to leave the past behind.[9] Although betrothed to Hermione, he is consumed by his passion for

---

8. "Oreste is all the more pathetic when we see that he has lost a sense of who he is and who he is destined to be. A significant part of his emerging madness, then, comes to light in how he situates himself with reference to preceding generations," notes Roland Racevskis, "Generational Transition in *Andromaque*," 67.

9. Many would contest this conclusion and view Pyrrhus as wholly unattached to the past because he is willing to embrace the cause of a historical enemy. As Racevskis points out in "Generational Transition in *Andromaque*," 65, both Oreste and Hermione see Pyrrhus as a rebel, even a traitor. Racevskis himself refers to him as the most liberated from genealogical imperatives. Roland Barthes, *Sur Racine* (Paris: Seuil, 1963), 78 also sees Pyrrhus as an emancipated character, as does Leo Bersani, *A Future for Astyanax: Character and Desire in Literature* (Boston: Little, Brown, and Co., 1976), 49. However, if we see the war as a unified mythological event, one that brings two opposing factions together in one glorious and unforgettable moment, Pyrrhus' embrace of the Trojan cause can be seen as the only means available to perpetuate the "event" itself. In other words, the goal for Pyrrhus is not treason, but to re-engage the battle. Heroism is a function of war, not peace, a fact of which Pyrrhus is only too aware.

Andromaque, a relationship that links him to his most recent victory in battle. Helplessly drawn to this living trophy whose imprisoned existence bears witness to his crowning achievement, Pyrrhus exhibits little enthusiasm for exchanging his glorious past for domesticated contentment as Hermione's husband. Hermione's wedding plans thus fall victim to Pyrrhus' nostalgia for his glory days. Neither her persuasive charms nor her threatened displeasure can persuade Pyrrhus to sever his connection to events that transformed him into a national hero. For Pyrrhus, the uncertain future is no match for the illustrious past wherein his heroism revealed itself on the world's stage. This allows Pyrrhus to view the war just ended with a certain nostalgia, even regret. Compared to the excitement of political mastery and conquest, the post-war peace is a pale substitute. Marriage to Hermione will only distance him further from his past triumphs, leaving Pyrrhus with only fond memories of his past glory. Andromaque, on the other hand, provides Pyrrhus with an opportunity to duplicate, rather than simply recollect, his battlefield exploits. Marriage to Andromaque will allow both to travel back in time to replay, if not re-write, history:

> Madame, dites-moi seulement que j'espère,
> Je vous rends votre fils, et je lui sers de père;
> Je l'instruirai moi-même à venger les Troyens;
> J'irai punir les Grecs de vos maux et des miens.
> Animé d'un regard, je puis tout entreprendre:
> Votre Ilion encor peut sortir de sa cendre. (325–30)

It will be noted that Pyrrhus' references to the war reveal an intoxicating fascination with the brutal art of slaughter:

> Sous tant de morts, sous Troie il falloit l'accabler.
> Tout étoit juste alors: la vieillesse et l'enfance
> En vain sur leur foiblesse appuyoient leur défense;
> La victoire et la nuit, plus cruelles que nous,
> Nous excitoient au meurtre, et confondoient nos coups. (208–12)

Pyrrhus the warrior finds stimulation in violence and mayhem, in conquering an opposing force. Arguably, his passion for Andromaque is fueled in part by her continued resistance, a refusal to surrender that evokes memories of Pyrrhus' defining moment in the heart of the battle. Andromaque becomes a metaphor for this enemy force and her resistance re-ignites his lust for conquest. Pyrrhus sees war and enemy resistance as tests of heroism, as a means to attain distinction by virtue of extraordinary achievements and excessive brutality ("Madame, je sais trop à quels excès de rage / La vengeance d'Hélène emporta mon courage" [1341–42]). The glory of conquest, the legendary battle with Troy, the exhilaration of slaughter and destruction, the thrill of victory prove too intoxicating to resist. Hoping perhaps to surpass his most recent triumph, Pyrrhus envisages the possibility of fighting on behalf of those he defeated, of usurping the role of the fallen warrior Hector himself. Eager to re-engage the conflict in which he so distinguished himself, Pyrrhus vows to duplicate his exploits during his exchange of vows with Andromaque:

> Andromaque, régnez sur l'Épire et sur moi.
> Je voue à votre fils une amitié de père;
> J'en atteste les Dieux, je le jure à sa mère.
> Pour tous mes ennemis je déclare les siens,
> Et je le reconnois pour le roi des Troyens. (1508–12)

In a context wherein historical precedent proves more compelling than the present or future, it is logical that the end of the drama bring us back to the beginning, to a rekindling of the very conflict that Pyrrhus' victory ostensibly resolved. Andromaque's final triumph constitutes a validation of her allegiance to history, her reverence for the past.[10] Of all the characters, she is the most tenaciously committed to refusing all negotiations with a future unlinked to the past. It is the hope of salvaging some remnant of Trojan history that drives Andromaque to consider suicide as a means to safeguard the historical record and to ensure the safety of Hector's living legacy, his child,

---

10. "Cette histoire, toute proche, fraîche et encore toute impregnée de l'odeur des 'murs fumants de Troie' (I, I), domine le texte dramatique d'*Andromaque* et l'enjeu de l'action mise en scène par Racine est, ni plus ni moins, que la possibilité de la resurrection de la citée troyenne," affirms Jean-Claude Vuillemin, "Troie/Buthrote: Problématique de l'origine dans *Andromaque*," 10.

Astyanax, Hector's mimetic reflection:

> C'est Hector, disoit-elle en l'embrassant toujours;
> Voilà ses yeux, sa bouche, et déjà son audace;
> C'est lui-même, cest toi, cher époux, que j'embrasse. (652–54)

His life must be preserved in order that history survive.[11] To keep the past alive, Andromaque commissions Céphise to make certain that the child is made to remember his past:

> Fais connoître à mon fils les héros de sa race;
> Autant que tu pourras, conduis-le sur leur trace.
> Dis-lui par quels exploits leurs noms ont éclaté,
> Plutôt ce qu'ils ont fait que ce qu'ils ont été;
> Parle-lui tous les jours des vertus de son père;
> Et quelquefois aussi parle-lui de sa mère. (1113–18)

Andromaque's commitment to preserving the past explains both her fidelity to Hector and her intense contempt for Pyrrhus. Although she is currently Pyrrhus' captive and the object of his sadistic threats and impossible ultimatums, Andromaque despises Pyrrhus more for past crimes than his present brutality. It is the recollection of Pyrrhus amidst the carnage of war that fuels her most bitter enmity towards her captor. Andromaque's most unyielding hatred is reserved for Pyrrhus the warrior, rather than Pyrrhus, the captor, or even Pyrrhus, the would-be child-killer:

> Songe, songe, Céphise, à cette nuit cruelle
> Qui fut pour tout un peuple une nuit éternelle.
> Figure-toi Pyrrhus, les yeux étincelants,
> Entrant à la lueur de nos palais brûlants,
> Sur tous mes frères morts se faisant un passage,
> Et de sang tout couvert échauffant le carnage.
> Songe aux cris des vainqueurs, songe aux cris des mourants,

---

11. In his article, *"Andromaque:* l'envers du discours racinien," *Stanford French Review* (1985), 125, John E. Jackson notes that the death of Hector is living theater: "Troie devient ainsi le théâtre, ou si l'on préfère la métaphore, de l'Autre, je veux dire le théâtre où la métaphore de la réalité *contre laquelle* tout l'art de Racine consiste à édifier sa pièce, le lieu où les paramètres qui guident sa façon d'écrire rencontrent leur limite et même leur envers."

Dans la flamme étouffés, sous le fer expirants.
Peins-toi dans ces horreurs Andromaque éperdue:
Voilà comme Pyrrhus vint s'offrir à ma vue;
Voilà par quels exploits il sut se couronner;
Enfin voilà l'époux que tu me veux donner. (997–1008)

In the end, Andromaque agrees to marry Pyrrhus to preserve the past that Astyanax represents. In order to ensure the survival of the historical record, she is willing to destroy herself, her present and future. When Pyrrhus' assassination renders her suicide unnecessary, she promises to avenge both Hector and Pyrrhus. The final image, then, is that of the past reincarnated, of the conflict between Greece and Troy re-igniting, with no visible end in sight:

Aux ordres d'Andromaque ici tout est soumis;
Ils la traitent en reine, et nous comme ennemis.
Andromaque elle-même, à Pyrrhus si rebelle,
Lui rend tous les devoirs d'une veuve fidèle,
Commande qu'on le venge, et peut-être sur nous
Veut venger Troie encore et son premier époux. (1587–92)

For Hermione, Andromaque's victory constitutes a tragic epiphany. Her attempt to make Pyrrhus pay for his infidelity with his life only demonstrates her persistent lack of influence and her inability to move the scenario forward, beyond the frame of history. Oreste's revelation that Pyrrhus dies in Greece's name rather than hers underscores definitively and irrevocably her own historical alienation, her lack of resemblance both to her mother, Hélène, and to her rival, Andromaque. Unlike Andromaque, whose power over Pyrrhus is total, and unlike her mother, whose singular beauty provoked an armed conflict of epic proportions, Hermione is unable to forge a personal legacy for future generations to appreciate. Oreste's affection for Hermione is tepid by the standard set by Pyrrhus for Andromaque. It is only with great reluctance that he finally agrees to commit an action that will at once rid him of his rival and place Hermione forever in his debt. Even then, he fails to honor his commitment to her. Oreste's men slay Pyrrhus after, rather than before, his marriage to Andromaque, and Hermione's role in the assassination is never even articulated. Pyrrhus, who shamelessly abandons Hermione for Andromaque, dies in Greece's name rather than hers. He dies wholly ignorant of her failed role in his assassination.

In the end, Hermione is isolated from the rest of her compatriots obsessed with the past and the important role they played in it. Pyrrhus' death serves only to further relegate Hermione to the margins of history by rekindling the war Hélène started in the first place. Worse yet, Hermione learns that her rival Andromaque is leading the re-enactment of history, moving Hermione even further away from the center stage she covets. Because Hermione has no immediate link to the legend that bonds the others, she is completely and irrevocably alienated as the play comes to an end. Despite her diligent efforts, Hermione finds herself on the verge of being eradicated from the very scenario in which she expected to play a central role.

Rather than accept scenic erasure, however, Hermione rushes to the scene of tragedy in order to establish some link, however contrived, to the past that so consumes the others. Her suicide, then, constitutes not a gesture of renunciation but rather a final effort to connect with the legend. Before Pyrrhus' body can be removed from the temple, and in full view of those who witnessed his marriage to Andromaque, Hermione stabs herself over the body of the man who betrayed her. Suicide offers Hermione one last opportunity to link her identity with Pyrrhus, to insert herself into the legend that defined him. This final gesture allows her to be united finally with her beloved. Her suicide, designed for maximum public exposure, guarantees Hermione at least a footnote in the historical record, a reference that Andromaque's and Pyrrhus' marriage very nearly effaced entirely.

The motive behind Hermione'suicide invites close scrutiny. Despite Hermione's efforts to recast Pyrrhus as an amorous rather than a political traitor, he dies as a result of his betrayal of Greece, not Hermione:

> A ces mots, qui du peuple attiroient le suffrage,
> Nos Grecs n'ont répondu que par un cri de rage;
> L'infidèle s'est vu partout envelopper. (1513–15)

She bears, therefore, no responsibility for his death. Consequently, remorse can hardly be ascribed as the motive for Hermione's suicide. Hermione can neither take, nor be assigned, any culpable role in the slaying. Oreste, the only soldier motivated by passion rather than patriotism, does not succeed in even touching Pyrrhus body ("Et je n'ai pu trouver de place pour frapper" [1516]). Nor is it likely that despair over the loss of Pyrrhus to Andromaque, an event she seems finally to accept as inevitable ("Achevez votre hymen, j'y consens" [1371]), motivates her action. Moreover, even if we were to accept that sorrow for the death of the man she loved, or repentance for having willed it so, constitute the main reasons for her suicide, this would still not explain the histrionic manner of her death. The decision to stab herself in such a public arena suggests that this gesture is more theatrical than repentant. On the very altar where she hoped to inaugurate her future with Pyrrhus, on the stage whereupon history is re-incarnated, Hermione makes a final and decisive attempt to avoid total irrelevance.

Having failed throughout to establish any credible link to the legendary past, Hermione surrenders to the power of history by publicly stabbing herself over Pyrrhus' corpse. On the sacred stage that was to usher in a new era uniting Pyrrhus and Hermione, Hermione elects to sacrifice her future in order to forge a permanent link to Pyrrhus' past. Hermione's suicide represents an acknowledgement of the triumph of history, its superiority to the present. Correlatively speaking, Hermione's death represents the failure of creative invention and innovation. Hermione's repeated attempts to re-create herself for the situation at hand convey an impression of volatility and instability that contrasts unfavorably with the durability and the comforting familiarity of history. Unable to realize her dream of a future with Pyrrhus, Hermione elects finally to commit suicide on the stage of his betrayal in order to weave her identity into the fabric of history. In death, Hermione can finally stake a claim within the coveted legend and its never-ending replay in theatrical eternity. Significantly, this self-destructive impulse, enacted in a public arena, metatextually establishes a link between history and theatrical legitimacy, one of the basic tenets of neo-classical dramatic theory.

CHAPTER 7

Phèdre or the Triumph of Law

Neo-classical doctrine was intended to discover and codify the precise aesthetic elements that would yield the highest quality aesthetic artefact. That ultimate goal convinced most playwrights to accept the necessity of incorporating dramaturgical rules into their works. Despite some resistance to theory, Pierre Corneille was the first successful dramatist to deliberately and successfully incorporate neo-classical aesthetic theories into the construction of his tragedies, a decision that changed the course of French theater and paved the way for his rival Racine's success. The rather harsh critique of *Le Cid* by members of the *Académie Française* seemed to put Corneille at odds with the academicians, distorting significantly Corneille's sincere commitment to the cause of regularizing French tragedy, that is to say, to minimizing its baroque tendencies. Compared to the tragedies preceding it, and even some penned by Corneille himself, *Le Cid* marks a turning point in the quest to perfect French tragedy. Arguably, it was because, rather than in spite of, Corneille's incorporation of dramatic theory into his early tragedies that *Le Cid* proved so popular with audiences. Had the author ignored the basic tenets of neo-classical theater, *Le Cid* would have found no zealous support from sophisticated theater-goers eager to dispute the harsh criticism of the Academy. Nevertheless, it is no less true that Corneille, certainly in comparison to Racine, seemed to be in a constant struggle with academic imperatives, even when surrendering to their necessity.

Corneille's belabored conformity is in sharp contrast to Racine's apparent ease with following neo-classical directives. Whereas Corneille's theater seemed always to betray the writer's difficulty reining in the creative spirit in order to respect dramaturgical rules, Racine's tragedies revealed no trace of revolt against prescribed regulations. The academic rules so problematic for Corneille were, by all appearances and accounts, embraced by Racine. In fact, his tragedies seemed to justify the Academy's conviction that theater benefitted when classical theory was coupled with successful contemporary dramatic practice. Clearly, the established dramatic principles worked in Racine's favor, and contributed significantly to augmenting his tragedies' merits. His plays demonstrated that respect for conventions yielded a heightened dramatic experience for spectators, and resulted in greater admiration and renown for the theaterician. In short, Racine owed his theatrical success to his respect for the rules of dramatic convention. Corneille's less regular tragedies may have paved the way for French neo-classical tragedy, but it is Racine's chiseled and flawless masterpieces that now serve as its most perfected example.

In the preceding chapter, Hermione's suicide was cast as a metatextual triumph of the dramaturgical doctrine of imitation (the obligation to repeat heralded texts of the past) over innovation (Hermione's fantasized scenario of an unscripted future with Pyrrhus). It was, I argued, a public surrender to the primacy of the past, and was in this sense not a renunciation *per se,* but rather an attempt by Hermione to inject herself into the legendary narrative that excluded her. Phèdre's suicide, too, can be interpreted as an attempt to renegotiate her legitimacy on center stage, a legitimacy she surrendered by violating conventional codes of conduct. It is from this vantage point that *Phèdre,* judged by many to be the pinnacle of French neo-classical theatrical achievement, can be read, like *Andromaque,* as a defense of neo-classical theatrical doctrine.[1] In *Phèdre,* a link can be forged between the rule of law established by Thésée, and the theatrical rules established by the *Académie.*[2] For both, imposed regulations are intended to keep the forces of chaos, political on the one hand, aesthetic on the other, at bay, far removed from the scenic center. The attempt to disregard or suspend these laws leads inevitably to political and scenic disorder.

1. In an extremely perceptive and interesting article, "Noble Deeds and the Secret Singularity: *Hamlet* and *Phèdre,*" *Canadian Review of Comparative Literature* 18 (1991), 281, Paul Morrison also links moral and theatrical decorum in *Phèdre:* "It is difficult to separate, however, the 'désordre' that the play dramatizes, the tension between Phèdre's desire and her moral restraint, from the conventions that govern dramatization itself."
2. Judd D. Hubert in "Les écarts de Trézène," *Relectures raciniennes: Nouvelles approches du discours tragique,* ed. Richard L. Barnett (Paris: PFSCL, 1986), 82, establishes a link between political and scenic order as well: "Or, Racine nous montre en Trézène le foyer même de l'ordre et de l'harmonie au sein d'une tragédie où dominent les thèmes conjugués de la monstruosité et de la violence."

The absence of order resulting from Thésée's reported death prompts Phèdre and Hippolyte to supplant legitimate and conventional practices with illicit fantasies.[3] When both learn that Thésée is no longer in control, they emerge from the shadows of power to propose rogue scenarios of their own design. Regulations previously enforced are relaxed, if not ignored outright. The rebel fantasies of Hippolyte and Phèdre, unstructured and unregulated, violate the letter and spirit of established moral, political, and even aesthetic conventions. Predictably, both scenarios prove wholly unrepresentable. The repudiation of laws, we are led to conclude, does not engender a more liberated, more just, or more satisfying spectacle, but results rather in unnecessary tragedy, chaos, and self destruction. Upon his return, Thésée is obliged to restore political, moral and aesthetic order by somehow transforming the fragmented fantasies of Hippolyte and Phèdre into legitimate theater. A repentant Phèdre comes before Thésée to commit suicide in atonement for her role in the tragic sequence of events. Her suicide purifies the scenic space and allows Thésée to rehabilitate Hippolyte's rebellious scenario by adopting Aricie into his political family. Phèdre's self-destructive *mea culpa,* then, is no more a gesture of renunciation than was Hermione's. It constitutes instead a deliberate theatrical gesture designed to re-legitimize her place on center stage. Phèdre's public suicide gives her access to an arena from which she would otherwise be barred as a result of her transgressions. Phèdre's final entrance allows her to denounce the transgressive disorder caused by her unregulated performance, and thereby transform the catastrophic consequences of her actions into redemptive, cathartic theater.

When news of Thésée's death reaches Trézène, Hippolyte is the first to enact a sequence of unauthorized scenarios that not only break existing laws, but that actually repudiate the necessity for the law as well.[4] His avowal of affection to Aricie constitutes a legal infraction;

---

3. Louise Horowitz notes in "Racine's Laws," *Dalhousie French Studies* 49 (1999), 132, that *Phèdre* demonstrates a fixation with the law and the disintegration of authority that results from Thésée's absence.
4. In the interpretation of Judd Hubert, "Les écarts de Trézène," 84, Hippolyte was looking for a "new role" even before he learned about his father's death.

his proposal that the two become political allies implies that Thésée erred in establishing the law in the first place. Thésée forbids Aricie to marry because he hopes to prevent the procreation of future rivals to the throne ("Jamais les feux d'hymen ne s'allument pour elle" [110])[5]. The Pallantides were overthrown by Thésée in his quest to control Athens, seat of political, and interestingly enough, aesthetic, authority. By destroying all descendants of the Pallantide family, Thésée can diminish the potential for political anarchy by safeguarding his political legitimacy. Hippolyte, however, does not share his father's concern for political order and security. In one impassioned moment, Hippolyte liberates the forces of potential chaos first by courting the family's political enemy, and then by offering to give her a share of the realm. Before confessing his love to Aricie, a woman legally prohibited from marrying anyone, he proposes a treasonous political alliance. Thésée's death leaves Greece with three competing and viable successors to the throne: Hippolyte, Phèdre's elder son, and Aricie herself. Hippolyte offers to withdraw from contention in order to allow his supporters to align themselves with Aricie's ("L'Attique est votre bien. Je pars, et vais pour vous / Réunir tous les voeux partagés entre nous" [507–08]).

Hippolyte attempts to justify his offer to restore Aricie's political legitimacy by maintaining that Thésée's law had no moral authority. What Thésée perceived as political security, Hippolyte sees as unjust cruelty. His own right to inherit the throne, like Aricie's, is threatened by unjust and discriminatory laws ("Je sais, sans vouloir me flatter, / Qu'une superbe loi semble me rejeter. / La Grèce me reproche une mère étrangère" [487–89]). Nevertheless, Hippolyte believes he is a worthy successor to Thésée :

> Mais si pour concurrent je n'avois que mon frère,
> Madame, j'ai sur lui de véritables droits
> Que je saurois sauver du caprice des lois. (490–92)

---

5. All references are to Racine, *Oeuvres* (Paris: Les Grands Ecrivains de la France), 1929.

Aricie's status as political outsider is cast as equally arbitrary. Consequently, the political alienation of Hippolyte and Aricie serves to unite these two outsiders, and prompts Hippolyte to liberate Aricie. In fact, the first action he takes upon hearing the news of Thésée's death is to declare an end to his father's sanctions against a potential political rival ("Je puis vous affranchir d'une austère tutelle. / Je révoque des lois dont j'ai plaint la rigueur" [474–75]).

After overturning an established legal interdiction, Hippolyte then proceeds to argue for an authority based on personal sentiment rather than national security. Not only does he assert that the law he set aside had no compelling relevance or justification, but he asserts further that passion rather than politics should determine the state's priorities. His commitment to passion suggests at first glance a link between father and son, but the resemblance is only apparent. Thésée is careful not to allow his sexual exploits to interfere with his political duties. Hippolyte makes no such distinction, and offers political power in exchange for physical satisfaction. For Hippolyte, when the laws of the heart enter into conflict with the laws of the state, he is fully prepared to assert the primacy of the former over the latter. It will be revealed that Hippolyte's suspension of Thésée's prohibition against Aricie's possible marriage has less to do with a passion for justice than passion for Aricie herself. Moreover, there is evidence to suggest that the intensity of his feelings derives in part from the forbidden nature of the relationship. The undisciplined Hippolyte, accustomed to living in an unregulated environment, appears ill-equipped to deal with external restraints of any sort. Even Théramène believes Hippolyte's passion is more the result of rebellious defiance than personal attraction:

Thésée ouvre vos yeux en voulant les fermer;
Et sa haine, irritant une flamme rebelle,
Prête à son ennemie une grâce nouvelle. (116–18)

Once Thésée's death is reported, Hippolyte makes no effort to subordinate his passion to political necessity. Although his feelings for Aricie are in conflict with legal statutes, patriotic principles, familial duty, prior responsibilities and pleasurable pastimes, he remains fully committed only to his emotional impulses. He even ceases tending his beloved horses:

> On vous voit moins souvent orgueilleux et sauvage,
> Tantôt faire voler un char sur le rivage,
> Tantôt, savant dans l'art par Neptune inventé,
> Rendre docile au frein un coursier indompté. (129–32)

More dangerous still, Hippolyte's infatuation causes him to abandon his spiritual commitments. Both Neptune ("Mon arc, mes javelots, mon char, tout m'importune; / Je ne me souviens plus des leçons de Neptune" [549–50]), and Diane, Goddess of the hunt and of chastity, are obliged to yield to Venus in the mind-set of an infatuated Hippolyte. What Hippolyte advocates by his surrender to passion is essentially the establishment of a lawless realm, one free from the constraints of oppressive regulations, from the necessity of self-discipline, from paternal influence, from order itself. His decision to ally himself with Aricie effectively supplants the legitimate rule of the father with the chaos of illicit passion. Indeed, he surrenders completely to his emotional impulses:

> Un frein plus légitime arrête mon audace:
> Je vous cède, ou plutôt je vous rends une place,
> Un sceptre que jadis vos aïeux ont reçu
> De ce fameux mortel que la terre a conçu. (493–96)

When Hippolyte first became aware of his feelings, his first reaction was one of shame. Hippolyte feared to present himself upon the sacred stage of political legitimacy where laws were based on historical precedent and where acting on impulse was deemed harmful to the society at large. Ashamed of his amorous feelings for Aricie, Hippolyte isolated himself on the outskirts of power in order to avoid Thésée's critical eye. Loathe to allow his unlawful desires to sully the integrity of Thésée's stage, he used his father's absence as a pretext for departure. His real goal, however, was to avoid further temptation by Aricie ("Je fuis, je l'avoûrai, cette jeune Aricie, / Reste d'un sang fatal conjuré contre nous" [50–51]).

At the report of Thésée's death, however, Hippolyte's shame

evaporates. Emboldened by his new-found freedom, he forms an alliance with Aricie, his father's enemy and the object of his affection. In his initial encounter with Aricie, he reveals by his naiveté and lack of sophistication his fundamental unsuitability for the intricate complexity of political theater. His awkwardness explicitly in evidence, he apologizes for his woefully apparent lack of experience as he tries to take his father's place on center stage:

> Songez que je vous parle une langue étrangère;
> Et ne rejetez pas des voeux mal exprimés,
> Qu'Hippolyte sans vous n'auroit jamais formés. (558–60)

Whereas the first consequence of Thésée's death was Hippolyte's political treason, the second is his rather primitive aesthetic effort. His poetic *coup d'essai* wherein passion takes precedence over duty is awash in neo-platonic figures and is overfreighted with literary clichés. He is love's prisoner ("Je vous laisse aussi libre, et plus libre que moi" [480]; "Aux fers de ses captifs" [532]); his love is in defiance of reason ("Je vois que la raison cède à la violence" [525]); he is love's wounded prey ("Portant partout le trait dont je suis déchiré" [540]). Hippolyte's discursive manner hearkens back to a prior literary age, a time before neo-classical constraints and prescriptive conformity.[6] His desire to serve the beloved situates him in the courtly love tradition rather than the neo-classical age. Hippolyte's love for Aricie, then, defies the rule of the father in both its political (Thésée's laws) and aesthetic (Aristotle's poetics) manifestations. From this vantage point, it is particularly significant that the woman selected by Hippolyte to preside over the new "deregulated" Athens, Aricie, is a purely fictional character with no mythological or literary pedigree whatsoever.

---

6. Even his offering the crown to Aricie suggests a return to the notion of pure origin, suggests Richard Goodkin in "Thomas Corneille's *Ariane* and Racine's *Phèdre:* The Older Sister Strikes Back," *Esprit Créateur* 38 (1998), 60–71. See also the article by Elissa Marder, "The Mother Tongue in *Phèdre* and *Frankenstein,*" *Yale French Studies* 76 (1989), 59: "The question of origins and the implicit impossibility of speaking about them is articulated through the figure of an absent mother who dictates and engenders the texts that circumscribe her absence."

Hippolyte's transgressions of Thésée's laws intersect with Phèdre's attempt to stage an illicit scenario of her own. For Phèdre, as for Hippolyte, Thésée's disappearance emboldens her to negotiate a more prominent place for herself in the developing crisis. Phèdre's decision to re-insert herself into the political fray constitutes a significant change of attitude. When the tragedy opened, Phèdre expressed only a desire for seclusion and shadows:

> Lasse enfin d'elle-même et du jour qui l'éclaire. (46)
> . . . .
> Elle veut voir le jour; et sa douleur profonde
> M'ordonne toutefois d'écarter tout le monde . . . (149–50)

She was particularly eager to avoid Hippolyte ("Je l'évitois partout" [289]). Ashamed of her illicit and immoral attraction to her step-son, she sought to elude the spotlight of public scrutiny and inevitable disgrace.

Phèdre regards her passion for Hippolyte as an unspeakable failing ("J'ai conçu pour mon crime une juste terreur" [307]), a fantasy so scandalous it requires darkness and isolation even to be contemplated. She labors, therefore, to keep her desire unseen and unspoken, even were such silence to cause her death ("Je meurs, pour ne point faire un aveu si funeste" [226]). Phèdre acknowledges that her attraction to Hippolyte violates all established legal and moral precepts, that her illicit passion renders her unfit to serve in her assigned role as Thésée's wife and queen. In consequence, she feels obliged to distance herself from the political limelight. Her unsuitability for her current role is metatextually affirmed by her discomfort with her theatrical garments and accoutrements:[7]

> Que ces vains ornements, que ces voiles me pèsent!
> Quelle importune main, en formant tous ces noeuds,
> A pris soin sur mon front d'assembler mes cheveux? (158–60)

Phèdre's initial motive for appearing on stage at all is to announce her imminent withdrawal from public view, to surrender, as it were, her

---

7. See also, Judd Hubert, "Les écarts de Trézène," 90.

"spectacle" status.[8] Weary of posturing, of performing a role for which she is no longer worthy or suited, she expresses the desire to retreat in order take private pleasure in a fantasy as intoxicating as it is taboo:

> Dieux! que ne suis-je assise à l'ombre des forêts!
> Quand pourrai-je, au travers d'une noble poussière,
> Suivre de l'oeil un char fuyant dans la carrière? (176–78)

The world Phèdre renounces, it bears repeating, is the legitimate world of inherited political power, marital fidelity, and moral rectitude. As Thésée's wife she is bound strictly by the laws of marriage and state ("Sous les lois de l'hymen" [270]), laws that require sexual and political fidelity. Her passion for Hippolyte is therefore triply transgressive in that it violates moral (it is incestuous), sexual (it is adulterous) and political regulations (Hyppolyte's foreign-born mother disqualifies him from sharing the throne with her). Moreover, her lust for Hippolyte constitutes a significant breach of paternal honor. Phèdre is the daughter of Minos whose judicious rationality earns him the right to determine verdicts and pronounce judgments. She shudders at the thought of her father's reaction to the report of his daughter's shameful conduct:

> Minos juge aux enfers tous les pâles humains.
> Ah! combien frémira son ombre épouvantée,
> Lorsqu'il verra sa fille à ses yeux présentée. (1280–82)

Phèdre's passion, like Hippolyte's, is unlawful. Only Phèdre's passion has the additional taint of being immoral and unnatural, however. Indeed, Phèdre's lust violates nature's laws more than man's. So morally repugnant is Phèdre's sexual fantasy that she is able to articulate it only upon the insistent probing of her confidante, Oenone. Oenone encourages Phèdre to verbalize what she has heretofore refused to acknowledge publicly. Surrendering finally to Oenone's pleas, Phèdre reveals her secret passion, only to discover that its linguistic

---

8. Elizabeth Berg also links Phèdre's renunciation of costume to a broader desire to usurp the masculine right of center stage in her article "Impossible Representation: A Reading of *Phèdre*," *Romanic Review* 73 (1982), 421–37.

rendition renders it even more offensive. The articulated representation of Phèdre and Hippolyte in amorous union disgusts even the indulgent Oenone. Her assurances of support give way to shrieks of horror. ("O désespoir! ô crime! ô déplorable race!" [266]).

The separate reactions to the confessions of love made by Hippolyte to Aricie and Phèdre to Hippolyte reveal an important distinction between the transgressions involved. Hippolyte's love for Aricie violates his father's law, but not the laws of nature. There is nothing inherently repugnant about his attraction to Aricie. Consequently, its discovery by Théramène provokes no howls of outrage. On the contrary, both Théramène and Aricie react rather positively to Hippolyte's revelation. Théramène even assures Hippolyte that his feelings are not only natural, but inevitable ("Ah! Seigneur, si votre heure est une fois marquée, / Le ciel de nos raisons ne sait point s'informer" [114–15]). Aricie, too, expresses approval for Hippolyte's declaration of affection ("Mais cet empire enfin si grand, si glorieux, / N'est pas de vos présents le plus cher à mes yeux" [575–76]). Hippolyte's love for Aricie may threaten to destabilize political security, and it may violate neo-classical ideology by subordinating reason to passion, but his declaration of affection does not offend his audience's sensitivities. Phèdre's, on the other, offends both Oenone, and Hippolyte as well.

The reported death of Thésée softens Oenone's opposition to Phèdre's fantasy-scenario. Oenone considers Thésée's death to be an exculpation of her mistress. Now that Phèdre is a widow, Oenone is of the opinion that a relationship between Phèdre and her step son is now feasible. In fact, Oenone maintains that a union is now not only possible, but ordinary ("une flamme ordinaire" [350]).[9] Oenone, like Théramène, believes that sexual attraction is wholly natural. Now that Phèdre's bonds to Thésée are broken, her love for Hippolyte must be considered from an entirely different perspective. Oenone

9. "C'est ainsi que, dans *Phèdre,* la 'mort' de Thésée pousse Oenone à transformer 'la flamme si noire' de sa maîtresse en une 'flamme ordinaire' (I, 5, v. 350). Elle trivialise, de la sorte, l'existence héroïque de Phèdre; elle 'démythologise' cette passion en la ramenant à l'anonymat," comments Ralph Albanese, Jr. in "Dramatrugie classique et codes idéologiques: Le cas racine," *Relectures Raciniennes: Nouvelles approches du discours tragique,* ed. Richard L. Barnett (Paris: PFSCL, 1986), 23.

counsels her mistress to consider new laws in response to her new situation ("Mais ce nouveau malheur vous prescrit d'autres lois" [340]). There is, she argues, no need to respect the laws of Thésée's reign in the absence of Thésée himself. The primary benefit of Thésée's death, then, at least from Oenone's perspective, is the behavioral anarchy it sanctions.

Oenone's reasoning has one significant and overriding flaw, however. Her arguments do not take into account the power of prejudice to override legality. The preoccupation with legal technicalities blinds Oenone to the more problematic judgment of public opinion. From a strictly legal perspective, Phèdre may now be free to marry another man, but marriage to this particular man, Hippolyte, has the taint of incest about it. The law may sanction such a union, but moral decency does not. What is legal and what is tolerable are clearly two very different entities, something the rules of the *bienséances* explicitly acknowledge. Despite Oenone's optimistic appraisal of Phèdre's changed situation, Thésée's death does not alter the public's attitude towards morality or propriety. The citizens remain as conservative as ever. In fact, shortly after Thésée's death is announced, his constituents affirm their commitment to his moral authority by supporting his and Phèdre's elder son as heir to the throne. Aricie's and Hippolyte's illegitimate status is affirmed by the public. The status quo is therefore enthusiastically reclaimed:

> Mais Athènes, Seigneur, s'est déjà déclarée.
> Ses chefs ont pris les voix de toutes ses tribus.
> Votre frère l'emporte, et Phèdre a le dessus. (722–24)

The distinction between the licit and the undecorous is significant, I believe, for it casts Phèdre's continuing pursuit of Hippolyte as an aesthetic, as well as a moral, transgression. Yielding to Oenone's rational assurances that she is now free to love Hippolyte, Phèdre decides to confront him. Phèdre's confession of love for her step-son violates not only established moral law (the prohibition against incest), but neo-classical aesthetic laws as well. By center-staging the common ("une flamme ordinaire") and the indecorous (incest), Phèdre sullies the noble character of the stage on which she has been called upon to perform. Even more serious aesthetic infractions are revealed by the poetic manner of the celebrated "aveu" itself. Not only is the subject of her discourse morally offensive, but its articulation violates established literary conventions. To begin with, Phèdre casts herself as Hippolyte's subordinate, an inversion of the courtly love tradition that Hippolyte's confession of love to Aricie exemplifies. The typical courtly lover is of course a male, like Hippolyte, who serves as "vassal" to a woman of superior rank, a woman he loves and admires, yet fears to approach. Phèdre's improperly submissive salutation to Hippolyte (whom she thrice calls her "Seigneur"), set off by poetic enjambement for heightened dramatic effect, inverts this paradigm. Phèdre is an impassioned woman who subordinates herself to an indifferent male, one who is in fact her political inferior. Whereas literary tradition sanctions the co-presence of heroism and subordination to the meritorious beloved in males, there is no corresponding literary model for a female heroine subordinating herself to an inferior male.[10] The role of the heroine is limited to inspiring passion, generally platonic, as a result of the nobility of her character. Phèdre's bold attempt to invert the courtly love paradigm by her sexual aggressiveness lays stress upon her aesthetic impropriety. Her frank eroticism defies all expectations for female behavior. It has no credible or respectable model in the literary arena.

Predictably, Hippolyte's reaction to Phèdre's discourse is one of stunned incredulity. The content of her message is so lacking in *bienséance* that it lacks verisimilitude as well, rendering her message virtually incomprehensible to her intended audience. Hippolyte labors at first to reinscribe Phèdre's audacious affirmations ("Si la haine peut seule attirer votre haine, / Jamais femme ne fut plus digne de pitié" [606–07]; "Il n'est point mort, puisqu'il respire en vous"

---

10. Jean Michel Pelous comments on the romanesque normality of Hippolyte's passion versus the abnormality of Phèdre's in "Métaphores et figures de l'amour dans la *Phèdre* de Racine," *Travaux de Linguistique et de Littérature*," 19, 2 (1981), 75: "La passion par une nécessité de sa nature viole toutes les règles du jeu de l'amour. L'aveu que Phèdre fait à Hippolyte, honteux et involontaire selon ses propres termes, achève de bouleverser l'économie du système. Ce manquement grave à la réserve féminine est l'aboutissement d'une scandaleuse inversion des rôles: Phèdre s'humilie sans profit parce qu'il n'appartient pas à son sexe de s'humilier."

[627]) into something less audacious. With each of Hippolyte's attempts to vacate Phèdre's words of their intended significance, she becomes ever more offensively explicit with each clarification. Hippolyte persists in misinterpreting her remarks until her lusty scenario explodes with paroxysmic clarity ("Et Phèdre au Labyrinthe avec vous descendue / Se seroit avec vous retrouvée, ou perdue" [661–62]). Even then, an embarrassed Hippolyte refuses to acknowledge fully the reality of what he hears ("Madame, pardonnez. J'avoue, en rougissant, / Que j'accusois à tort un discours innocent" [667–69]). Ultimately, Phèdre's discourse becomes too explicit to re-script, however. His shocked reaction to her *aveu* underscores the degree to which Phèdre's offensive discourse violates acceptable standards of decorum. Frustrated in turn by Hippolyte's reaction, Phèdre commits a final sequence of even more blatant "theatrical" transgressions. She invites Hippolyte to commit a violent act on stage ("Voilà mon coeur. C'est là que ta main doit frapper" [704]); she violates the sanctity of his theatrical space by reaching for his sword, and she commits an infraction against the rules of the *bienséances* by brandishing this unsheathed weapon of destruction in full view of the spectators.[11]

Despite Hippolyte's obvious dismay, Phèdre is not quite ready to concede defeat. Although Oenone is quick to interpret Hippolyte's reaction as a non-negotiable condemnation ("Avec quels yeux cruels sa rigueur obstinée / Vous laissoit à ses pieds peu s'en faut prosternée!" [777–78]), Phèdre remains committed to the scenario. Perhaps, she theorizes, the avant-garde nature of her discourse proved too unsettling for her unsophisticated audience ("Peut-être sa surprise a causé son silence" [785]). In other words, Phèdre believes it was not so much the content of her message that proved distasteful, but rather the naiveté of the recipient or even the manner of delivery. She believes that if the same message were to be presented in a different

11. "In Racine, however, hands never quite touch the body, although the sense of a taboo nearly violated, contact nearly made, accounts for the intense erotic energy of the scene. But the question remains: precisely what taboo? The prohibition against incest, and thus a psycho-sexual taboo? Or the prohibition against touching on stage, and thus a theatrical taboo?" ponders Paul Morrison, "Noble Deeds and the Secret Singularity," 281.

format, it would have a more pleasing effect ("Cherchons pour l'attaquer quelque endroit plus sensible" [794]). Phèdre therefore commissions Oenone to re-script the scenario using a more conventional format and a more restrained delivery:

> Tes discours trouveront plus d' accès que les miens.
> Presse, pleure, gémis; plains-lui Phèdre mourante;
> Ne rougis point de prendre une voix suppliante. (808–10)

Thésée's reappearance puts an abrupt end to Phèdre's efforts to rescript her audacious scenario. His return serves to reinstate the legal ordinances and moral authority that were in place prior to his departure, the same laws and moral codes that both Hippolyte and Phèdre have been attempting to overturn. His unanticipated reappearance leaves Oenone with the difficult task of legitimizing Phèdre's transgressive behaviors. Fearful that Hippolyte will reveal Phèdre's actions to Thésée, Oenone and Phèdre invent a fictional scenario intended to counter reality. The fictional scenario proposed, unlike the reality it is designed to mask, relies heavily on conventional literary assumptions to make the point. In Oenone's constructed version of events, Hippolyte becomes the aggressor, and Phèdre the unwilling victim, a scenario more in line with courtly love traditions. Because this fictional construct is so much more credible than the reality it supplants, Oenone is convinced that the success of their strategy is assured:

> Qui vous démentira? Tout parle contre lui:
> Son épée en vos mains heureusement laissée,
> Votre trouble présent, votre douleur passée,
> Son père par vos cris dès longtemps prévenu,
> Et déjà son exil par vous-même obtenu. (888–92)

In Oenone's scenario, Hippolyte is assigned the more believable role of impassioned courtier rather than the reluctant suitor he actually was. Phèdre, too, is transformed into a more traditional and believable figure. She is now the virtuous, yet inaccessible, heroine responsible for inspiring the step-son's illicit passion. Because

Oenone's proposed scenario is designed to appeal to popular prejudices (Hippolyte is, after all, the offspring of an uncivilized Amazon and a lusty father), it is, certain to persuade. Oenone argues further that the reliance on convention will not only protect Phèdre, but Hippolyte as well. The powerful bond linking father and son, she argues, ensures that Hippolyte's punishment will be mild ("Un père en punissant, Madame, est toujours père" [901]).

Thésée's return prompts only Phèdre to abandon her illicit and immoral scenario. Hippolyte, on the other hand, remains committed to his plan to marry Aricie, even in defiance of his father's laws. Hyppolyte's continued pursuit of Aricie demonstrates yet again a fundamental distinction between the transgressive nature of the unsanctioned unions (Hippolyte/Phèdre versus Hippolyte/Aricie). Although Thésée's return once again renders both couplings illegal, only one remains immoral. Therefore, while Phèdre takes desperate measures to suppress her undecorous scenario, Hippolyte remains committed to his. Because the only obstacle to Hippolyte's future happiness with Aricie is the legal interdiction, Hippolyte believes his scenario can yet be realized. He will, however, be required to find an alternate stage on which to perform the marriage ceremony, an arena outside the jurisdiction of his father's arbitrary laws:

> L'hymen n'est point toujours entouré de flambeaux.
> Aux portes de Trézène, et parmi ces tombeaux,
> Des princes de ma race antiques sépultures,
> Est un temple sacré, formidable aux parjures.
> C'est là que les mortels n'osent jurer en vain. (1391–95)

The marriage is to be performed just beyond the Athenian borders, beyond the limits of conventional politics and aesthetics. Hippolyte is convinced his marriage to Aricie will find sanction where his father's influence ends. The gods who monitor the purity of heart of those who perform on this sacred stage will surely approve of his performance:

> Nous prendrons à témoin le dieu qu'on y révère;
> Nos le prîrons tous deux de nous servir de père.

Des dieux les plus sacrés j'attesterai le nom.
Et la chaste Diane, et l'auguste Junon,
Et tous les Dieux enfin, témoins de mes tendressses,
Garantiront la foi de mes saintes promesses. (1401–06)

Hippolyte learns at his peril, however, that a scenario in the absence of legal sanction remains fundamentally flawed. Beyond the father's law, beyond imposed regulations, beyond disciplined self control and self-denial, no performance can please. Hippolyte's self-indulgent scenario threatens the political stability of his family, center-stages passion over reason, and glorifies an emotional attachment that Théramène has dismissed as common, ordinary. The lawless scenario proposed by Hippolyte results in his own destruction and compromises his heroic legacy.[12] Although he slays the frightening (and baroque) monster, he dies as a result of the disorder he himself engendered. His horses no longer recognize his voice as one of authority, and Hippolyte is dragged ignominiously to his death in their unimpeded flight to freedom. Hippolyte's quest for unregulated theater costs him his life, and the scenario he envisaged culminates in baroque fragmentation. Neptune's agitation of the horses ("Un Dieu qui d'aiguillons pressoit leur flanc poudreux" [1540] signifies celestial support for respecting the law and disapproval for deregulated scenarios.[13]

After Hippolyte is dragged to his death by runaway horses (emblematic of the passion that led him so astray in the first place), it will be up to Théramène to recast the tragedy in the measured poetics of classical textuality. The length of Théramène's récit underscores how difficult it is to transform the disordered exuberance of non-regular theater back into a poetics of elevated tragedy. Hippolyte's transgressive scenario is so unruly that it requires the lengthy and measured perfection of Théramène's récit to convey the magnitude

12. The récit does manage to transform Hippolyte into theatrical spectacle, the metatextual goal of Thésée's son from the outset according to Judd Hubert, "Les écarts de Trézène," 85.
13. Notes Paul Morrison, "Noble Deeds and the Secret Singularity," 283, the rules do not allow for the representation of such violence: "And it is here that Racine is both deeply faithful to and deeply in conflict with 'les tragédies des Anciens,' at least as explicated by Aristotle."

of the damage wrought by Hippolyte's unregulated theater.[14]

Hippolyte's death definitively ends Phèdre's lustful fantasies, but it does nothing to remove the fictional invention she and Oenone created for self-protection. It is therefore imperative that Phèdre take the stage one last time in order to publicly admit the error of her ways, and to offer her life in atonement for her part in the tragedy. Her suicide is a *mea culpa* of sorts, although she is careful to place most of the blame on the Gods and Oenone ("Le ciel mit dans mon sein une flamme funeste; / La détestable Oenone a conduit tout le reste" [1625–26]). Arguably, Phèdre's presence in the last scene is necessary to confirm Thésée's growing suspicions that his son was an innocent victim after all. Yet, Phèdre's on stage death is a little too histrionic, too theatrically contrived, to convey genuine moral remorse. In fact, a more ostentatious finale could hardly be envisaged. Phèdre's intrusive and flamboyant entrance in the last scenes of the tragedy commands the sustained and unwavering focus of all in witness. Her decision to commit suicide on center stage reveals a significant change of heart from the opening scenes of the tragedy. Whereas she initially shunned the spotlight in order to nurse her illicit scenarios of adultery and incest, she now makes a deliberate and ostentatious spectacle of herself. In her final appearance on stage and in contradistinction to everything she maintained during the last five acts, Phèdre pledges allegiance to traditional values and affirms the necessity of conforming to conventional moral codes. Confessing to the man who must now restore the moral and political order she sought to undermine, Phèdre subordinates herself finally to her husband Thésée and to his laws.

---

14. "Avec ce célèbre morceau de bravoure, la tragédie racinienne semble amener à un point de non-retour—comme est appelé à le faire tout chef-d'oeuvre qui s'honore—les lois du genre qui sont les siennes: elle réussit ce tour de force de produire encore une représentation à travers l'abolition des formes de représentation qui lui étaient jusqu'alors imparties," argues Olivier Pot in "La Mort d'Hippolyte ou la défiguration silencieuse du langage," *Papers on French Seventeenth-Century Literature* 23 (1996), 601–02. In a related observation, Eric Gans in "Racine et la fin de la tragédie," *Relectures raciniennes: Nouvelles approches du discours tragique,* ed. Richard L. Barnett (Paris: PFSCL, 1986), 62, establishes a similar link between illicit desire and scenic unrepresentability: "Le labyrinthe ne peut jamais être mis en scène, seulement en discours. Que la petite-fille du Soleil y situe son désir, qu'elle puisse formuler le désir qui convient à ce lieu, c'est le signe d'un dépassement, ou pour mieux dire d'un débordement de la scène tragique."

Although Phèdre's tragedy is often interpreted from a Jansenist perspective, her suicide actually offers more in the way of aesthetic rather than spiritual guidance. Her final words make pointed reference to the scenic purification her death will facilitate:

> Et le ciel et l'époux qe ma présence outrage;
> Et la mort, à mes yeux dérobant la clarté,
> Rend au jour, qu'ils souilloient, toute sa pureté. (1642–44)

Moreover, the manner of death, a poison introduced into Athens by Médée, has metatextual overtones. The reference to Médée calls attention certainly to the familial links between Phèdre and Médée, but it also recalls Corneille's baroque tragedy of the same name.[15] *Médée,* unlike *Le Cid,* did not incorporate neo-classical theory into its construction, and it actually has more in common with the French tragedies that preceded it than his many masterpieces that followed. With the poison of Médée, then, Phèdre removes herself, slowly and ostentatiously, from the regulated stage, purifying it of its baroque resonances, and leaving it free for neo-classical representations. It is in this sense that Phèdre's suicide can be read, not simply as an ethical *mea culpa,* but as a gesture of submission to the necessity of neo-classical dramaturgical imperatives.[16] Phèdre's on-stage suicide constitutes a repudiation of the irregular, the undisciplined, the unconventional, the undecorous, the baroque. Her decision to take her final breaths on stage constitutes a public surrender to the rules of neo-classical dramaturgy she so aggressively, but so unsuccessfully, contested. Significantly, her aesthetic surrender serves both a

---

15. Muriel Gutleben takes note of some similarities between Phèdre and Médée in "Faste et pompe, monstres et sublime dans *Médée* de Corneille et *Phèdre* de Racine," *Papers on French Seventeenth-Century Literature* 27 (2000), 153–61. The poison that links the two is also a focus of attention for A. G. Branan, "Dramatis res and couleur mythologique in Racine's *Phèdre,*" *Romance Notes* 23 (1982), 30 and Ronald Tobin "Les Trachiniennes et Phèdre: D'un poison à l'autre," *Ouverture et Dialogue,* ed. Ulrich Doring (Tubingen: Narr, 1981), 426. Tobin, however, believes the comparison between the two heroines is designed to underscore Phèdre's humanity.
16. See also, Eric Gans, "Racine et la fin de la tragédie," 64: "La famille humaine ne serait alors qu'une métaphore de la scène originaire où le centre est figuré par la puissance paternelle, puissance que le fils ne peut acquérir sans détruire la structure scénique qui lui donne son sens."

political and an aesthetic purpose: it unites Thésée with his former enemy, Aricie, and it provides spectators/readers with the illusion of a final and cathartic sense of justice.[17]

The Academy maintained in theory, and Racine confirmed in practice, that effective theater always involved the suppression of instinct, the careful bracketing of creativity, the stifling of invention in deference to public tastes and tolerances. Racine's more maverick rival Corneille rebelled against these rules, in part because he saw them as arbitrary and theatrically "irrelevant." What *Phèdre* demonstrates, I argue, is that Academic rules were not arbitrary at all; they merely codified what centuries of theatrical representations had consistently borne out. Aesthetic rules are essential precisely because they allow the writer to respect the one tenet that Corneille, and later Molière, and even Racine himself deemed inviolable: providing a pleasurable theatrical experience to viewers. The illicit and immoral fantasies proposed by Hippolyte and Phèdre do not meet this criterion, and both remain unrepresentable and unrepresented. Both Hippolyte and Phèdre die as failed or flawed heroes/heroines, their deaths a result of their own lack of discipline and repudiation of order. Hippolyte's attempt to find an alternate stage outside Athens ends with his dismemberment; Phèdre acknowledges that she can occupy the legitimate stage only if her performance conforms to establish moral codes, if it does not offend public prejudices. Hippolyte's death and Phèdre's suicide, then, can be read as metaphorical stagings of the death of irregular or baroque theater.[18] The irony of this message is that unbeknownst to Racine, his *Phèdre* represents the death of neo-classical theater as well.

17. The observations of Eric Gans, "Racine et la fin de la tragédie," 52–53, prove particularly illuminating in this context: "Le désir racinien menace l'intégrité scénique d'une manière bien plus radicale que celui de Shakespeare ou de Sophocle. Cette menace n'est pas celle de l'effrondrement des différences fondatrices de la vie humaine—destruction sacrificielle pour laquelle la scène tragique est le lieu tout désigné—mais celle de l'affaissement de la forme tragique, de son glissement vers le mélodrame, l'opéra ou le roman."
18. See the remarks of Sara Melzer in "Myths of Mixture in *Phèdre* and the Sun King's Assimilation Policy in the New World," *Esprit Créateur* 38 (1998), 79 where she sees Racine's theater as a theater of purity, or more precisely, a condemnation of the baroque.

CHAPTER 8

Racine's *Athalie* or the Power of Precedent[1]

In *Bérénice, Andromaque and Phèdre,* the death or exile of the Racinian heroine can be read as a sign of the author's support for academic regulation and the need to purge the text of its baroque tendencies. The death of one of his last heroines, however, points to a possible shift in perspective. *Athalie* stands as Racine's dramatic swan song, but this ultimate chant, this tragic finale, invokes no consonant resolution and much dissonant bewilderment. On the most superficial (and least interesting) level, the presumably didactic thrust renders *Athalie* naively simplistic, perhaps even uncharacteristically transparent in motivation, design, and execution. Created for the edification of young girls in a religious convent (who also participated as members of the dramatic "chorus of maidens"), the play appears to convey a divine message at once transparent and unambiguous. The God of Israel, the God of uncompromising and eternal truth, demonstrates his superiority over irreverent modernity, symbolically represented by the heretical Athalie. Consequently, *Athalie* has traditionally been regarded as a biblical drama conveying an orthodox religious premise: divine truth is immutable, timeless, and inflexible; those arrogant enough to contravene God's law incur inevitably the wrath of an avenging God. The fact that Athalie is a heroine with a decidedly Jesuit attitude lends contemporary flourish to the presumably motivated and encoded message.

This simplistic overview fails to take into account a number of textual dilemmas, not the least of which is locating the play's "tragic" center. If this is a Christian drama wherein evil reaps its just reward, Athalie's execution can only be seen as a triumphant cause for celebration. In a biblical reading, Athalie has no heroic standing at all and represents merely a heretical foil to the play's real hero, God himself.[2] Her destruction then, should evoke no sense of pity. Even for those who prefer to read

---

1. This article first appeared in *Les épreuves du labryrinthe: Essais de poétique et d'herméneutique raciniennes: Hommage tricentenaire,* ed. Richard-Laurent Barnett, *Dalhousie French Studies* 49 (1999), 182–92.
2. Claude Abraham, *Jean Racine* (Boston: G.K. Hall, 1977), 152.

the play more secularly, Athalie represents a flawed heroine whose hubris blinds her to the divine truths defended by Joad and the true believers. Both these readings, however, prove equally unsatisfying. Despite her irreverent defiance, Athalie remains sympathetic to viewers, and her execution is in no way perceived as an exemplary case of final justice. Indeed, the sense of futility evoked at the final curtain diminishes whatever instructive religious purpose the tragedy might have intended to convey. Joad's prophetic vision at the end of Act Three confirms that the dramatic rescue of baby Joas is all for naught. Although Joas' existence provides the Israelites with renewed faith in the messianic promise, divine intervention reveals that Joas, like those before him, will stray from the straight and narrow of the sacred path. In consequence, the coronation of Joas, a triumph on which the tragedy closes, is hardly cause for righteous jubilation. More significantly perhaps, the drama cannot be interpreted as the dramatization of God's triumph over Athalie because in the end, as John Trethewey notes in a recent article, Athalie's and God's will both coincide.[3] Using this argumentation, the only terror evoked at the final curtain is the unrelenting obstinacy of religious fanatics who assign holy pretexts to acts motivated by personal grudges. On the secular side, if the didactic message of the play were intended to denigrate hubristic arrogance, Athalie's lucid remorse for having allowed this character flaw to destroy her political future would be requisite. Racine's heroine, however, remains obstinately unrepentant and vehemently defiant, even as she is dragged forcibly from the stage.

The dilemmas posed by this supposedly self-explanatory and didactic tragedy are sufficiently intriguing to propose a radical re-reading, one that focuses less on the overt religious significance than on the more subtle aesthetic codes hidden just beneath the biblical overlay.[4] The central antagonists, Joad and Athalie, clearly occupy

---

3. "Anti-Judaism in Racine's *Athalie*," *Seventeenth-Century French Studies* 18 (1996), 173.
4. "The network of conflicting signals is sustained by a plot designed to produce the greatest dramatic effect, and a denouement, actively precipitated by Joad, which both fulfills and frustrates his claim to be acting under divine guidance. The whole is enough to leave us uncomfortably conscious of the uncertainties which hedge about any simple interpretation of the play," notes John Campbell in "The Exposition of *Athalie*," *Seventeenth-Century French Studies* 12 (1990), 157. Significant also is his conclusion that the exposition exposes the aesthetic problem of *vraisemblance* (157).

different extremes of the religious spectrum, and these polar perspectives appear logically to situate them within the Jansenist/Jesuit polemic of the period.[5] In this reading, the uncompromising and conservative Joad, who remains loyal to traditional religious law, appears to represent the minority Jansenist viewpoint. The heretical Athalie, who introduces the people to a more liberal and permissive deity ("Enfin au Dieu nouveau, qu'elle avoit introduit, / Par les mains d'Athalie un temple fut construit" [945–46]),[6] seems to embrace more popular Jesuit values. The didactic intention motivating the play's design and representation lends additional support to this interpretation. Commissioned by the devout Madame de Maintenon, *Athalie* is seen as the repentant offering of a born-again writer eager to expiate the errors of his misspent career. In his "retirement," Racine, like Pascal, appeared ready to commit his considerable talents to the advancement of a higher cause.

While the Jansenist/Jesuit polarity serves to elucidate some aspects of the tragedy, it is not the only signification that can be assigned to the tragedy's opposing ideologies. Racine was first and foremost, a man of the theater. As such, he was inevitably more concerned with dramaturgy than with liturgy. It is possible, if not likely, that the same poetic impulses that motivated the author's tragedy *Phèdre* infiltrated the dramas of the "biblical" period as well. Consequently, religion is not necessarily either the entire, nor even the primary preoccupation underpinning *Athalie*. On the contrary, I argue that on some unconscious level, *Athalie* is more about dramatic theory than religious dogma, more about the effectiveness of neo-classical imperatives than about the legacy of the Old Testament. In fact, I believe the contemporary debate in evidence is not the Jesuit/Jansenist controversy so surfacially apparent, but the more secular contemporary debate pitting the Ancients against the Moderns.

---

5. This allegorical interpretation is in fact effectively refuted by Stanley F. Levine in his article "Exotism and the Jew: Racine's Biblical Tragedies,"*Cahiers du Dix-Septième* 3 (1989), 62–63. Even though his argument that "no public or private testimony, either from supporters of any of these causes or from their enemies, indicates that Racine's contemporaries saw such allusions in the plays," the polarity between conservative and progressive views of religious dogma are too striking to be totally ignored.
6. References are to Racine, *Oeuvres* (Paris: Les Grands Ecrivains de la France, 1929).

Richelieu's mimetic imperative was intended to lead French neo-classical literature into the promised land of literary renown. It is not without significance and a certain irony that Racine's work almost single-handedly fulfilled that promise. But the void that followed in the wake of Racine's silence demonstrated, perhaps, the futility of the quest after all. At the time of *Athalie*, the literary landscape was evolving rapidly. Opera was increasingly popular, and its visual and sensory lavishness made neo-classical theater look barren in contrast. The theater of Antiquity, it appeared, much like the Old Testament, belonged to the distant past, its narratives interesting, but no longer wholly relevant. It is in this context that Athalie's death acquires metatheatrical significance. Her attempt to forge new scenarios to better reflect contemporary reality was cut short by narrow-minded reactionaries who refused to assign merit to anything not scripted in narratives of the past. Athalie's final assertion conveys the notion that in the future, merit will be determined not by the degree of mimetic exactitude, but by the power to persuade others to embrace innovation and leave the past behind.

There is ample evidence to support this secularized reading. Joad's insistent demands for conformity to past models provide an aesthetic dimension to the play. The call for imitation echoes the Academy's professed belief in the supremacy of the Ancients and the concomitant demand for mimetic fidelity to Greek and Roman models. In *Athalie*, the conflict between the Israelites who pledge allegiance to immutable and textually inscribed laws on the one hand, and the Baal worshipers willing to renounce that past in order to forge representations more reflective of current "reality" on the other, mirrors the perspectives and arguments around which the much-celebrated literary debate swirled. In essence, the tragedy's conflict involves precisely these opposing viewpoints. Athalie's quest for the freedom to enact practical reforms that respond to a changed and changing environment is countered by Joad's mimetic imperative requiring fidelity to tradition:

> Et nous, dont cette femme impie et meurtrière
> A souillé les regards et troublé la prière,

Rentrons; et qu'un sang pur, par mes mains épanché,
Lave jusques au marbre où ses pas ont touché. (747–50)

For Joad, the *Apostle's Creed* can only be conjugated in past tense.
His literal interpretation of biblical law allows for neither variation nor
ideological nuance. Form overrides meaning; tradition substitutes for
faith. More concerned with the rule of ritual than with moral rectitude,
Joad measures faith by the degree of mimetic exactitude. The intrinsic
validity of an act of faith is irrelevant; fidelity to textual precedent
constitutes its own tautological justification. Indeed, the past determines propriety in all conceivable spheres, from ritualistic celebration
to political leadership. Athalie's reign, though politically successful, is
dismissed as tyranny by Joad who regards her as an unfit leader. Joad
refuses to recognize any authority figure without scriptural validation.
For this reason, Joas' rescue is vital. Without a direct descendant from
the house of David, Joad cannot continue to rely on textual precedent
to justify his faith ("Songez qu'en cet enfant tout Israël réside" [1342]).
Indeed, if David's blood-line is severed, scriptural truth will be transformed into inconsequential fiction.

Joad's dogmatic preoccupation with scriptural fidelity, with the
formal rule and not the spirit of biblical law, is one of the reasons he
and his followers appear so unsympathetic despite their pious blus-
ter. One of his most striking characteristics is an extremely technical
approach to matters of faith, a preoccupation with form over substance. For the Jewish faithful, religious worship is a ritualistic ceremony strictly controlled by textual laws and precedents. As the drama
opens, worshippers are in fact preparing to attend the ceremony that
will replicate liturgical celebrations of the past, a ceremony in praise
of the cyclical nature of life and fundamentally unchanged from its
initial staging:

Oui, je viens dans son temple adorer l'Éternel.
Je viens, selon l'usage antique et solennel,
Célébrer avec vous la fameuse journée
Où sur le mont Sina la loi nous fut donnée. (1–4)

But if the ceremony itself has not varied through the ages, the

number of worshippers in witness has decreased precipitously, and
the diminished number of spectators is cause for concern.

> Que les temps sont changés! Sitôt que de ce jour
> La trompette sacrée annonçoit le retour,
> Du temple, orné partout de festons magnifiques,
> Le peuple saint en foule inondoit les portiques;
> Et tous devant l'autel avec ordre introduits,
> De leurs champs dans leurs mains portant les nouveaux fruits,
> Au Dieu de l'univers consacroient ces prémices.
> Les prêtres ne pouvoient suffire aux sacrifices. (5–12)

Curiously enough, it is not fear of religious persecution from Athalie
that explains the drop in attendance, but rather simple spectator preference. Athalie's religion of Baal offers a more compelling spectacle,
and is attracting a number of converts:

> Le reste pour son Dieu montre un oubli fatal,
> Ou même, s'empressant aux autels de Baal,
> Se fait initier à ses honteux mystères,
> Et blasphème le nom qu'ont invoqué leurs pères. (17–20)

The initial scenes thus establish the conflict as one between competing styles of liturgical celebration, one traditional (and losing support), one improvised (and attracting converts). In other words, *Athalie*
is structured principally around an aesthetic disagreement. From the
very outset, then, the battle between Joad and Athalie revolves around
ceremonial practices. Joad's ritual is based on textual tradition;
Athalie's is highly improvised. Casting himself as the voice of religious authority, Joad maintains that only those rituals rooted in the
textual past have moral validity. The problem is, this moral validity
is insufficient to sustain parishioners' interest. They have migrated to
Athalie's liturgical dramas. Public opinion, then, is at odds with the
dictates of traditional authority. The metatextual significance of this
fact cannot be overlooked. Athalie's and Joad's competition for viewer
allegiance calls to mind one of the major literary debates of the century. The *querelle du Cid* was instrumental in establishing separate
but not equal juries for determining the theatrical worth of a dra-

matic event. In this battle, the *Académie* emerged victorious over the people. Richelieu and his *Académie* condemned Corneille's play, widely appreciated by the contemporary audience, for its transgressions of theory, theories gleaned from sacred documents written in the distant past. Not unlike Corneille, Athalie, too, creates a spectacle that violates tradition, yet pleases the audience. Joad, like Richelieu, remains committed stubbornly to precedent.

   Joad's reactionary attitude is not the only reason he fails to elicit spectator sympathy. His religious hypocrisy, that is to say, his eagerness to employ unholy means to achieve divine ends, is equally distasteful. He uses, and without apology, machiavellian manipulation and deceptive language to provoke, and then entrap, an unarmed woman. The inherent contradiction implied by the use of deceptive strategies to confirm biblical truth inevitably serves to diminish Joad's self-proclaimed moral supremacy, if not discredit him outright.[7] For a man so preoccupied with locating truth, Joad's communiqués are unexpectedly oblique:[8]

> Je ne m'explique point. Mais quand l'astre du jour
> Aura sur l'horizon fait le tiers de son tour,
> Losque la troisième heure aux prières rappelle,
> Retrouvez-vous au temple avec ce même zèle. (153–56)

   Moreover, there is something ostensibly odious about a holy man who claims to valorize truth, yet who does not hesitate to use deception to accomplish his goals. Clearly, it is difficult to commiserate with a religious leader who behaves with such machiavellian abandon, who uses hypocrisy in the name of truth, who masks personal spite beneath a pose of moral outrage, who confuses private revenge with divine justice. Nor does he have any qualms about desecrating a holy temple by transforming it into a potential slaughter-

---

7. Indeed, none of the "saintly" characters in *Athalie* appears particularly admirable. In his encounter with Athalie, the disrespectful Eliacin rejects the concepts of respect, courtesy, and charity that constitute essential elements of Christian humility.

8. Notes John Campbell, Joad even refuses to communicate sincerely with his wife, which has the effect of increasing, rather than allaying, her fears. See his article, "The Exposition of *Athalie*," *Seventeenth-Century French Studies* 12 (1990), 152.

house. Joad manifests a particularly violent and aggressive brand of religious fervor :

> Par de stériles voeux pensez-vous m'honorer?
> Quel fruit me revient-il de tous vos sacrifices?
> Ai-je besoin du sang des boucs et des génisses?
> Le sang de vos rois crie, et n'est point écouté.
> Rompez, rompez tout pacte avec l'impiété,
> Du milieu de mon peuple exterminez les crimes,
> Et vous viendrez alors m'immoler vos victimes. (86–92)

Additionally, Joad and his followers are ever ready to attack verbally those who do not share their faith. Athalie acknowledges and denounces their unjust portrayals:

> Je sais sur ma conduite et contre ma puissance
> Jusqu'où de leurs discours ils portent la licence. (595–96)

However, since much, if not all, of the spectators' reaction to Athalie derives from the negative assessments put forth by the religious zealots, and since we are predisposed to accept their view as being synonymous with God's, our opinion of Athalie is subjectively shaped (and hence distorted), by their vitriolic affirmations. Eager to justify his antipathy and his aggressive campaign to destroy her, Joad depicts Athalie as a demonized and denatured being, one who preys relentlessly on the vulnerable, the innocent, and the virtuous. She is portrayed as a savage despot questing unlimited power. At times, Joad appears more concerned with the destruction of his enemy and rival Athalie than with the more Christian concepts of humility and charity.

A biblical reading of the play would perhaps attempt to justify spectator antipathy towards the High Priest by using arguments put forth by the Jansenists themselves to explain their own social and political disfavor. The persecution they were forced to endure was deemed proof of how fundamentally antithetical were spiritual and worldly values. It is therefore understandable, if not inevitable, that worldly theater-goers would sympathize with Athalie rather than defend the stringent orthodoxy of Joad and the true believers. Alienation and public scorn are, after all, the customary rewards for the pious who refuse to jeopardize their eternal soul by pursuing perishable pleasures. Presumably, the pure of heart at Saint-Cyr would have been immune from such judgmental errors.

Attempts to justify the heroism of Joad based on his uncompromising religiosity do little to explain why Racine slants the textual bias in Athalie's direction, however. She is, after all, the titular heroine.[9] Arguably, that designation is not in and of itself indicative of authorial favor. She finds herself in the company of a number of other less than heroic characters who figure prominently in previous titles. Even so, in the battle between dichotomized protagonists representing extremist notions of good and evil, Athalie appears the more sympathetic character. Consequently, despite the verbal assaults of Joad and his followers, Athalie commands respect and sympathy throughout, and the spectator/reader experiences an unmistakable twinge of regret, a sense of fundamental injustice, at her defeat. In fact, Joad's bitter enmity towards Athalie appears to have no continuing basis in fact. On the contrary, textual evidence belies the identity imposed upon her. We witness not a monomaniacal despot, but an innovative stateswoman who has brought peace to a region steeped formerly in violence:

> Le ciel même a pris soin de me justifier.
> Sur d'éclatants succès ma puissance établie
> A fait jusqu'aux deux mers respecter Athalie.
> Par moi Jérusalem goûte un calme profond. (470–73)

Under her able reign, religious tolerance has replaced bigotry ("Vos prêtres, je veux bien, Abner, vous l'avouer, / Des bontés d'Athalie ont lieu de se louer" [593–94]). Despite Abner's expressed fears, Athalie has made no attempt to persecute the Israelites ("Ils vivent cependant, et leur temple est debout" [597]). Unlike her en-

---

9. Racine's attempt in his preface to the play to justify the title on the basis of the heroine's infamy relative to the less recognizable character Joas only underscores the fact that the author himself sees the heroine as the more powerful character. It is significant also, that Racine in his *Préface* admits to an infraction against codified rules ("j'aurois dû dans les règles l'intituler *Joas*" [593]). As my thesis suggests, and Racine here supports, *Athalie* is a play about breaking traditional rules.

emies, she is secure enough to allow for multiple worship, to leave Joad's followers free to respect any God they choose:

> Je sais que dès l'enfance élévé dans les armes
> Abner a le coeur noble, et qu'il rend à la foi
> Ce qu'il doit à son Dieu, ce qu'il doit à ses rois. (456–58)

Indeed, one of the more intriguing aspects of *Athalie* is that in the ideological battle at hand, the spectator is compelled to side with Athalie rather than Joad, the spiritual leader who aligns himself directly with God. In contradistinction to Joad, Athalie appears less villain than victim, a capable queen for whom progress imports more than precedent. Unlike Joad who reveres the past, Athalie disdains it ("Je ne veux point ici rappeler le passé" [465]). She prefers instead to stay focused on the future. Athalie's commitment to destroying the past can be witnessed in the infamous slaughter of her own clan, her very heritage:

> Enfin de votre Dieu l'implacable vengeance
> Entre nos deux maisons rompit toute alliance.
> David m'est en horreur; et les fils de ce roi,
> Quoique nés de mon sang, sont étrangers pour moi. (727–30).

Athalie was from birth deemed textually irrelevant; no prior document or precedent sanctions her legitimacy. Her solution is to nullify the past in order to allow for the possibility of progressive reform:

> Où serois-je aujourd'hui, si domptant ma foiblesse,
> Je n'eusse d'une mère étouffé la tendresse,
> Si de mon propre sang ma main versant des flots
> N'eût par ce coup hardi réprimé vos complots? (723–26)

But Athalie has not been wholly successful in erasing that past. Joas was rescued and survives unbeknownst to her. She is alerted in a dream, however, that the past is not so easily destroyed. The dream conveys the past as a ghoulish and virtually indestructible entity. The fundamental hideousness of the past is symbolized by the image of Jezebel whose attempts to conceal the tired traces of her longevity, to appear ever youthful, repel rather than attract:

> Même elle avoit encor cet éclat emprunté
> Dont elle eut soin de peindre et d'orner son visage,
> Pour réparer des ans l'irréparable outrage. (494–96)   ·

Not only is the past represented as visually repugnant, but it is without palpable substance as well. When Athalie reaches out to embrace the past, she is left with nothing but torn flesh and bloody fragments:

> Et moi, le lui tendois les mains pour l'embrasser.
> Mais je n'ai plus trouvé qu'un horrible mélange
> D'os et de chair meurtris, et traînés dans la fange,
> Des lambeaux pleins de sang, et des membres affreux
> Que des chiens dévorants se disputoient entre eux. (502–06)

The dream conveys finally an even more frightening detail about the past: its vindictive nature. The child and the past that Athalie thought she had conquered are now poised to destroy her instead.

Rather than heed the explicit warnings represented ("un songe vain" [584]), she decides to take refuge in the very past the dream cautioned against. In a gesture of self-renunciation, she enters the temple of her persecutors:

> Dans le temple des Juifs un instinct m'a poussée,
> Et d'apaiser leur Dieu j'ai conçu la pensée:
> J'ai cru que des présents calmeroient son courroux,
> Que ce Dieu, quel qu'il soit, en deviendroit plus doux. (527–30)

Once inside the temple, terror rather than comfort is the consequence. Here she discovers the very child portrayed in the dream as the agent of her demise. Again, however, Athalie disregards the dream's warnings and allows herself to be beguiled by this presumably orphaned prodigy. Conventional arguments explain Athalie's vulnerability as a result of either divine intervention, or maternal weakness. I believe, however, that her attachment to Joas is an extension of her modernist quest. What draws Athalie to this child of illusion is his averred lack of any heritage. He is an orphan with no ancestral roots that can link him to any historical precedent or prejudice. This child without a past, then, is free to make judgmental decisions without imposed biases. Athalie hopes to mold this child in her own image, to found a dynasty of modernists, thereby validating her own example. She will thus establish herself as an archetypal model who inspires imitations of her own:

> Vous voyez, je suis reine, et n'ai point d'héritier.
> Laissez là cet habit, quittez ce vil métier.
> Je veux vous faire part de toutes mes richesses;
> Essayez dès ce jour l'effet de mes promesses.
> A ma table, partout, à mes côtés assis,
> Je prétends vous traiter comme mon propre fils. (693–98)

The child is not without a past, however. On the contrary, he defines himself by it. Joas represents everything that Athalie denounces: an unflinching allegiance to historical and scriptural traditions ("Pourrois-je à cette loi ne me pas conformer?" [1383]). His very existence succeeds in rescripting the past that Athalie endeavored to eradicate. Consequently, in the conflict between past and present that underpins *Athalie,* Joas' survival heralds the triumph of Joad over Athalie. On that point, there is little disagreement. It is, however, the symbolic significance of Joad's victory that is open to debate. We learn in Act Three that Joas will transgress the sacred laws that sanction Athalie's murder and restore his crown. Consequently, the messianic promise on which Joad's faith is founded is revealed to be, if not false, undecipherably cryptic and therefore, useless.

That point is significant because it establishes that "truth" in *Athalie* resides not in the texts of the past but rather in the creative visions of the future: Athalie's nightmare and Joad's prophecy. Had Athalie placed her faith in the truth of her dreams, she would have continued to survive and prosper. She was specifically warned in the dream to beware of the past repeating itself. She even discovers in the dream the face of the child who will be responsible for her death. Nevertheless, Athalie refuses to believe in the creative spirit. Consequently, she is condemned to the same fate that befell her ancestors.

Like her mother Jezebel, Athalie falls victim to the Israelites.[10]

Joad's prophetic vision, like Athalie's, also foretells a frightening scenario. His divinely inspired vision reveals that the future reality contradicts his "reading" of it ("Comment en un plomb vil l'or pur s'est-il changé? / Quel est dans le lieu saint ce pontife égorgé?" [1142–43]). Joad remains curiously unconflicted by the message conveyed to him directly by God, however, and he continues to pursue undeterred his vendetta against Athalie. In light of the evidence transmitted to him, the end (the restoration of Joas to the throne) can hardly be said to justify the means (Athalie's entrapment and murder by armed priests inside a holy temple). Joad's prophecy problematizes any religious reading of the play because it reveals, if not the falsehood, at least the uncertainty, of scriptural truths. A final irony related to the divine message is the indication that the traditional practices so strictly enforced by Joad will lose their relevance:

> Ton encens à ses yeux est un encens souillé.
> Où menez-vous ces enfants et ces femmes?
> Le Seigneur a détruit la reine des cités.
> Ses prêtres sont captifs, ses rois sont rejetés.
> Dieu ne veut plus qu'on vienne à ses solennités.
> Temple, renverse-toi. Cèdres, jetez des flammes. (1147–52)

Additionally and equally disturbing, Joad encounters in his vision a whole new theater of spectators, unfamiliar faces with no apparent link to the past:

> D'où lui viennent de tous côtés
> Ces enfants qu'en son sein elle n'a point portés? (1164–65)

This focus on new rituals and unfamiliar celebrants is but one of many metadramatic references that drench the play from the opening scenes. Indeed, the overtly "theatrical" nature of this play is too conspicuous to be inconsequential. The very decision to reinstate the

---

10. See also, Marcel Gutwirth, "Jéhu, le fier Jéhu: La Métaphorisation du tragique" in *Relectures raciniennes: Nouvelles approches du discours tragique,* ed. Richard L. Barnett (Paris: PFSCL, 1986), 71: "Telle mère, sommes-nous bien fondés à dire, telle fille."

traditional chorus situates the play in the Greek tradition that French
neo-classical dramatists so dutifully revered.[11] And with good reason. Respect for theatrical rules, like obedience to liturgical law, meant
the difference between acceptance or ex-communication from Academic favor. Just as the law in *Athalie* is seen as God's primary gift
("Mais sa loi sainte, sa loi pure / Est le plus riche don qu'il ait fait
aux humains" [330–31]),[12] theoretical rules in the neo-classical age
were considered sacrosanct imperatives. *Athalie*'s numerous on-stage
rituals convey also a metatheatrical message, as do Athalie's persistent interruptions of these performances. It is in fact her interruption
of the Pentecostal celebration, a traditional ceremony meticulously
prescribed by religious law, that prompts Joad to accelerate the representation of Joas' coronation, the main theatrical event:

> Déjà, selon la loi, le grand prêtre mon père,
> Après avoir au Dieu qui nourrit les humains
> De la moisson nouvelle offert les premiers pains,
> Lui présentoit encore entre ses mains sanglantes
> Des victimes de paix les entrailles fumantes. (384–88)

This early interruption constitutes a symbolic representation of
Athalie's commitment to destroying rituals of the past, to revive and
transform ceremonial practices that no longer inspire faith in the parishioners. The need for spectacular performances is averred even by
Athalie's enemies to be requisite to sustain spiritual conviction. The
paucity of revitalizing scenarios is cited as a reason for the wane in
traditional fervor:

> Dieu même, disent-ils, s'est retiré de nous:
> De l'honneur des Hébreux autrefois si jaloux,
> Il voit sans intérêt leur grandeur terrassée;
> Et sa miséricorde à la fin s'est lassée.
> On ne voit plus pour nous ses redoutables mains

11. *"Athalie,* de par ses rapports au mythe et au rituel, serait-elle la plus grecque des
oeuvres de Racine?" asks Jacques-Jude Lepine in "La Barbarie à visage divin: mythe et
rituel dans *Athalie,*" *The French Review* 64, 1 (1990), 19.
12. See also Erica Harth's remarks in "The Tragic Moment in *Athalie,*" *Modern Language
Quarterly* 33 (1972), 389.

De merveilles sans nombre effrayer les humains;
L'arche sainte est muette, et ne rend plus d'oracles. (97–103)

Significantly, it is Joad's promise of an extraordinary and innovative spectacle that prompts Abner's sudden renewal of faith ("Dieu pourra vous montrer par d'importants bienfaits / Que sa parole est stable et ne trompe jamais" [157–58]).

These metatheatrical insertions pale in comparison to the staged revelation of Joas, however. The thoroughly theatricalized manner in which Joas' "resurrection" is revealed to the faithful is the most potent indication of the degree to which dramaturgical preoccupations infiltrate this text.[13] Everything in this scene conspires to ensure that the coronation of Joas is cast as high drama.[14] There is respect for traditions ("Et vous, à cette loi, votre règle éternelle, / Roi, ne jurez-vous pas d'être toujours fidèle?" [1381–82]); dramatic suspense ("Je vous veux devant elle expliquer sa naissance: / Vous verrez s'il le faut remettre en sa puissance, / Et je vous ferai juge entre Athalie et lui" [1663–65]); appropriate costuming ("Princesse, quel est donc ce spectacle nouveau? / Pourquoi ce livre saint, ce glaive, ce bandeau?" [1247–48]);[15] elaborate stage directions from Joad, the metteur en scène ("Suivez de point en point ces ordres importants" [1674]); theatrical illusions ("Surtout qu'à son entrée et que sur son passage / Tout d'un calme profond lui présente l'image" [1675–76]); the need for an audience ("Appelez tout le peuple au secours de son roi, / Et faites retentir jusques à son oreille / De Joas conservé l'étonnante merveille" [1686–88]). All these references confirm that the coronation of Joas is designed to be viewed as a theatrical event. Fittingly, the public revelation of Joas' identity takes place at the drawing back

13. It is, notes John Campbell in "The God of Athalie," *French Studies* 43, 4 (1989), 395, "the most theatrical recognition-scene in all of Racine's theater."
14. Notes John Campbell in "The Unity of Time in *Athalie*," *Modern Language Review* 86, 3 (1991), 575: "The High Priest actively stage-manages a production where only he knows how much every second counts."
15. For information regarding the symbolism of these "stage props," one can consult the articles by Jack Yashinsky, " 'Pourquoi ce livre saint, ce glaive, ce bandeau?' Commentaires textuels sur *Athalie*," *Lettres Romanes* 38 (1984), 65–75, and by David Maskell, "The Hand of God in French Religious Drama: Racine, Boyer and Campistron," *Seventeenth-Century French Studies* 14 (1992), 126.

of the theatrical curtain, a stage prop that separates Joad's "fiction" from Athalie's reality.[16] But as the stage magically transforms from temple into fortress, illusion rather than celestial truths can claim a victory. Though the past is proclaimed triumphant ("Tous chantent de David le fils ressuscité" [1765]), we know that the Old Testament's truths will not prevail. Joas will fail to keep the messianic promise.[17]

∾

If Athalie's death can be made to symbolize the redemption of the Moderns, it is because one can draw a parallel between the laws of Moses and the laws of Richelieu and his *Académie*. Such a hypothesis clarifies too many of the text's oft-cited problems to be summarily dismissed. Indeed, displacing the text from its religious plane to an aesthetic one explains more than a few of its more troubling aspects: the overtly "theatrical" nature of the drama; Athalie's rejection of the past to the point of parricide and infanticide; the ambiguity of good and evil as manifested by both protagonists; Athalie's incomprehensible attachment to the orphan child. In this reading, Athalie's death is interpreted not as a sacrificial execution intended to redeem the supremacy of ancient Law, but as a futile attempt to blunt the creative spirit and block aesthetic progress. Joad's final victory is hollow, and he recognizes it as such. His hallucination foretells the inevitable failure of the scriptural prophecy on which his faith depends. The heroic rescue of baby Joas which was to confirm the infallibility of God's Law exposes instead its fraudulence. Joas will not lead the Chosen People to final redemption; his salvation postpones, but does not alter, the inevitable fall of the House of David. Notes Claude Abraham, "the end of the play is far from being the end of the story."[18] Athalie's execution affords a momentary re-establishment of traditional religious practices, but in the end, the textual truths on which Joas' supremacy is established will be totally transformed

16. Notes Pierre Clarac in "*Athalie:* La Prophétie de Joad," *L'Information Littéraire* 14, 5 (1962), 228: "L'heureux dénouement est, en effet, illusoire."
17. In John Campbell's view, "The God of Athalie," 398, both the God of Athalie and the God of Joad constitute similar fictions or errors.
18. *Jean Racine,* 149.

by modern scripture, the New Testament.

Athalie is then very much an aesthetic parable. It is the dramatization of the failure of the mimetic enterprise, the end of the theater of imitation, the end of old testaments. Raymond Picard notes that *Athalie* "marque, à tous sens, la fin de Racine",[19] which is tantamount to saying, the end of neo-classical theater. And perhaps therein lies the play's tragic focus. Racine created his last masterpiece with the instinctive awareness that neo-classical theater, the theater his name virtually defines, would not survive his efforts, that an aesthetic revolution was imminent.[20] Like Joad, Racine witnesses the endpoint of his own legacy, but like his stubborn protagonist, he decides to stage one more ancient tragedy, one more dramatization of scriptural precedent, before surrendering to the inevitable.

19. Racine, *Oeuvres complètes,* ed. Raymond Picard (Paris: Gallimard, 1951), 888.
20. Indeed, Raymond Picard, 416, suggests that Racine was already attempting to develop a new genre here, the *opéra sacré.*

CHAPTER 9

The Imaginary as Protagonist:
Les Lettres portugaises

Although Richelieu's theoretical regulations applied primarily
to the genres of poetry and theater, narrative, too, struggled for legitimacy in the neo-classical age. There were, however, few rules to guide
prose writers other than the rules of the *bienséances* and
vraisemblance. In prose, as in drama, it was essential for the author
to offer a credible illusion of reality. One such author, Guilleragues,
proved so effective at creating a realistic illusion that his work was
presumed for years to be wholly authentic. From that perspective at
least, his work can be deemed an unqualified success. Guilleragues'
Lettres portugaises, tainted and taunted, largely untended and forever enigmatic, invite the very brand of sustained critical attention
that has eluded them since formal publication in the classical age.
The work thus constitutes a veritable playground for the contemporary literary critic, in that it places at once in relief and in question
textual conundrums of a timely and significant ilk. More intriguingly
still, the surfeit of unresolved issues intersects and, in the process of
criss-crossing, gives way to a new set of resultant queries. At the core
of this literary enterprise stand the problematics of epistolarity, rife
and riddled: the very nature of the genre requires the absence that
renders this text so problematic, and so relevant for a study involving
the death, in this case, the disappearance, of the heroine.

In a real sense, the *Lettres* trace the tale of female excision, but
do so through a complex maze of textual events that would deflect us
from such a nucleus. This would-be novel, we have been forewarned,
is a recounting of love and of unrequited love, a novel of despair, a
telling of woe and a poetic transcription of solitude. But can the mono-
phonic voice that we hear convincingly sanction and authorize such
classification? Can a single, unanswered voice represent the duality
that love implies? Does the relentless pounding of the verbal fist at-
test to the current absence of a former presence or does it rather index the eternal wantingness that such ongoing distance implies? And
if we accede to the latter theory of a single voice contriving its re-

spondent, how does such matter mean? We are carried along by the spaces left by the explicit silence of the interlocutor. To theorize the interlocutor as contrivance, then, is not to fill the heedless ellipses, but to efface them. That is, the spaces between segments, spaces to have been swamped with significance by the intentional, cruel, significant refusal of the lover to respond, become meaningless and make, then, of the text, one long diatribe divided reiteratively and deconstructively into five artificial entities. The ontology and epistemology of absence are no longer functional: all that remains is the single voice relaying and replacing the same monolithic melody and complexifying the dichotomy between fact and fiction by exponentializing fictional fictions and in the end by basing a work on a level of untruth once more removed.

If, as consequence, we concede to the breaking of the work's primary paradigm and begin to envisage the principal actant as the reciter of a self-obsessed monologic refrain and no more, then we are drawn into a new whirlwind of constraints and contortions. For, in essence, Mariane, the female protagonist of the series, is devolved and annihilated by the image of an un-present being, decimated by the unauthentic reference to the absent male figure, whose non-reality and non-substance, however, shed new light on the very constitution and orchestration of the text. It is, then, the concept, not the fact, of the dominating, all embracing male, absent or present, real or contrived, potent or im-potent, to which all femaleness is subjected, by which it is subsumed and ultimately dismantled. The text does not merely allow such defeat, it paves the way for it, facilitates it and beckons us to attend the spiritual demise of its dilapidated heroine.

From a feminist perspective, this is a telling itinerary. The erasure of the male from the novel's weave, except by way of reference *in absentia,* is orchestrated and spoken by a female. As is the dissolution of the heroine via the very discourse that she, Mariane, wields. It is a discourse, in effect, that as in misplaced and hyperbolic deference to male dominance and power, strips her ultimately of her very identity and attributes to her a kind of marginal status. All is deception: the male author masked as female writes-in a female character who in turn invents a male adversary. The male adversary, a contrived figure from the start, never shows up, of course, but is represented as the agent of ultimate destruction. So, then, a male invents a female who invents a male such that, in the end, the female is undone and rendered suicidal by the power of a male who is not and never was.[1]

How then is this strategy of ignominious decease encoded from the outset? The requisite concept of absence, coupled with the interlocutor's silence, provide perhaps the most accessible points of departure. Susan Lee Carrell notes that one of Guilleragues' important innovations to the love-letter genre is his representation of letters from a solitary writer, a narrative strategy that effectively underscores the heroine's solitude and isolation.[2] The absence of letters in response to hers has the narrational function of provoking the continuing discourse. Confronted with the lover's silence, Mariane attempts to confirm her desirability in the mind of the soldier by writing ever more poignant and desperate letters in an attempt to oblige or shame him into responding. The soldier's silence remains largely, though not totally, unbroken, despite Mariane's efforts, and Mariane elects ultimately to put an end to both discourse and desire. This widely held interpretation of Guilleragues' novel casts the epistolary enterprise as a narrative documentation of the heroine's emotional evolution from dependency to liberation, from *déraison* back to rationality.[3] With each successive unanswered letter, Mariane becomes increasingly aware of the unworthiness of her lover, of the delusions of her romantic fantasy, of the need to detach herself from an all-consuming and destructive passion.

---

1. Some interesting insights into the male author's decision to disguise himself as a female, and thereby, deliberately accept a "lesser status" are offered by Nancy K. Miller in "'I's' in Drag: The Sex of Recollection," *Eighteenth-Century: Theory & Interpretation* 22, 1 (1981), 47–57. One possibility proposed is that Guilleragues, like the pornographic writer, is depicting the effect males wish they had on their abandoned lovers. Whatever the reason for the disguise, the literary effect is the same: the fiction of authenticity is demolished by denying the subject her authorial prerogative (57).

2. *Le Soliloque de la passion féminine ou le dialogue illusoire* (Tubingen: Gunter Narr, 1982), 39.

3. See Carrol, *Le Soliloque de la passion,* 45 and Elizabeth McArthur, *Extravagant Narratives: Closure and Dynamics in the Epistolary Form* (Princeton: Princeton University Press, 1990), 79.

The desire to provoke a response, however, is not the only possible motive for Mariane's continuation of the one-sided correspondence. In fact, a closer investigation into her motivational impulses provides additional depth and complexity to the text. Elizabeth MacArthur suggests that at least part of Mariane's motivation to write letters in the absence of any response derives from an internal desire to give order and structure to an emotional experience that has moved beyond her limited ability to control it.[4] In MacArthur's view, Mariane's epistolary project originates as much from a need to reclaim the identity she lost when she surrendered her body and soul to irrational passion as to engage into a meaningful dialogue with the distant lover. In her view, the letters allow Mariane to slow the steady descent into emotional collapse, to regain some rational measure of self-determination. The act of writing letters, especially unanswered letters, allows her to structure the experience as she desires, to maintain an active role in controlling the relationship, to forestall by the continuing discourse, the imposed closure that the soldier's definitive rejection would otherwise accomplish.[5]

In this chapter, I would like to explore more fully yet another possible motive for the letters: the need to construct an aesthetic identity, a fictional alter-ego of sorts, that is unlinked to the flesh and blood persona that creates it.[6] The letters can be read as fictional embellishments to lived experience, texts designed to transport the bored and unfulfilled heroine to a more exciting, albeit imaginary, plane of existence via the hyperbolic rhetoric of an essentially unauthentic discourse. While there is evidence in a number of different letters and narrative strategies to support this reading, the myth of their authenticity effectively dissuades readers from fully exploiting the notion of an insincere Mariane.

---

4. "Extravagant Narratives," 79.
5. "Extravagant Narratives," 79–82. See also, Elizabeth Berg, "Iconoclastic Moments: Reading the *Sonnets for Hélène,* Writing the *Portuguese Letters,*" *The Poetics of Gender,* eds. Nancy K. Miller and Carolyn Heilbrun (New York: Columbia University Press, 1986), 214–17.
6. For more on the aesthetic dimension of the *Lettres portugaises,* see M. J. Muratore, *Mimesis and Metatextuality in the French Neo-Classical Text* (Geneva: Droz, 1994), 75–90.

This is partly the result of Guilleragues' narrative manner. One of the innovations Guilleragues brings to the love letter genre is the writer's baroque and erratic rhetorical style, a reflection, presumably, of the heroine's genuine distress and her inability or unwillingness to control the discursive rendering of her emotional dismantling. Mariane's careless, unheeded style is what so persuaded readers of their authenticity.[7] This authenticity, it will be noted, is in inverse proportion to the letters' "literariness". The unconstructed style of the letters seems to reflect mimetically and accurately the unbridled emotionality of a distraught and abandoned woman who has been manipulated and scorned by an indifferent lover. This emotional distress prevents, necessarily and logically, the distraught heroine from respecting the codified rules of conventional and classical epistolarity.[8]

This link between female authorship and non-literary discourse has the advantage of combining an array of prevailing prejudices about gender and genre. Women were perceived as being generally unable to control either their passion or their rhetoric, and in consequence, excelled in only one aesthetic effort: the love letter.[9] Mariane's overly exuberant and spontaneous writerly manner serves to alienate her from the literary establishment as much as her sexual indiscretion isolates her from those inside the convent. In consequence, Mariane is a marginalized figure in both the literary and fictional contexts in which she operates.

We know now, however, that there is nothing natural about this "feminine" discourse. The letters are the fictional construct of a man pretending to write "as a woman" about the effects of a passion he

7. Jonathan Mallinson, "Writing Wrongs: *Lettres portugaises* and the Search for an Identity," in *Writers and Heroines: Essays on Women in French Literature,* eds. Shirley Jones Day and Annette Lavers (Bern: Peter Lang, 1999), 31. Claire Goldstein, "Love Letters: Discourses of Gender and Writing in the Criticism of the *Lettres portugaises,*" *Romanic Review* 88 (1997), 571–90, also points out that women were considered superior to men in the art of writing love letters because women were so emotional, so needy, so dependent on love to provide them with any identity or function at all. This point is also made by Jean-Michel Pelous in "Une Heroine romanesque entre le naturel et la rhétorique: Le langage des passions dans les *Lettres portugaises,*" *Revue d'Histoire Littéraire de la France* 77 (1977), 557.
8. See Mallinson, "Writing Wrongs," 31.
9. See the remarks of Gabrielle Verdier, "Gender and Rhetoric in Some Seventeenth-Century Love Letters," *Esprit Créateur* 22 (1983), 45–57.

was by all accounts, incapable of experiencing.[10] The letters are nothing but aesthetic constructions and do not constitute, as it was believed at the time, an actual documentation of genuine sentiments. But the prejudices associated with feminine writing, the general consensus that it is a fundamentally emotional and careless manner of expression, persuade readers even today of the mimetic exactitude of these "female" letters. The attribution of authorship to Guilleragues, in other words, has failed to alter dramatically readers' impressions or perceptions of the heroine's sincerity. While most critics now accept that Guilleragues is the voice of Mariane, most readers continue to view Mariane as a sincere narrator, one whose words constitute a faithful reflection of the narrated experience.

If, however, we are willing to draw the same distinction between Mariane, the writer, and Mariane the character that we use to distinguish Guilleragues, the male author from his fictional, female heroine, we can provide the text with added depth. By focussing on Mariane as a writing subject separate from Mariane the fictional character, we call attention to the theoretical issues surrounding the distinction between created character and creative writer, between the Mariane who authors the letters, and the Mariane who constitutes their subject. The separation between narrator and narrative subject offers insights into Guilleragues' perspectives on literary aesthetics, aspects generally sacrificed or subordinated to discussions focussing on the psychological state of the heroine. By separating Mariane into two different entities, writing subject and textual subject, we can postulate that the effacement of the heroine from the text, both literally (in the sense that her letters progressively deteriorate and culminate in silence) and figuratively (in the sense that "she" is actually a product of a male writer's imagination) is a deliberate narrative strategy designed to underscore the fictional nature of all literary discourse, its fundamentally artificial (non-mimetic) essence. As we will

---

10. Much of the credit for discrediting the authenticity goes to Leo Spitzer's analysis of the "poetic" style found in Guilleragues' work in "*Les Lettres portugaises*," *Romanische Forschungen* 65 (1953), 94–135. See also his remarks in *Essays on Seventeenth-Century French Literature* (Cambridge: Cambridge University Press, 1983), 255–58, where he notes that all art is contrived. Otherwise it would not be art.

see, this is essentially the conclusion reached by the heroine herself, whose letters, rather than document a textual voyage from emotional dependency to independence (the widely held view of her epistolary evolution), trace her textual voyage from literary mimesis ("Il me semble que je fais le plus grand tort du monde aux sentiments de mon coeur, de tâcher de vous les faire connaître en les écrivant" [p. 151]) to literary liberation ("suis-je obligée de vous rendre un compte exact de tous mes divers mouvements?" [177]).[11] Severing the link between mimetic exactitude and aesthetic production constitutes, I believe, the text's most innovative characteristic, and establishes the *Lettres portugaises* as an early apology for the art of fiction, a kind of theoretical manifesto in drag.[12]

The distinction between rhetoric and reality is established almost from the outset. On the surface, Mariane's letters seem to underscore the letter's fundamental insufficiency vis à vis the reality it is called upon to supplant. The letters (the text) are depicted as a poor substitute for the reality they mimic. Initially, the letters echo the widely held presumption that rhetorical encounters between letter writers are intrinsically less satisfying than the physical conjoinings they are designed to replace. The fact that Mariane's letters are often none other than a metatextual commentary on the shortcomings of the epistolary exchange itself suggests that Mariane, like most letter-writers, appears to view the letter as a decidedly poor substitute for the flesh and blood encounter:

> Quoi? cette absence, à laquelle ma douleur, tout ingénieuse qu'elle est, ne peut donner un nom assez funeste, me privera donc pour toujours de regarder ces yeux dans lesquels je voyais tant d'amour, et qui me faisaient connaître des mouvements qui me comblaient de joie, qui me tenaient lieu de toutes choses, et qui enfin me suffisaient? (147)

11. All references are to the Frédéric Deloffre and Jacques Rougeot edition, Guilleragues, *Chansons et Bons Mots Valentins. Lettres Portugaises* (Geneva: Droz, 1972).
12. Theory being the domain of the masculine writer, the articulation of aesthetic concerns via the pen of a female writer is an effective camouflage indeed.

Adieu, je ne puis quitter ce papier, il tombera entre vos mains,
je voudrais bien avoir le même bonheur: hélas! insensée que je
suis, je m'aperçois bien que cela n'est pas possible. (150)
. . . .
Hélas! il n'est pas en mon pouvoir de m'y résoudre, il me semble
que je vous parle, quand je vous écris, et que m'êtes un peu plus
présent. (167)

In reality, this diminished view of the epistolary act is not a
wholly accurate depiction of Mariane's genuine attitude. Despite her
scripted anguish over her lover's absence, Mariane reveals surprisingly a decided preference for letters over clandestine encounters.
Mariane affirms in letter five that the actual relationship created nothing but anxiety for her, that the presence of the lover in her room in
the convent generated more panic than passion:

Je mourais de frayeur que vous ne me fussiez pas fidèle, je
voulais vous voir à tous moments, et cela n'était pas possible,
j'étais troublée par le péril que vous couriez en entrant dans ce
couvent; je ne vivais pas lorsque vous étiez à l'armée . . . (173–74)

In point of fact, Mariane does not regard the epistolary exchange
as a diminished experience at all, but rather as a more secure, even
more satisfying mode of connecting with her lover.[13] In contradistinction to the physical encounter, the act of writing letters causes
her no fear or anxiety. On the contrary, she has difficulty bringing the
letters to a close, so pleasurable does she find the activity. More significantly perhaps, from the outset she envisages the epistolary exchange with a sense of anticipatory enthusiasm:

J'avoue cependant que l'occasion que mon frère m'a donnée de
vous écrire a surpris en moi quelques mouvements de joie, et qu'elle
a suspendu pour un moment le désespoir où je suis. (149–50)

---

13. Peggy Kamuf, *Fictions of Feminine Desire* (Lincoln: University of Nebraska Press,
1982), 43 also suggests that because the epistolary love affair is immune to the dangers of
real erotic encounters, it provides Mariane with a protected, more secure, relationship
than the real encounter.

Rather than bemoan the absence that the epistolary project is designed to supplant and in some way alleviate, Mariane appears to anticipate and welcome the absence that will necessitate the less threatening mode of contact provided by the epistolary exchange. Clearly more comfortable with letters than with clandestine rendez-vous, Mariane contemplates with eagerness the frequent exchange of long and passionate letters that will replace secret encounters.

As it happens, expectation and reality do not coincide, a turn of events that prompts her to bemoan the "espérances trompeuses" that constitute the only yield of her failed epistolary project:

> Je me trouve bien éloignée de tout ce que j'avais prévu: j'espérais que vous m'écririez de tous les endroits où vous passeriez, et qu vos lettres seraient fort longues; que vous soutiendriez ma passion par l'espérance de vous revoir, qu'une entière confiance en votre fidélité me donnerait quelque sorte de repos, et que je demeurerais cependant dans un état assez supportable sans d'extrêmes douleurs. (155)

The failure, it must be underscored, is not the fault of the epistolary project in and of itself. It is not the letter-writing activity that is flawed, but the quality (even more than the lack) of her partner's responses. Mariane's initial frustration, we quickly learn, derives neither from the partner's physical absence or lack of responses, but from his re-fusal to write the type of impassioned love letter her imagination anticipates. She finds the few letters she has received to be woefully inadequate to meet her needs. Dissatisfied with the lover's dispas-sionate rhetoric, Mariane liberates herself from the necessity of writing "responses" at all, and her letters become increasingly monologic.

Arguably, Mariane's vocation pre-disposes her to prefer mono-logue to dialogue. Her pious existence conditions her to privilege solitary meditation over dialogic exchange, and it is therefore not illogical that her letters tend towards soliloquy rather than towards genuine communicative efforts. This tendency, coupled with the lover's disappointing epistolary manner, prompts Mariane to dispense with the need for a writing partner, and to simply create freely, in the

absence of his input. As we noted above, the lover's early letters
disappoint because they do not correspond precisely to the scripted
dialogue she imagines and anticipates. His letters represent faith-
fully a psychological reality, that of his fundamental indifference.
Such a depiction has no place in Mariane's fantasized scenario, and
explains her preference for solitary musings over a dialogue that falls
short of expectation.[14] Indeed, at one point Mariane admits to having
no need for an actual addressee at all ("j'ecris plus pour moi que
pour vous" [168]). Mariane's decision to write letters in the absence
of a response provides her with the opportunity to embellish at will,
to nurture and sustain verbally a deliberate self-construction without
fear of contradiction. In effect, the lover's reluctance to respond constitutes a decided advantage for the fantasy prone heroine. The spaces
of silence function like a blank canvas on which to project whatever
image she desires. Mariane's oft-repeated complaint about the lover's
non-responsiveness, then, is nothing but rhetorical posturing. She at
one point admits she never believed he read her letters in the first
place:

> Ingrat, je suis encore assez folle pour être au désespoir de ne
> pouvoir me flatter qu'elles ne soient pas venues jusques à vous,
> et qu'on ne vous les ait pas rendues! (171)

The lover's reluctance to answer Mariane's letters obliges the
reader to accept by default Mariane's version of events. The more his
silence persists, the more emboldened the heroine becomes. His silence provides her with the motive and opportunity to take increasing poetic license with a view of reality that she alone controls, thereby
effecting a kind of rhetorical revenge. The soldier's shameless seduction of the virtuous heroine is effectively countered by her subse-
quent rhetorical domination. It is significant that the heroine is
reluctant to reveal specific details about the relationship until it is
established that no contradictory information is forthcoming. Only
then does her narration become ornamented with an array of belated

---

14. Consult Carrell, *Le Soliloque de la passion*, 42–45.

specifics, examples that have no discernible function beyond that of rendering her account more credible in the continued absence of a corroborating witness. Ironically, however, the continuing silence of the lover subversively creates sympathy for the man whose version of events we never hear. Correlatively, Mariane's control of the scenario becomes increasingly annoying. Nevertheless, in the absence of any rebuttal, readers have little choice but to accept as truthful Mariane's statements. We simply have no other testimony available. Mariane's monopoly of the rhetorical evidence deprives her lover of voice and pen, and effectively victimizes, indeed, castrates, the soldier, just as she claims to have been physically and emotionally dominated by him.

Mariane's inability to substantiate her account with the lover's corroborating documentation obliges the readers to place their trust exclusively in a narrator whose grasp of reality is loosening. Her inconsistent recounting of events and increasingly fragile state of mind cast doubt on her ability to determine precisely where existence ends and invention begins. The heroine's narrative isolation contributes inevitably to the suspicion that the letters do not so much recount reality as reconstruct it from Mariane's own distorted perspective. The frequent internal contradictions contained in these five brief letters have been adequately documented.[15] Less commonly cited is the degree to which these contradictions erode the reader's trust in the narrator's fundamental credibility. These documented inconsistencies suggest that Mariane's sense of reality is irretrievably flawed, that she may in fact be incapable of discerning fact from fiction, or at the very least, not particularly willing to

---

15. For a perceptive analysis of the "deconstructive" nature of this text, see Richard-Laurent Barnett's masterful essay, "Excising the Text: Narrative Ablation in Guilleragues' *Lettres portugaises,*" *Romanic Review* 88 (1997), 364–84. Notes Barnett, "We, as readers, are thus confronted with, entrapped within, defied by a web of essentially self-effacing rhetoric, a textual lattice loomed of its own prescriptive annulment; that which it appears to assert, it rescinds; that which it avers to validate, it belies; its subsistence is rooted in its dissolution, in the contortions of its verbal grid whose countervailing terms, steeped in a pit, in a "fistula" of selfness and sameness (to return to the premonitory "propos" of our earlier considerations) engender a self-annihilating resultant, a totalized reduction heeding nothing short of the Barthesian 'degré zéro de l'écriture'" (376).

make a distinction.[16] It will be noted that as the letters progress, Mariane appears increasingly prone to equate fantasy with fact. She asserts at one point, without either provocation or justification, that the messenger waiting to deliver her letter is pressuring her to finish quickly in order to more hastily abandon some tiresome mistress ("il abandonne sans doute quelque malheureuse en ce pays" [167]). Giving her imaginative faculties full reign, she imagines her lover amidst a parade of willing and nubile mistresses :

> Je ne puis me reprocher d'avoir souhaité un seul moment de ne vous plus aimer: vous êtes plus à plaindre que je ne suis, et il vaut mieux souffrir tout ce que je souffre, que de jouir des plaisirs languissants que vous donnent vos maîtresses de France. (152–53)

She sees herself taking on other lovers in order to spite the unworthy soldier ("Je suis persuadée que je trouverais peut-être, en ce pays, un amant plus fidèle et mieux fait" [172]); she writes of taking a fantasized revenge ("Si quelque hasard vous ramenait en ce pays, je vous déclare que je vous livrerai à la vengeance de mes parents" [175]). Conversely, as her imagination flourishes, her ability to recall the factual details of mundane reality vanishes outright: ("tous ceux qui me parlent croient que je suis folle, je ne sais ce que je leur réponds . . ." [153]; "ma mère m'en a parlé avec aigreur, et ensuite avec quelque bonté, je ne sais ce que je lui ai répondu, il me semble que je lui ai tout avoué" [163]). Mariane's reliability is eroded further by a textual insistence on images of blindness:

> Hélas! les miens [ces yeux] sont privés de la seule lumière qui les animait . . . (147)
> . . . .
> J'attribue tout ce malheur à l'aveuglement avec lequel je me suis abandonee à m'attacher à vous . . . (151)

---

16. In the end, notes Mallinson, "Writing Wrongs," 46, we can longer tell the "constructed" from the spontaneous, the real from the role.

... je sens bien plus de disposition à m'abandonner aveuglément
à ma passion, qu'aux raisons que vous me donnez de me plaindre
de votre peu de soin. (160)

. . . .

Vous n'étiez point aveuglé, comme moi; pouquoi avez-vous donc
souffert que je devinsse en l'état où je me trouve? (161–62)

Her account is rendered equally suspect by a tendency to offer contradictory affirmations,[17] and by the strikingly insular nature of her existence. Her cloistered solitude contributes significantly to a textual product overridden by rhetorical questions and self-refutations ("mais non"), stylistic characteristics which, in conjunction with the unyielding silence of her partner, lend credence to the notion that Mariane may have lost touch with all reality beyond the convent walls, or, worse yet, that her discourse is no longer tethered to any reality at all.

Mariane's relentless engagement with an absent and silent partner suggests that making actual contact with the soldier is less the motive for the continuing discourse than a convenient pretext, a narrative strategy invoked to justify the heroine's continuing tale. Beyond his status of addressee, he has no other role to play. He functions as a literary construct, but nothing more. It is perhaps for this reason that the author makes no effort to contour his character or give him any substantive reality beyond that of anonymous addressee. From the opening apostrophe addressed to an abstract concept rather than a living being ("Considère, mon amour"), the lover appears too vague to contemplate.[18] The few details that emerge only further cloud the

17. Frédéric Deloffre (*Chansons,* 141–42), outlines some of the major contradictions.
18. The opening apostrophe has generated its fair share of discussion. Although a leading critic of the work, Frédéric Deloffre, "Les *Lettres portugaises,*" *L'Information Litteraire* 41 (1989), 11 insists that the opening is directed to the absent lover, an affirmation he restates again in "A propos des *Lettres portugaises,*" *Romanische Forschungen* 77 (1965), 351–52, a number of critics disagree, in particular Wolfgang Leiner. In a series of articles, Leiner demonstrates that Mariane addresses herself to the abstract concept rather than a flesh and blood partner. See for example, "De Nouvelles considérations sur l'apostrophe initiale des *Lettres portugaises,*" *Romanische Forschungen* 78 (1966), 548–66; "Ex Visceribus causae. Passion, rhétorique, littérature. Aspects rhétoriques de la formule initiale des *Lettres portugaises,*" *PFSCL* 3 (1975), 33–46; "L'amour de Mariane, du plaisir et la rhétorique du sentiment: Cheminements de la critique entre mythes et texte," *Oeuvres et Critiques* 1 (1976), 125–45.

reader's ability to envisage the solder as a living, breathing entity. He has few if any physical traits that might serve to identify him, and the behavioral portrait sketched out by Mariane is too inconsistent to confer any real sense of identity upon him. He is described as both distant ("N'aurez-vous de charmes que pour moi, et ne paraîtrez-vous pas agréable à d'autres yeux?" [165] and social ("des plaisirs languissants que vous donnent vos maîtresses de France" [152–53]); inconstant ("qui est en France au milieu des plaisirs" [148]) and faithful ("Mais non, je ne puis me résoudre à juger si injurieusement de vous" [148]); sincere ("avec toute l'ardeur et tout l'emportement que vous me faisiez voir" [152]); and hypocritical ("mais qui n'aurait été abusée, comme moi, par tant d'empressements, et à qui n'eussent-ils paru sincères?" [161]); communicative ("Ne remplissez plus vos lettres de choses inutiles, et ne m'écrivez plus de me souvenir de vous" [149]) and silent ("Pourquoi en est-il mieux informé, et enfin pourquoi ne m'avez-vous point écrit?" [160]). In fact, it is difficult to determine with any degree of precision whether he is the aggressive seducer or the passively seduced:

> . . . enfin je m'intéressais secrètement à toutes vos actions, je sentais bien que vous ne m'étiez point indifférent, et je prenais pour moi tout ce que vous faisiez. (164–65)

That the addressee constitutes nothing but a narrative pretext for Mariane is borne out by the masochistic pleasure the heroine takes in her own impassioned rhetoric. It has been noted that Mariane's reiteration of the same basic complaint serves to aggravate, rather than diminish, her frustration and anguish. Mariane seems to take perverted pleasure in recounting the emotional turmoil provoked by the lover's absence and prolonged silence:

> Cependant il me semble que j'ai quelque attachement pour des malheurs dont vous êtes la seule cause: je vous ai destiné ma vie aussitôt que je vous ai vu, et je sens quelque plaisir en vous la sacrifiant. (147)

Adieu, aimez-moi toujours; et faites-moi souffrir encore plus de maux. (150)

. . . .

. . . j'aime mieux souffrir encore davantage que vous oublier. (152)

. . . .

. . . cependant je vous remercie dans le fond de mon coeur du désespoir que vous me causez, et je déteste la tranquillité où j'ai vécu avant que je vous connusse. (159)

. . . .

. . . cependant je ne me plains point de toute la violence des mouvements de mon coeur, je m'accoutume à ses persécutions, et je ne pourrais vivre sans un plaisir que je découvre, et dont je jouis en vous aimant au milieu de mille douleurs. (163)

Whereas traditional letters are motivated in part by the hope of alleviating the void of solitude by providing discursive access to the absent partner, Mariane's letters appear designed not to attenuate or blunt the pangs of desire, but rather to inflame them. The reiterated focus on the unjust nature of her plight, on the unworthiness of the soldier, on the heroine's own inability to live up to personal expectations of the ideal "abandoned" lover, edge the heroine ever closer to dementia. With each successive letter, Mariane appears increasingly inflamed by her own avowals of affection, by the account of her impassioned self-sacrifice, by her rhetoric of unbridled desire.[19] Dominated as much by her impassioned discourse as by the lover himself ("J'ai éprouvé que vous m'étiez moins cher que ma passion" [170]), the heroine ultimately loses the will to live in the real world at all and retreats ever further into her discursive fantasies. The more she writes, the more she needs to write in order to escape the cloistered confines of her sterile reality and inhabit the imaginary world of discourse. The letters function no longer as the means to reestablish communication or to arrange an eventual reunion with the lover but to intensify her outrage and frustration by focusing on the lover's absence and indifference. What motivates the letters, then, is not the desire

19. "Indeed there are moments when Mariane realizes that her different emotions are not so much expressed, but are perhaps even created by the words on the page," notes Mallinson, "Writing Wrongs," 43.

for ultimate fulfillment that the lover's physical presence or epistolary responses would theoretically realize, but the desire for eternal
deferral, the promise of future satisfaction ever delayed, and in consequence, ever denied. In other words, the heroine writes not only in
the knowledge, but in the fervent desire, that she will not be answered,
because it is the lover's silence that provides her with the narrational
liberty to recast events in her own image, and to reiterate them indefinitely. This never-ending tale of abandonment functions in turn
to deliver her from the death-in-life existence of the convent wherein
she is destined to remain eternally confined.

Entrapped within a constructed web of fantasies, Mariane the
character disappears behind the dramatic rhetoric of Mariane the
writer.[20] Unfortunately, the fictional pose collapses with the arrival
of an unexpected response from the lover. The soldier's letter confirms his patent indifference, a truth established at the expense of
Mariane's fictions. With the unwelcome intrusion of reality into the
fictional construct, this particular epistolary project comes to an end.
But Mariane the writer claims to have learned much from the experience, and one of these lessons is that narrative discourse is safest the
greater the distance between rhetoric and reality. Her next literary
project will be neither so mimetic ("suis-je obligée de vous rendre un
compte exact de tous mes divers movements" [177]) nor so spontaneous ("Je veux vous écrire une autre lettre, pour vous faire voir que
je serai peut-être plus tranquille dans quelque temps" [176]).[21] Her
next opus will, in other words, be a much more deliberated, more
fictional, and less mimetic, account.

Just as the successful seduction requires that the speaker divorce sentiment and statement, so does the successful literary enterprise require words to be more studied, more contoured, more
constructed, than the reality they depict. It is in this sense that

20. "It is, nonetheless, via the never-absent, auto-erotic exertion of language, a friction of
fiction, as it were, object of its own contorted pleasure, that the text is, that dialectic meets
with disrepair, communication with castration, discourse with destruction" asserts Barnett,
"Excising the Text," 381.
21. A view that is shared by Mallinson, "Writing Wrongs," 46 who argues that language
cannot express reality in this work, and that beneath the apparent attempt to reveal truth,
there may only be fiction.

Guilleragues' text reveals its most cogent theoretical assertion. Mariane the character, depicted through the eyes of a male author, is constructed from an amalgam of prejudiced assumptions: that women are more passionate and less able to suppress their emotional impulses than males; that women are less able to control discourse than their male counterparts; that women naively equate the act of articulation with truth itself; that female identity is derived from the male's perception and reaction. Mariane, the character, is in every sense a literary stereotype confirming all these gendered presumptions. But Mariane the stereotypical character is the construct of Mariane, the writer, who like Guilleragues, may be deliberately duping her readers in order to create a work of fiction, which, by catering to prejudice, will persuade them of its veracity. It is in this sense that the character Mariane's excision from the text by two separate writers, one real (Guilleragues), one textual (Mariane, the letter writer), can be interpreted as a metatextual affirmation of the essentiality of aesthetic distance, and of the requisite distinction between experience and art. Classical writers believed that art must improve upon nature by controlling and refining it. Guilleragues' *Lettres portugaises* suggest that art is at its most persuasive when it supplants reality outright.

Few "constructed" texts have appeared as credible to the reading public as the *Lettres portugaises*, five short letters whose authorial source preoccupied readers for centuries. That these letters were for so long presumed authentic when they were in fact so wholly invented attests not to the naïveté of their readership but to the sophisticated narrative strategy of the author whose "textual effacement" serves to render his text more credible, more truth-seeming, more natural. Mariane's final excision from the text, her promise to write another text whose existence we cannot confirm, fortifies Mallinson's argument that beneath the attempt at truth, there may only be fiction; that language may be incapable of revealing any solid substance.[22] Mariane's disappearance (not unlike that of the author hiding behind his female invention) and her final silence distance the

---

22. "Writing Wrongs," 46. Consult also Elizabeth Berg, "Extravagant Narratives," 217, who proposes that the final question poses the very writerly dilemma of how to write in the state of tranquility, in the absence of inspiring and motivational events.

text from its ostensible author. This technique results in fictions that appear more compelling than truth. Guilleragues' *Lettres portugaises* demonstrate that the text that survives its fraudulent origins can also transcend reality itself and claim a spot in the a-temporal sphere of literary renown, thereby forever escaping the confining boundaries of the historical record.

CHAPTER 10

The Triumph of Illusion: *La Princesse de Clèves*[1]

Credibility was for Madame de Lafayette, as it was for Guilleragues, fundamental to the narrative enterprise. She hoped to achieve this goal in *La Princesse de Clèves* through a fascinating interweave of historical fact and creative fiction. The heroine, one of the novel's rare invented characters, intrudes upon the lives of historical figures. This fusion of fictional and historical elements, it is widely presumed, was intended to render the invented material more believable. The resulting achievement, however, renders this assumption less certain. At stake in this negotiation between art and history is the very status and legitimacy of the fictional construct. As the novel closes, readers are left to ponder a number of unresolved dilemmas, not the least of which is an aesthetic conundrum: is art called upon to imitate or idealize, to mimic or enhance, to document or distort reality? More significantly perhaps, what is, or what should be, the precise relationship between art and fiction and what is the relative status of each?

The contemporary literature of France, notably that birthed during the second half of the twentieth century, has been, since its postwar incipience, largely defined by critical voices whose object remains to distinguish that corpus from all textual antecedents. Thus do we encounter cumulative depictions which cast light upon what is averred to be a new brand of out-of-frame timing: a purposeful incorporation of non-sequentiality; the express depletion of character development; the eradication of story line, plot or theme; the "middleness" of matter adrift in a kind of aporia void of outset or conclusion; the image unhinged and without referent, slipping, as it were, from grasp; and, too, the problematics of disarticulation, a newly-turned language that harbors no stabilized meaning and that, by refuting the fixedness of the word, seeks to embrace the reader in a universe of mangled significance, of unmeaning refrain.

---

1. A briefer version of this article, "Historical Imposters, Fictional Truths: *La Princesse de Clèves*," appeared in *Symposium* 54, 4 (2001), 245–58.

At first or second glance, such codified portrayals of difference strike as lucid, insightful and, above all perhaps, as markedly precise. Yet, on closer scrutiny, the non-initiate must ultimately conclude that each and every would-be attribution so posited is a derivative of historical homologues that surface readings simply fail to illuminate. How does one chart the coordinates of temporality or sequentiality in Pascal's *Pensées* or in the *Maximes* of La Rochefoucauld? Could any personages prove less fully rounded, or obstinately resistant to rational exegesis, than Guilleragues' Mariane or Molière's Jourdain? Are Descartes' *Passions de l'âme,* La Bruyère's *Caractères,* Madame de Sévigné's epistolary efforts founded on, or faithful to, any brand of conventional plot, theme or even "reality"? And Phèdre's shrieks of agony hurled from within: are they not the vocalization of one who recoils in dread before a language that eludes her and that will not yield or mean as it should, a language that betrays and ultimately dismantles she who speaks it? Such reflections point, if little else, to the need for a re-enucleation of modernity or, perhaps all the more daringly and enduringly, for an altered consensus that would purport, at last and none too soon, the reiterative mode of all literary endeavor, whose unicity and grandeur reside without the too readily contrived matrices of catalogued features and sweeping generalizations.

Perhaps no other mark of difference has been more concertedly posited as the cornerstone of virtually all post-proustian endeavor than that of the binarily-inscribed enigma of presence and absence, terms invoked to ascertain modernity via its reconciliation of the familiar and the other, that which is and that which is not, the blunted demarcation between fiction and reality, the concrete and the abstract, the virtual and the real. I invoke these very dichotomies as the untold key to one of classicism's earliest, most widely read and least understood works of fiction, *La Princesse de Clèves.* For what has been traditionally evoked as France's first psychological novel turns out to be, in fact, a three hundred year old prefiguration of contemporary enterprise, a text strewn with structural, aesthetic and metaphysical riddles, complexities rarely adduced and patently unresolved.

In sum and contrary to critical tradition, this is a novel not merely born of absence, but focused upon it, a novel in which it is the un-said, the undone, the unexecuted, the un-realized that become the generators, if not the blatant glorification, of the fictional reality in which the authoress would have us engage.[2] More pointedly still, the work proliferates a meta-subtext, at once commonly un-perceived and yet forever over-riding, as a function of which motives and meanings are the product not of action underpinned by historical fact but of deliberate inaction, not of deeds but of fundamental deed-less-ness.[3] And thus it is that the narrative is propelled, indeed all but exclusively, by the very essence of *manque,* non-occurrence, by that which, in sum, never has and never will come to pass because its locus of existence resides exclusively in the imaginative domain. The question, then, is not the one oft celebrated of whether to be or not to be, but rather, a layered variant thereof: namely, how to grapple with a construct whose internal unfolding is the yield of all that is brutally absent, of all that is not.[4]

For Madame de Lafayette, the figuration of absence issues into an integration of antithetical narratives within one text, a juxtaposition that provides the basis for articulating an aesthetic principle: the autonomy of the fictional enterprise. Here, fictional discourse not only establishes its independence from historical reality, but in certain cases, actually triumphs over it.[5] Whereas the reality-based and

2. Lafayette's elliptical style is the subject of two outstanding articles by Joan DeJean, "Lafayette's Ellipses: The Privileges of Anonymity,"*An Inimitable Example: The Case for the Princesse de Clèves,* eds. Patrick Henry and John D. Lyons (Washington D.C.: Catholic University of America Press, 1992), 39–70 and "*La Princesse de Clèves:* The Poetics of Suppression," *Papers on French Seventeenth-Century Literature* 10,18 (1983), 79–97. "Lafayette's reader must quite literally read between the lines: she must interpret (verbalize) the unsaid and even the unsayable, for the language of the heroine is a language of lack, of silence, of gaps, of repression" (*"La Princesse de Clèves,"* 80).
3. See also, James R. McGuire, "La Princesse de Clèves dé-nouant *La Princesse de Clèves,"* *The French Review* 66, 3 (1993), 385.
4. Naomi Shor subjects Zola's heroine Nana to a similar analysis in order to argue the thesis that the woman in this novel constitutes the eternal enigma. "In a word, Nana is the enigmatic, which is to say hermeneutic object par excellence," *Breaking the Chain* (New York: Columbia University Press, 1985), 35.
5. On the triumph of fiction over history, see Erica Harth, *Ideology and Culture in Seventeenth-Century France* (Ithaca: Cornell University Press, 1983), 219 and Jean Rousset, *Forme et Signification: Essais sur les structures littéraires de Corneille à Claudel* (Paris: Corti, 1962), 20–21.

detail-rich historical text, grounded by the compelling virtue of truth, might logically be expected to represent the privileged site of reality, it is here portrayed as a fundamentally parasitic and static narrative form, one destined to remain ever subservient and inferior to the reality it passively re-constructs. Moreover, the essentially iterative function of historical discourse corresponds to the inherent nature of its subject of inquiry. In *La Princesse de Clèves*, history itself is presented as a fundamentally repetitive phenomenon. Despite the exceptional nature of the courtiers inhabiting this particular court ("La magnificence et la galanterie n'ont jamais paru en France avec tant d'éclat que dans les dernières années du règne de Henri second." [241]; "Jamais cour n'a eu tant de belles personnes et d'hommes admirablement bien faits" [242]),[6] there is little to suggest that the day to day experience at the court of Henri II is in any fundamental way distinguishable from life in previous courts.[7] On the contrary, the historical dimension of the novel conveys the idea of a court calcified by the routine and the habitual. This ritualistic conformity establishes a cultural link between the court of Henri II, center-staged in *La Princesse de Clèves*, to that of François I preceding it, and to the court of Louis XIV succeeding it. The information contained in the novel's embedded narratives also suggests that history repeats itself. These narrative subtexts underscore the cyclical nature of history by revealing the quest for love and power to be habitual courtly pursuits. Manners, customs, pastimes, even style of dress appear relatively unchanged across the generations:

> . . . les couleurs et les chiffres de Mme de Valentinois paraissaient partout, et elle paraissait elle-même avec tous les ajustements que pouvait avoir Mlle de la Marck, sa petite-fille, qui était alors à marier. (241)

6. All references are to Madame de Lafayette, *Romans et Nouvelles* (Paris: Garnier Frères, 1961).
7. I find Alain Niderst's assertion that the years 1557–1559 were not seen as the apogée of courtly elegance to be particularly noteworthy. Consult his article, "Pour une interprétation allégorique de *La Princesse de Clèves*," *Actes de Davis* (Paris: PFSCL/Biblio 17, 1988), 15.

The uniformity of life at court is paralleled by a fundamental resemblance of the courtiers to one another. Despite, perhaps even because of, their hyperbolic perfection, the characters appear largely indistinguishable one from the other.[8] Indeed, the initial cataloguing of courtiers, intended to acquaint readers with the characters, turns out to be more confusing that clarifying. Where hyperbole constitutes the norm, individual identities all tend to coalesce into one hazy mass of superlative humanity.[9] Like the historical periods that contain them, then, the characters appear more similar than different.

With two exceptions, of course. Even in an arena overfreighted with superlatives, Mlle de Chartres and the Duc de Nemours stand out in stark relief. What is significant, however, is that their noteworthy singularity has the effect of "fictionalizing" both protagonists, even the historically real Nemours, by placing emphasis on their historical non-conformity, that is to say, on their valorization of difference over resemblance.[10] As we have seen, history in *La Princesse de Clèves* is repetitive and imitative: courtiers of the present tend to resemble courtiers of the past, who in turn resemble courtiers of the future. These similarities are the result of deliberate patterning rather than accidental coincidence. The older generation provides an example to be reverently imitated by the younger, the latter imitating dutifully behavioral models of the past. The Duc de Nemours, however, breaks the pattern by defying replication:[11]

> Mais ce prince était un chef-d'oeuvre de la nature; ce qu'il avait
> de moins admirable, c'était d'être l'homme du monde le mieux

8. Ralph Albanese Jr. suggests that hyperbole and litote both bespeak a refusal of the mimetic mode by avoiding the concrete and the precise in "Classical Discourse in *La Princesse de Clèves*," *Romance Notes* 35, 1 (1994), 35.

9. See also, Jules Brody, "*La Princesse de Clèves* and the Myth of Courtly Love," *University of Toronto Quarterly* 38 (1969), 133.

10. Consult Laurence A. Gregorio, "Husserl, History and Historiography: A Phenomenological Approach to *La Princesse de Clèves* in *Racine; Fontenelle; Entretiens sur la pluralité des mondes; Histoire et Littérature,* ed. Charles Williams (Paris: PFSCL/ Biblio 17, 1990), 214.

11. "In a social arena where imitation and repetition yield homogeneity, Nemours alone seems to stand out as incomparable and unique," notes Byron R. Wells, "The King, the Court, the Country: Theme and Structure in *La Princesse de Clèves*," *Papers on French Seventeenth-Century Literature* (1985), 553.

fait et le plus beau. Ce qui le mettait au-dessus des autres était
une valeur incomparable, et un agrément dans son esprit, dans
son visage et dans ses actions que l'on n'a jamais vu qu'à lui
seul; il avait un enjouement qui plaisait également aux hommes
et aux femmes, une adresse extraordinaire dans tous ses
exercices, une manière de s'habiller qui était toujours suivie de
tout le monde, sans pouvoir être imitée, et enfin un air dans
toute sa personne qui faisait qu'on ne pouvait regarder que lui
dans tous les lieux où il paraissait. (243–44)

The heroine likewise eludes duplication by exhibiting unprec-
edented, even eccentric, behaviors. It is widely acknowledged that
no other woman behaves as she does, and her aberrational nature is a
constant focus of attention:

... il n'y a que vous de femme au monde qui fasse confidence
à son mari de toutes les choses qu'elle sait. (327)
. . . .
Eh bien, monsieur, lui répondit-elle en se jetant à ses genoux, je
vais vous faire un aveu que l'on n'a jamais fait à son mari; mais
l'innocence de ma conduite et de mes intentions m'en donne la
force. (333)
. . . .
Il [Nemours] trouva de la gloire à s'être fait aimer d'une femme
si différente de toutes celles de son sexe; enfin, il se trouva cent
fois heureux et malheureux tout ensemble. (337)

Her behavior has no documentable precedent ("La singularité d'un
pareil aveu, dont elle ne trouvait point d'exemple, lui en faisait voir
tout le péril" [337]); it engenders no enthusiastic following.[12] Alienation is in fact her singular legacy:

12. "In terms of literary history, Madame de Lafayette is effecting a shift from the generally
familiar (the *mémoire* or chronicle or *histoire secret*) to something quite novel, a novel of
the idiosyncratic and unpredictable. She frustrates expectations by replacing *déjà lu* with
jamais lu, advancing a narrative which avoids assumed continuities, shared maxims,
collective experience," notes David Mickelsen in "You Can Never Tell: *Déjà Vu* and *Jamais
Vu* in *La Princesse de Clèves,*" *Romance Languages Annual* 6 (1994), 139.

... et sa vie, qui fut assez courte, laissa des exemples de vertu inimitables. (395)

Although the Princesse and the Duc are alike in that both defy imitation, they dwell in two distinct textual dimensions, one historical, one fictional. Indeed, this blending of history (factual data) with romance (invented incredulities) into "novella" (the secret underside of historical reality)[13] constitutes the text's most oft-cited innovation. What is curious, however, is that the historical dimension does not result in an appreciable "de-fictionalization" of the invented material. On the contrary, argues Erica Harth, the fiction dehistorizes past realities.[14] Jean Rousset, too, notes that the historical dimension is actually subsumed by the fictional account.[15] This triumph of fiction is the result of deliberate narrative manipulation and premeditated authorial intent. Madame de Lafayette takes care to center-stage the heroine's invented status by underscoring her apartness from her historical peers. In so doing, she exacerbates rather than dissipates the tensions devolving from a fictional narrative pivoting on history. The polarization of historical and fictional value systems, one valorizing conformity, the other innovation, serves to isolate the fictional heroine within her historical milieu.[16] Characterized by a tendency to refrain from speech or actions in situations where both are generally deemed requisite, the heroine remains separate and superior to her grounding environment, an estrangement that is a primary factor in the oft-cited charge of *invraisemblance*.[17]

13. See Erica Harth, *Ideology and Culture,* 190.
14. *Ideology and Culture,* 219: "Love does not so much revise history as it dehistorizes fiction."
15. *Forme et Signification,* 20–21.
16. The Princesse's anti-mimetic nature has been documented by Gérard Genette (who refers to her as a "personnage sans maxime") in "Vraisemblance et motivation," *Figures II* (Paris: Seuil, 1969), 75; Ralph Albanese Jr., "Classical Discourse in *La Princesse de Clèves," Romance Notes* 35, 1 (1994), 44; Jules Brody, "*La Princesse de Clèves* and the Myth of Courtly Love," 133; Sylvie de Larimore de Lara, "*La Princesse de Clèves* ou l'invention de 'l'individu' féminin," *Romance Notes* 35, 1 (1994), 63; and Odette Virmauz, *Les Héroines romanesques de Madame de Lafayette* (Paris: Klincksieck, 1981), 39.
17. The heroine's implausibility was of course one of Valincour's principal condemnations in his *Lettres à Madame la Marquise *** sur le sujet de La Princesse de Clèves,* (Paris: Sébastien Mabre-Cramoisy, 1678; Université de Tours, 1972), 40–43.

The Princesse's contempt for the mimetic emulation so cherished by the other courtiers translates most often into a refusal to act at all.[18] The heroine equates action with imitation, and imitation with mediocrity, even vulgarity:

> C'est pourtant pour cet homme, que j'ai cru si différent du reste des hommes, que je me trouve, comme les autres femmes, étant si éloignée de leur ressembler. (352)

The litany of her non-responsiveness begins even before her marriage to the Prince de Clèves, a relationship characterized by the Princesse's dispassionate indifference. Her self-acknowledged frigidity ("Mlle de Chartres répondit qu'elle lui remarquait les mêmes bonnes qualités; qu'elle l'épouserait même avec moins de répugnance qu'un autre, mais qu'elle n'avait aucune inclination particulière pour sa personne" [257–58]) is in itself a distinguishing characteristic in a context overdetermined by impassioned alliances:

> L'ambition et la galanterie étaient l'âme de cette cour, et occupaient également les hommes et les femmes. Il y avait tant d'intérêts et tant de cabales différentes, et les dames y avaient tant de part que l'amour était toujours mêlé aux affaires et les affaires à l'amour. (252)

It is, however, her continuing reluctance to reveal any outward sign of affection towards her new husband that renders her wholly enigmatic:

18. "Même si la *Princesse de Clèves* appartient à la représentation classique et forcément mimétique, il n'empêche que le roman fait intervenir des éléments fictionnels qui déjà remettent en question un tel système," observes Sylvie Larimore de Lara, "*La Princesse de Clèves* ou l'invention de 'l'individu,'"63. See also, Odette Virmauz, *Les Héroïnes romanesques de Madame de Lafayette,* 39 and Ralph Albanese Jr., "Classical Discourse in *La Princesse de Clèves,*" 41. Also noteworthy is the remark by James McGuire, "La Princesse de Clèves dé-nouant *La Princesse de Clèves,*" 385: "Ce refus, qui est en effet représenté dans les actes singuliers de la Princesse, ne se manifeste pas comme une sorte d'écriture propre à la Princesse, mais plutôt dans des actes de silence et de détachement."

> Il voyait avec beaucoup de peine que les sentiments de Mlle de
> Chartres ne passaient pas ceux de l'estime et de la reconnais-
> sance et il ne pouvait se flatter qu'elle en cachât de plus
> obligeants, puisque l'état où ils étaient lui permettait de les faire
> paraître sans choquer son extrême modestie. (258)

In this particular instance, the heroine's non-responsiveness signals a corresponding lack of affection. However, the Princesse's non-
responsiveness is often not linked to any external reality at all. In
fact, for the inscrutable Princesse, silence and stasis can signal a pleni-
tude as well as a dearth of emotion. The initial encounter between
the Duc de Nemours and the Princesse provides a case in point. Although she pleads ignorance as to the identity of her dancing partner
("Je vous assure, madame, reprit Mme de Clèves, qui paraissait un
peu embarrassée, que je ne devine pas si bien que vous pensez" [262]),
the sincerity of this denial is effectively disputed: ("Vous devinez
fort bien, répondit Mme la dauphine; et il y a même quelque chose
d'obligeant pour M. de Nemours à ne vouloir pas avouer que vous le
connaissez sans l'avoir jamais vu" [262]). On this occasion, silence
communicates information the Princesse prefers to conceal, as it does
again when she chooses not to reveal her feelings towards Nemours
to her mother:

> Elle ne se trouva pas la même disposition à dire à sa mère ce
> qu'elle pensait des sentiments de ce prince qu'elle avait eue à
> lui parler de ses autres amants; sans avoir un dessein formé de
> lui cacher, elle ne lui en parla point. (270)

Absence of evidence, then, does not necessarily signify evidence
of absence. Both the heroine and Nemours succeed in communicat-
ing quite effectively in silence.[19] Although Nemours remains uncharacteristically reserved about his feelings for the Princesse ("Il n'en

19. "Le langage non verbal est peut-être l'expression des sentiments les plus profonds et
les plus sincères, il est peut-être celui auquel on doit se fier; mais il a l'inconvénient d'être
singulièrement imprécis," notes Christian Garaud in "Le Geste et la parole: Remarques
sur la communication amoureuse dans *La Princesse de Clèves*," *XVIIᵉ Siècle* (1978), 262.

parla pas même au vidame de Chartres" [270]), she successfully interprets his unspoken yearnings ("elle aurait eu peine à s'en apercevoir
elle-même, si l'inclination qu'elle avait pour lui ne lui eût donné une
attention particulière pour ses actions, qui ne lui permît pas d'en
douter" [270]). The Princesse in turn uses silence to communicate
covertly with Nemours:

> Il demeura quelque temps sans pouvoir parler. Mme de Clèves
> n'était pas moins interdite, de sorte qu'ils gardèrent assez
> longtemps le silence. (293)
> . . . .
> Elle demeurait donc sans répondre, et M. de Nemours se fût
> aperçu de son silence, dont il n'aurait peut être pas tiré de
> mauvais présages si l'arrivée de M. de Clèves n'eût fini la con-
> versation et sa visite. (294)

Silence also conveys information the heroine is reluctant to reveal to her husband, and he rightly assumes silence provides proof of
culpability:

> Mme de Clèves ne répondit point; et son silence achevant de
> confirmer son mari dans ce qu'il avait pensé:
> —Vous ne me dites rien, reprit-il, et c'est me dire que je ne me
> trompe pas. (333)
> . . . .
> Comme il vit qu'elle ne lui nommait point M. de Nemours, il
> lui demanda, en tremblant, si c'était tout ce qu'elle avait vu,
> afin de lui donner lieu de nommer ce prince et de n'avoir pas la
> douleur qu'elle lui en fît une finesse. (361)

These silences that communicate are accompanied in turn by a
number of non-actions that signify. The first example is the Princesse's
decision not to attend the Maréchal de Saint-André's ball. In order to
appease an unsuspecting Duc de Nemours, she feigns illness to avoid
attending a reception that the Duc is obliged to miss as well. A second, more egregious, non-sign of affection occurs during the theft of

her portrait. Although she discovers Nemours in the act of stealing the miniature belonging to her husband, she chooses not to react, thereby allowing Nemours to interpret her passivity as tacit approval:

> Enfin, elle jugea qu'il valait mieux le lui laisser, et elle fut bien aise de lui accorder une faveur qu'elle lui pouvait faire sans qu'il sût même qu'elle la lui faisait. M. de Nemours, qui remarquait son embarras, et qui en devinait quasi la cause, s'approcha d'elle et lui dit tout bas:
> —Si vous avez vu ce que j'ai osé faire, ayez la bonté, madame, de me laisser croire que vous l'ignorez; je n'ose vous en demander davantage. (302)

Likewise, her refusal to grant Nemours an audience is taken for a sign of her simmering passion ("Ce prince ne fut pas blessé de ce refus: une marque de froideur, dans un temps où elle pouvait avoir de la jalousie, n'était pas un mauvais augure" [323]). Even the much-criticized "aveu", one of the few actions for which she can claim active responsibility, is made in order to prolong her inactivity by remaining self-exiled from court, and therefore, less vulnerable to Nemours' seductive charms.[20]

The function of these non-actions and non-verbal communiqués is two-fold. On one level, inactivity underscores the heroine's alienation and hence her fictionality amidst historical realities. Madame de Clèves is cast as the consummate stranger. Nameless, raised outside the court and therefore unfamiliar with its history and routine protocols, she is unable to navigate successfully the landscape she now inhabits. She remains throughout an incongruous participant, an enigmatic composite of prudish restraint and passive indulgence. Even her emblematic colors, those carried by Nemours during the tournament and intended to represent her, are a "fictional" construct in that they constitute colors that she refuses to wear:

---

20. Harriet Stone offers some extremely cogent insights into the distinction between fiction and history in her article "Exemplary Teaching in *La Princesse de Clèves*," *The French Review* 62, 2 (1988), 251: "The princess's move to inhabit a private space must be understood to be a move away from history and imitation."

> M. de Nemours avait du jaune et du noir; on en chercha
> inutilement la raison. Mme de Clèves n'eut pas de peine à la
> deviner: elle se souvint d'avoir dit devant lui qu'elle aimait le
> jaune, et qu'elle était fâchée d'être blonde, parce qu'elle n'en
> pouvait mettre. Ce prince crut pouvoir paraître avec cette couleur,
> sans indiscrétion, puisque, Mme de Clèves n'en mettant point,
> on ne pouvait soupçonner que ce fût la sienne. (355)

This poetics of absence has the additional effect of shifting reader dependency away from the limited knowledge of the narrator and on to the individual reader's imagination. The frequency with which Mme de Lafayette exploits the reader's need to rely on imaginative speculation is too striking to be aesthetically irrelevant. By conspicuously abandoning narrative responsibility at key moments in the text, the narrator obliges the reader to supply the missing data. This displacement from the evidence supplied in the text to the speculative imaginings of the reader forefronts yet another distinction between historical and fictional discourse. Whereas historical truth can be corroborated by documentation, fictional truth relies on inference. To make sense of the narrative, one must often interpret the data between the lines, and on occasion, supply it outright.[21] It is, for example, significant that although the heroine's stunning beauty is what supposedly distinguishes her from the rest of the beautiful women at court, her physical description is noticeably abridged, even in a novel notoriously short on descriptive embellishments:[22]

> La blancheur de son teint et ses cheveux blonds lui donnaient
> un éclat que l'on n'a jamais vu qu'à elle; tous ses traits étaient
> réguliers, et son visage et sa personne étaient pleins de grâce et
> de charmes. (248)

This stunted description of the court's most beautiful woman endows the newly-introduced character with an imprecise, ephemeral qual-

---

21. See also, Joan DeJean, "Lafayette's Ellipses: The Privileges of Anonymity," 51.
22. See also Albanese, "Classical Discourse in *La Princesse de Clèves*," 38.

ity and forces the readers to construct a mental image with few clues to guide them. As if to render her existence even more enigmatic, the courtiers are initially reluctant to lend credence to the report of her existence:

> Madame lui dit qu'il n'y avait point de personne comme celle qu'il dépeignait et que, s'il y en avait quelqu'une, elle serait connue de tout le monde. (250)

The paucity of detail attached to the Princesse's description constitutes but one of a number of examples where the narrator surrenders control of the text. During the course of the novel, the reader is often invited to imagine what the narrator suppresses:

> L'on peut juger ce que sentit Mme de Chartres par la rupture d'une chose qu'elle avait tant désirée, dont le mauvais succès donnait un si grand avantage à ses ennemis et faisait un si grand tort à sa fille. (255)
> . . . .
> L'on ne peut exprimer la douleur qu'elle sentit de connaître, par ce que lui venait de dire sa mère, l'intérêt qu'elle prenait à M. de Nemours: elle n'avait encore osé se l'avouer à elle-même. (275)
> . . . .
> Ces paroles . . . lui causèrent une douleur qu'il est aisé de s'imaginer. (344)
> . . . .
> Il est aisé de s'imaginer en quel état ils passèrent la nuit. (350)
> . . . .
> On ne peut exprimer ce que sentit M. de Nemours dans ce moment. (367)
> . . . .
> L'on ne peut exprimer ce que sentirent M. de Nemours et Mme de Clèves de se trouver seuls et en état de se parler pour la première fois. (382)

Most noteworthy of all, perhaps, the author fails even to provide a satisfactory denouement to the story. Only the barest outline of what befalls the Princesse in the aftermath of her rejection of Nemours is provided, obliging readers to speculate on their own.[23]

The narrator's surrender of discursive power to the reader takes on additional significance when contrasted with the narrative manner of the digressions. Although a common subject of critical inquiry, these sub-texts are generally either denounced as intrusive, or reconciled to the primary text as examples of parallel narratives that lend thematic and allegorical support to the fictional macro-structure.[24] There is, however, another possible explanation, one more consistent with the historical/fictional polarity on which the text is structured. These digressions may be intended to function not as parallel, but as counter-narratives. In point of fact, the embedded tales reveal far more differences with than similarities to the framing narrative. The digressions are predominately historical, whereas the primary narrative recounts the imagined exploits of an invented heroine. The embedded narratives are textually motivated, offered in response to specific requests; the fictional frame has no apparent intent or motive. The digressions serve an essentially didactic purpose, the moral instruction of the heroine; the lessons of the fictional tale are averred to be of minimal applicability due to the "inimitable" nature of the heroine's actions.[25] The

23. For further clarification and insights, consult Roland Racevskis, "Solitary Pleasures: Creative Avoidance of Court and Convent in *La Princesse de Clèves*," *French Review* 70 (1996), 24, and Richard Moye, "Silent Victory: Narrative, Appropriation, and Autonomy in *La Princesse de Clèves*," *MLN*, 104, 4 (1989), 860: "Simply by narrating the story and by undercutting the apparent closure of the conclusion, Lafayette invites us to appropriate the story and, in effect, to complete it by passing judgment upon the Princesse's final decision." See also, Joan DeJean, "*La Princesse de Clèves:* The Poetics of Suppression," 94: "Lafayette's novel has never ceased generating the desire Bussy experienced, the desire to fill in its gaps, to give it the continuity considered "natural," to appropriate the Princesse's story just as the Reine Dauphine did."

24. For a discussion of these embedded narratives, consult Stirling Haig, *Madame de Lafayette* (New York: Twayne, 1970), 110–13; Alain Niderst, *La Princesse de Clèves: Le Roman paradoxal* (Paris: Larousse, 1973), 137–45; and J. W. Scott, "The 'Digressions' of *The Princesse de Clèves*," *French Studies* 11 (1957), 315–22.

25. "An example that defies imitation is no longer a historical model: the rhetoric of history, gives way to a rhetoric of fiction" affirms Harth, *Ideology and Culture,* 220. See also, Nancy K. Miller, "Emphasis Added: Plots and Plausibilities in Women's Fiction" in *An Inimitable Example,* 31–32: "Thus in the end, Mme de Clèves herself becomes both the impossibility of an example for others 'in life' and its possibility in fiction." See also, Richard H. Moye, "Silent Victory," 859: "But it is not simply her physical death; it is also her narrative death, for the example, the *exemplum* the Princesse ultimately provides is unrepeatable, '*inimitable.*'"

detail-rich intrusions are delivered as monologues to a captive audience; the aporia-laden fictional account invites readers to participate in the task of textual construction. The embedded narratives require patience and concentration for full comprehension; the simplistic plot of the primary narrative holds readers' attention effortlessly. The embedded narratives, objective and factual, contain minimal stylistic embellishments; the primary narrative is rich in poetic effects. In sum, attempts to integrate the functions of the embedded and primary narratives would appear to be counterproductive. The two discursive events exemplify contrasting narrative manners, means and goals.

More significantly, perhaps, these contrasting narrative modes are not presented as equally effective discursive structures.[26] On the contrary, in *La Princesse de Clèves,* fiction proves unequivocally more compelling than fact. It is generally postulated that the historical digressions are designed to fortify by example Mme de Chartre's pedagogical fables to her daughter outlining the perils of extra-marital passion. If that is their function, they are surprisingly ineffective. The Princesse's growing attachment to Nemours is largely undeterred by these anecdotal accounts. The inability of the embedded narratives to fulfill their assigned instructional function establishes by default the limits of a discourse whose endpoint is the slavish documentation of an authentic reality. To elucidate the heroine, imaginative speculation, not historical example, provides the insight of final consequence. Indeed, one of the great originalities of this novel is that fiction wields more influence than fact. Only a "fictional" text, the Vidame's love letter mistakenly attributed to the Duc de Nemours, succeeds finally in enlightening the heroine.[27]

The letter's fictional status derives from its disputed authorship, a confusion that renders the assigned meanings wholly imaginary.

---

26. The remarks of Dalia Judovitz in "The Aesthetics of Implausibility: *La Princesse de Clèves,*" *MLN* 99, 5 (1984), 1054–55, are particularly relevant: "As we have shown, the novel, through its extensive play of intertextuality and narration, has posited the privileged role of representation (fiction) in the novel." The novel, she argues further, is a plea for a new concept of fiction where the implausible becomes a new criterion for aesthetic sensibility.

27. See Harriet Stone, "Exemplary Teaching in *La Princesse de Clèves,*" 253: "Ironically, fiction alone persuades the princess of her feelings for Nemours."

The missive's fictionality, however, in no way diminishes its impact. By introducing an alternate scenario into the heroine's consciousness, a destructive and unwelcome fantasy that challenges the visual evidence of lived experience, the letter enables the Princesse to conceptualize clearly the veiled warnings contained within the historical digressions. Forced suddenly to acknowledge two competing versions of "truth" (the Duc's apparent devotion now belied by the epistolary "evidence" of his infidelity), the Princesse elects to locate reality in the realm of her imaginary fears:

> Elle voyait, par la fin de la lettre, que cette personne se croyait aimée: elle pensait que la discrétion que ce prince lui avait fait paraître, et dont elle avait été si touchée, n'était peut-être que l'effet de la passion qu'il avait pour cette autre personne à qui il craignait de déplaire. (311)

Even after the Duc's innocence is established and the rightful author identified, the emotional bond to Nemours is critically fractured.[28] The Princesse has only to remember the distress occasioned by her jealousy to strengthen any weakening of her resolve:

> Mais, ce qu'elle pouvait moins supporter que tout le reste, était le souvenir de l'état où elle avait passé la nuit, et les cuisantes douleurs que lui avait causées la pensée que M. de Nemours aimait ailleurs et qu'elle était trompée. Elle avait ignoré jusqu'alors les inquiétudes mortelles de la défiance et de la jalousie; elle n'avait pensé qu'à se défendre d'aimer M. de Nemours et elle n'avait point encore commencé à craindre qu'il en aimât une autre. Quoique les soupçons que lui avait donnés cette lettre fussent effacés, ils ne laissèrent pas de lui ouvrir les yeux sur le hasard d'être trompée et de lui donner des impressions de défiance et de jalousie qu'elle n'avait jamais eues. (330)

---

28. After the letter, notes Vincent Gregoire in "*La Princesse de Clèves* ou le roman de la méprise," *Papers on French Seventeenth-Century Literature* 23, 44 (1996), 250 "Les effets en seront irréversibles."

The Princesse's decision to place her faith in phantom anxieties has no realistic justification. The hero has yet to reveal the flaws of reckless indiscretion (repeating the overheard "aveu") and destructive egocentrism (blaming the husband for the indiscretion) that discredit him later in the eyes of readers. The fantasy of an inconstant Nemours persuades, then, not because it resembles fact, but because it resembles fiction, or to be more precise, the fictions used by Mme de Chartres to keep her daughter morally pure.[29] Her mother's tales of doomed relationships condition the Princesse to interpret reality through the grid of fiction, to trust unsubstantiated fictions rather than visual evidence. Early in the novel, the Princesse blindly accepts her mother's motivated rumor linking Nemours and the Dauphine. Confronted again with the necessity of choosing between her mother's carefully crafted fabrications (portraying men as fickle brutes) and the evidence contradicting these claims (the King's unwavering attachment to the Duchesse de Valentinois), the Princesse elects to place her faith in illusory speculations.[30]

The thematic burdens of the letter are not limited to demonstrating the superiority of the imagination over historical example. The letter also serves to place the entire love affair in mextatextual relief. It is significant that the events uniting the historical Nemours and the fictional Princesse constitute aesthetic rather than physical encounters.[31] The dance that brings them together is followed by another aesthetic exchange, Nemours' theft of her portrait. The Princesse in turn appropriates court portraits of Nemours to decorate the walls of her retreat at Coulommiers. The relationship is metaphorically "consummated" when the couple moves from passive participants to fraudulent authors attempting to duplicate the contents of the Vidame's love letter. This intimate forgery (an act of aesthetic transgression)

---

29. This is suggested also by Peggy Kamuf, *Fictions of Feminine Desire: Disclosures of Heloise* (Lincoln: University of Nebraska Press, 1982), 96, when she refers to the Princesse as a product of her mother's fantasy.
30. John D. Lyons in "Narrative Interpretation and Paradox: *La Princesse de Clèves,*" *Romanic Review* (1981), 390, sees the Diane de Poitiers episode as "an exception to the rules of love."
31. "The ethical claims of the novel thus reflect the true character of classical aesthetics: the will to power as art," notes Judovitz, "The Aesthetics of Implausibility," 1055.

committed within the secured confines of the Princesse's bedroom
constitutes the climax of what to this point is an innocent and gaze-
based relationship. After the epistolary transgression, even the
Princesse considers her behavior as akin to marital infidelity:

> . . . elle trouvait qu'elle était d'intelligence avec M. de Nemours,
> qu'elle trompait le mari du monde qui méritait le moins d'être
> trompé, et elle était honteuse de paraître si peu digne d'estime
> aux yeux même de son amant. (330)

The move from aesthetic appreciation to active plagiarism, from
harmless gaze to illicit forgery articulates the novel's most cogent
and consistent metatextual point: the explicit condemnation of the
mimetic enterprise.[32] The Princesse is first seen attempting to match
precious stones, an attempt that fails. The portrait, presumably the
most mimetic of art forms, fails also to translate accurately the reality it ostensibly reflects. It is because the Princesse is obliged to request a retouching in order to bring static image and ever-changing
reality into closer congruence that Nemours manages to appropriate
the portrait. The attempt to duplicate the contents of the Vidame's
love letter proves equally ineffective. Even though the Princesse has
re-read the letter many times over, the attempt to re-construct it is
nothing short of catastrophic:

> Enfin à peine, à quatre heures, la lettre était-elle achevée, et elle
> était si mal, et l'écriture dont on la fit copier ressemblait si peu
> à celle que l'on avait eu dessein d'imiter qu'il eût fallu que la
> reine n'eût guère pris de soin d'éclaircir la vérité pour ne la pas
> connaître. (328–29)

Nemours' evolution within the novel also reveals the deficiencies of the mimetic endeavor. In the closing moments of the narrative, he is discovered attempting to escape his own historical reality
for the purpose of assuming a place in the more aesthetic realm of

---

32. See also, John D. Lyons, "Narrative Interpretation and Paradox," 400.

the Princesse. The court's most notable figure elects to exchange his historical reality, wherein deliberate imitation and generational repetition are paramount, for aesthetic anonymity. Disguised as an artist, he is caught casting stolen glances at the Princesse in retreat at Coulommiers:

> Le maître répondit qu'il n'en avait pas la clef et qu'elle était occupée par un homme qui y venait quelquefois pendant le jour pour dessiner de belles maisons et des jardins que l'on voyait de ses fenêtres. (379)

The significance of Nemour's historical betrayal is metatextually relevant. It constitutes a denunciation of historical reality in favor of the fictional dimension.[33]

The emphasis on the primacy of the aesthetic in *La Princesse de Clèves* serves to clarify what three centuries of debate have not yet fully resolved: the motivational impulse behind the widowed Princesse's refusal to marry Nemours.[34] Sexual frigidity, moral integrity, even feminist self preservation[35] have all been offered as possible motives for a decision that confounds reason:

> . . . mais ce ne sont point de véritables raisons. (385)

> Ah! madame, lui dit M. de Nemours, quel fantôme de devoir opposez-vous à mon bonheur? Quoi! madame, une pensée vaine et sans fondement vous empêchera de rendre heureux un homme que vous ne haïssez pas? (385–86)

---

33. "In establishing fiction as a standard for imitation, the narrative denies referentiality as a criterion for ordering knowledge within the novel," notes Stone, "Exemplary Teaching in *La Princesse de Clèves,*" 252.

34. Patrick Henry, *An Inimitable Example,* 11, views this enigmatic final renunciation as a twentieth-century obsession.

35. For more on this essentially "feminist" interpretation, consult, among others, the articles by Jules Brody, "*La Princesse de Clèves* and the Myth of Courtly Love," 131–34; Michael Danahy, *The Feminization of the Novel* (Gainesville, University of Florida Press, 1991), 101–25; Nancy K. Miller, "Emphasis Added: Plots and Plausibilities in Women's Fiction," 23; Domna C. Stanton, "The Ideal of Repos in Seventeenth-Century French Literature," *Esprit créateur* 15 (1975), 79–104; and A. Kibédi Varga, "Romans d'amour, romans de femmes à l'époque classique," *Revue des sciences humaines* 168 (1977), 524.

Her renunciation, I argue, appears incomprehensible only from a historical or real-world perspective. Narratively speaking, her decision is not only logical, but textually requisite. The Princesse's defining trait is her apartness from the historical reality attempting to assimilate her.[36] Her final incomprehensible gesture is therefore consistent with her overall behavior. To counter her refusals with rational alternatives is to suggest that the historical and fictional worlds operate under similar laws and principles, when in fact, they do not. Her decision cannot be persuasively justified or defended on the basis of logic because it is not a rational decision at all. It is a narrative strategy designed to endow the heroine with poetic coherence. Even the Princesse concedes she has no credible defense to offer:

> Il est vrai, répliqua-t-elle, que je sacrifie beaucoup à un devoir
> qui ne subsiste que dans mon imagination. (389)

If the novel is destined, like theater and poetry, to instruct as well as please, the lessons will derive not from the representation of reality, but from power of the imagination to invent solutions that have yet to be tried. "In the light of the darkness made visible in the obscure clarity of this novel," notes John Campbell, "the only appropriate answer perhaps comes not from Pascal, but from his ally and adversary: Que sais-je."[37] This sentiment is echoed by Dalia Judovitz who notes that in this novel, the "implausible enters the domain of the real only to change both our definition of the novel and that of reality."[38] Madame de Lafayette's novel, then, achieves its most satisfying unity when read as an apology for the liberating creativity of the fictional enterprise. When a discourse allows the patterns of expectation to become so entrenched that any deviation is dismissed as implausible, that discourse becomes irrelevant and impotent. It is for this reason that the astrologer's prediction is summarily dismissed.

---

36. "C'est une femme incompréhensible" was the early conclusion of Jean Baptiste Valincour, *Lettres à Madame la Marquise*, 50.
37. "The Cloud of Unknowing: Self-Discovery in *La Princesse de Clèves*," *French Studies* 48, 4 (1994), 413.
38. "The Aesthetics of Implausibility," 1054.

The prediction deviates too radically from anticipated realities, and is consequently disregarded. To benefit from the prediction, the King would have to reconcile the disparate images of fiction and reality by subjecting known reality (political security) to the laws of unknown fictions (the astrologer's implausible prediction). His survival depends on his ability to imagine the unimaginable, and he is clearly unprepared to do so.[39]

If in the end, we acknowledge the reversal of paradigms, if we ply to the altered prototype that the novel, however tentatively, thrusts upon us, what then, is really at stake? Can art subsume history any more effectively than it can represent it? Is it not so that life and art, like truth and fiction, are perpetually and necessarily at odds, that neither aptly bespeaks, conquers, alas even signifies, the other? Mimesis, like semiosis, is a contrivance, an attempt to harmonize and ultimately to hierarchize two "objects," two "realities" that can at best pretend to imitate each other. A participant in this enterprise of imitation and emulation, Madame de Lafayette merely inverts the ostensible rules of the game, the would-be outcome of the ensuing battle. As such, she creates an atypical fictional heroine (one "who marries neither God nor Man")[40] just as she contrives a history destined to subserve the needs of fiction.

39. See Lyons, "Narrative Interpretation and Paradox," 396.
40. Suzanne Relyea, "Se manquer ou se prononcer: Presence and Self-Possession in the *Princesse de Clèves*," *Papers on French Seventeenth-Century Literature* 10, 18 (1983), 45.

BIBLIOGRAPHY

Abel, Elizabeth, Marianne Hirsch, and Elizabeth Langland, eds. *The Voyage In: Fictions of Female Development.* Hanover: University Press of New England, 1983.

Abraham, Claude. *Jean Racine.* Boston: G. K. Hall, 1977.

———. *The Strangers: The Tragic World of Tristan L'Hermite.* Gainesville: University of Florida Press, 1966.

———. *Tristan L'Hermite.* Boston: G. K. Hall, 1980.

Albanese, Ralph Jr. "Classical Discourse in *La Princesse de Clèves.*" *Romance Notes* 35. 1 (1994): 35–43.

———. "Dramaturgie classique et codes idéologiques: Le cas Racine." *Relectures raciniennes: Nouvelles approches du discours tragique.* Ed. R. L. Barnett. Paris: PFSCL 16 (1986): 15–29.

Allentuch, Harriet. "Reflections on Women in the Theatre of Corneille." *Kentucky Romance Quarterly* 21 (1974): 97–111.

Apostilidès, Jean-Marie. "Corneille, Tite-Live et la fondation de Rome." *Poétique* 21 (1990): 203–22.

Bach, Ray. "Fatal Identity: Parents and Children in Racine's *Andromaque.*" *Stanford French Review* 16 (1992): 9–18.

Barthes, Roland. *Sur Racine.* Paris: Seuil, 1963.

Barnett, R. L. "Excising the Text: Narrative Ablation in Guilleragues' *Lettres portugaises.*" *Romanic Review* 88 (1997): 364–84.

———. ed. *Les Epreuves du labyrinthe: Essais de poétique et d'herméneutique raciniennes. Hommage tricentenaire.* Dalhousie French Studies 49 (1999).

———. "Of Discourse Subverted: Metonymic Dysfunction in Corneille's *Horace.*" *Romanic Review* 81 (1990): 1–10.

———. ed. *Relectures raciniennes: Nouvelles approches du discours tragique.* PFSCL 16 (1986).

Benstock, Shari, ed. *Feminist Issues in Literary Scholarship.* Bloomington: Indiana University Press, 1987.

Berg, Elizabeth. "Iconoclastic Moments: Reading the *Sonnets for Hélène,* Writing the *Portuguese Letters.*" *The Poetics of Gender.* Eds. Nancy K. Miller and Carolyn Heilbrun. New York: Columbia University Press, 1986. 208–21.

———. "Impossible Representation: A Reading of *Phèdre.*" *Romanic Review* 73 (1982): 421–37.

Bersani, Leo. *A Future for Astyanax: Character and Desire in Literature.* Boston: Little, Brown and Co., 1976.

Bertaud, Madeleine, and Alain Niderst, eds. *Onze études sur la vieillesse de Corneille dédiées à la mémoire de Georges Couton.* Boulogne: ADIREL, 1994.

Branan, A. J. "Dramatis res and Couleur mythologique in Racine's *Phèdre.*" *Romance Notes* 23 (1982): 29–33.

Brody, Jules. "*La Princesse de Clèves* and the Myth of Courtly Love." *University of Toronto Quarterly* 38 (1969):105–35.

Campbell, John. "The Cloud of Unknowing: Self-Discovery in *La Princesse de Clèves.*" *French Studies* 48. 4 (1994): 402–15.

———. "The God of Athalie." *French Studies* 43.4 (1989): 385–404.

———. "The Exposition of *Athalie.*" *Seventeenth-Century French Studies* 12 (1990): 149–57.

———. "The Unity of Time in *Athalie.*" *Modern Language Review* 86 (1991): 573–79.

Campbell, Joseph. *The Hero with a Thousand Faces.* New York: Pantheon, 1949.

Carrell, Susan Lee. *Le Soliloque de la passion féminine ou le dialogue illusoire.* Tubingen: Gunter Narr, 1982.

Clarac, Pierre. "*Athalie:* La Prophétie de Joad. *L'Information Littéraire* 14 (1962): 224–28.

Clarke, David. *Pierre Corneille: Politics and Political Drama under Louis XIII.* Cambridge: Cambridge University Press, 1992.

Cloonan, William. "Love and Gloire in *Bérénice:* A Freudian Perspective." *Kentucky Romance Quarterly* 22 (1975): 517–25.

Corneille, Pierre. *Rodogune.* Ed. Jacques Schérer. Paris: Droz, 1946.

———. *Théâtre complet.* Ed. Maurice Rat. Paris: Garnier Frères, 1960.

Dalle Valle, Daniella. *Il teatro di Tristan l'Hermite.* Torino: Giappichelli, 1964.

Dainard, J. A. "The Power of the Spoken word in *Bérénice.*" *Romanic Review* 67 (1976): 157–71.

Danahy, Michael. *The Feminization of the Novel.* Gainesville: University of Florida Press, 1991.

Defaux, Gérard. "Titus ou le héros tremblant." *French Forum* 10 (1985): 271–94.

DeJean, Joan. "Lafayette's Ellipses: The Privileges of Anonymity." *An Inimitable Example: The Case for the Princesse de Clèves.* Eds. Patrick Henry and John Lyons. Washington D.C.: Catholic University of America Press, 1992: 884–902.

———. "*La Princesse de Clèves:* The Poetics of Suppression." *Papers on French Seventeenth-Century Literature* 10.18 (1983): 79–97.

Deloffre, Frédéric. "A propos des *Lettres portugaises.*" *Romanische Forschungen* 77 (1965): 351–52.

———. "Les *Lettres portugaises.*" *L'Information Littéraire* 41 (1989): 7–12.

Deloffre, Frédéric and Jaques Rougeot, eds. *Chansons et Bons Mots* Valentins. *Lettres portugaises.* Geneva: Droz, 1972.

———. "Les *Lettres portugaises.*" *L'Information Littéraire* 41 (1989): 7–12.

Duchêne, Roger and Pierre Ronzeaud, eds. *Ordre et contestation au temps des classiques, I.* Paris: PFSCL/Biblio 17, 1972.

Ferguson, Mary Anne. "The Female Novel of Development and the Myth of Psyché." *The Voyage In: Fictions of Female Development.* Eds. Elizabeth Abel, Marianne Hirsch and Elizabeth Langland. Hanover: University Press of New England, 1983. 228–43.

Forestier, Louis. *Pierre Corneille: Trois discours sur le poème dramatique.* Paris: Société d'Enseignement Supérieur, 1963.

Forestier, Geroges. *Essai de génétique théâtrale: Corneille à l'oeuvre.* Paris: Klincksieck, 1996.

———. "Où finit *Bérénice* commence *Tite et Bérénice.*" *Onze études sur la vieillesse de Corneille dédiées à la mémoire de Georges Couton.* Eds. Madeleine Bertaud and Alain Niderst. Boulogne: ADIREL, 1994. 53–75.

Gans, Eric. "Racine et la fin de la tragédie." *Relectures raciniennes: Nouvelles approches du discours tragique.* Ed. R. L. Barnett. Paris: PFSCL 16 (1986). 49–67.

Garaud, Christian. "Le Geste et la parole: Remarques sur la communication amoureuse dans *La Princesse de Clèves.*" *XVIIe Siècle* (1978): 257–68.

Genette, Gérard. *Figures II.* Paris: Seuil, 1969.

Girard, René. *La Violence et Le Sacré.* Paris: Grasset, 1977.

Goldmann, Lucien. *Le Dieu caché.* Paris: Gallimard, 1959.

Goldstein, Claire. "Love Letters: Discourses of Gender and Writing in the Criticism of the *Lettres portugaises.*" *Romanic Review* 88 (1997): 571–90.

Goodkin, Richard. *The Tragic Middle: Racine, Aristotle, Euripides.* Madison: University of Wisconsin Press, 1991.

———. "Thomas Corneille's Ariane and Racine's Phèdre: The Older Sister Strikes Back." *Esprit créateur* 38 (1998): 60–71.

Greenberg, Mitchell. *Canonical States, Canonical Stages: Oedipus, Othering and Seventeenth-Century Drama.* Minneapolis: University of Minnesota Press, 1994.

———. *Corneille, Classicism and the Ruses of Symmetry.* Cambridge: Cambridge University Press, 1986.

———. "Racine's *Bérénice:* Orientalism and the Allegory of Absolutism." *Esprit créateur* 32 (1992): 75–86.

Grégoire, Vincent. "*La Princesse de Clèves* ou le roman de la méprise." *Papers on French Seventeenth-Century Literature* 23. 44 (1996): 249–62.

Gregorio, Laurence A. "Husserl, History and Historiography: A Phenomenological Approach to *La Princesse de Clèves." Racine; Fontenelle; Entretiens sur la pluralité des mondes; Histoire et Littérature.* Ed. Charles Williams. Paris: Papers on Seventeenth-Century Literature, 1990. 209–16.

Guilleragues. *Chansons et Bons Mots Valentins: Lettres Portugaises.* Eds. Frédéric Deloffre and Jacques Rougeot. Geneva: Droz, 1972.

Gutleben, Muriel. "Faste et pompe, monstres et sublime dans *Médée* de Corneille et *Phèdre* de Racine." *Papers on French Seventeenth-Century Literature* (2000): 153–61.

Gutwirth, Marcel. "Jéhu, le fier Jéhu: La Métaphorisation du tragique." *Relectures raciniennes: Nouvelles approches du discours tragique.* Ed. R. L. Barnett. Paris: PFSCL 16 (1986). 69–80.

Haig, Stirling, *Madame de Lafayette.* New York: Twayne, 1970.

Harth, Erica. *Ideology and Culture in Seventeenth-Century France.* Ithaca: Cornell University Press, 1983.

———. "The Tragic Moment in *Athalie." Modern Language Quarterly* 33 (1972): 382–95.

Henry, Patrick and John D. Lyons, eds. *An Inimitable Example: The Case for the Princesse de Clèves.* Washington, D.C.: Catholic University of America Press, 1992.

Hirsch, Marianne. "Spiritual Bildung: The Beautiful Soul as Paradigm." *The Voyage in: Fictions of Female Development.* Eds. Elizabeth Abel, Marianne Hirsch, and Elizabeth Langland. Hanover: University Press of New England, 1983. 23–48.

Horowitz, Louise. "Racine's Laws." *Dalhousie French Studies* 49 (1999): 132–44.

Hubert, Judd D. "Les Écarts de Trézène." *Relectures raciniennes: Nouvelles approches du discours tragique.* Ed. R. L. Barnett. Paris: PFSCL 16 (1986). 81–97.

Jackson, John. E. "*Andromaque:* L'envers du discours racinien." *Stanford French Review* 9 (1985): 121–36.

Judovitz, Dalia. "The Aesthetics of Implausibility: *La Princesse de Clèves." MLN* 99.5 (1984): 1037–56.

Kamuf, Peggy. *Fictions of Feminine Desire.* Lincoln: University of Nebraska Press, 1982.

Koch, Philip. "*Horace:* réponse cornélienne à la querelle du *Cid." Romanic Review* 76 (1985): 148–61.

Lafayette, Madame de. *Romans et Nouvelles.* Ed. Emile Magne. Paris: Garnier Frères, 1970.

Larimore de Lara, Sylvie de. "*La Princesse de Clèves* ou l'invention de 'l'individu.'" *Romance Notes* 35.1 (1994): 63–69.

Le Hir, Jeanne. "Puissance et prestige du passé dans *Andromaque* de Racine." *Etudes Classiques* 33 (1965): 401–11.

Leiner, Wolfgang. "L'Amour de Mariane, du plaisir et la rhétorique du sentiment: Cheminements de la critique entre mythes et texte. *Oevures et critiques* 1 (1976): 125–45.

———. "De Nouvelles considérations sur l'apostrophe initiale des *Lettres portugaises.*" *Romanische Forschungen* 78 (1966): 548–66.

———. "Ex Visceribus causae. Passion, rhétorique, littérature. Aspects rhétoriques de la formule initiale des *Lettres portugaises.*" *PFSCL* 3 (1975): 33–46.

Lepine, Jacques-Jude. "La Barbarie à visage divin: Mythe et rituel dans *Athalie.*" *French Review* 64 (1990): 19–31.

Levine, Stanley F. "Exotism and the Jew: Racine's Biblical Tragedies." *Cahiers du Dix-Septième* 3 (1989): 51–70.

Lyons, John D. "Narrative Interpretation and Paradox: *La Princesse de Clèves.*" *Romanic Review* 72.4 (1981): 383–400.

Mall, Laurence. "Dire le départ, ou comment faire quelque chose de rien: Etude sur *Bérénice.*" *Neophilologus* 75 (1991): 41–55.

Mallinson, Johnathan. "Writing Wrongs: *Lettres portugaises* and the Search for an Identity." *Writers and Heroines: Essays on Women in French Literature.* Eds. Shirley Jones Day and Annette Lavers. Bern: Peter Lang, 1999. 31–47.

Marcus, Jane. "Still Practice, A/Wrested Alphabet. Toward a Feminist Aesthetic." *Feminist Issues in Literary Scholarship.* Ed. Shari Benstock. Bloomington: Indiana University Press, 1989. 79–97.

Marder, Elissa. "The Mother Tongue in *Phèdre* and *Frankenstein.*" *Yale French Studies* 76 (1989): 59–77.

Maskell, David. "The Hand of God in French Religious Drama: Racine. Boyer and Campistron." *Seventeenth-Century French Studies* 14 (1992): 119–31.

McArthur, Elizabeth. *Extravagant Narratives: Closure and Dynamics in the Epistolary Form.* Princeton: Princeton University Press, 1990.

McGregor, Gordon D. "Rodogune, Nicomède and the Status of History in Corneille." *Stanford French Review* 11. 2 (1987): 133–56.

McGuire, James R. "La Princesse de Clèves dé-nouant *La Princesse de Clèves.*" *The French Review* 66.3 (1993): 381–92.

Melzer, Sara. "Myths of Mixture in *Phèdre* and the Sun King's Assimilation Policy in the New World." *Esprit créateur* 38 (1998): 72–81.

Micklesen, David. "You Can Never Tell: *Déjà Vu* and *Jamais Vu* in *La Princesse de Clèves.*" *Romance Languages Annual* (1994): 135–40.

Miller, Nancy K. "Emphasis Added: Plots and Plausibilities in Women's Fiction." *An Inimitable Example: The Case for the Princesse de Clèves.* Eds. Patrick Henry and John Lyons. Washington D.C.: Catholic University of America Press, 1992. 15–38

———. "'I's' in Drag: The Sex of Recollection." *Eighteenth-Century: Theory and Interpretation* 22 (1981): 47–57.

Morrison, Paul. "Noble Deeds and the Secret Singularity: *Hamlet* and *Phèdre. Canadian Review of Comparative Literature* 18 (1991): 263–88.

Moye, Richard. "Silent Victory: Narrative, Appropriation, and Autonomy in *La Princessse de Clèves.*" *MLN* 104. 4 (1989): 845–60.

Muratore, Mary Jo. *Cornelian Theater: The Metadramatic Dimension.* Birmingham: Summa, 1990.

———. "Historical Imposters, Fictional Truths: *La Princesse de Clèves.*" *Symposium* 54. 4 (2001): 245–58.

————. *Mimesis and Metatextuality in the French Neo-Classical Text.* Geneva: Droz, 1994.

————. "Racine's *Athalie* or the Power of Precedent." *Les Epreuves du labyrinthe: Essais de poétique et d'herméneutique raciniennes: Hommage tricentenaire.* Ed. R. L. Barnett. *Dalhousie French Studies* 49 (1999): 182–92.

————. "Strategies of Containment: Repetition as Ideology in *Horace.*" *Romanische Forschungen* 109 (1997): 252–63.

————. "The Gender of Truth: Rhetorical Privilege in Tristan's *Mariane.*" *Papers on French Seventeenth-Century Literature.* Ed. Francis Assaf. 102 (1997): 145–53.

————. "The Pleasures of Re-Enactment in *Andromaque. Dalhousie French Studies* 24 (1993): 57–70.

Murphy, Bernadette Lintz. "Du désordre à l'ordre: Le rôle de la violence dans *Horace.*" *The Existential Coordinates of the Human Condition.* Ed. Anna-Teresa Tymieniecka. Dordrecth: Reidel, 1984: 435–47.

Niderst, Alain and Georges Couton, eds. *Pierre Corneille.* Paris: Presses Universitaires de France, 1985.

————. *La Princesse de Clèves: Le Roman paradoxal.* Paris: Larousse, 1973.

————. "Pour une interprétation allégorique de *La Princesse de Clèves.*" *Actes de Davis.* Paris: PFSCL (1988): 5–19.

Norman, Dorothy. *The Hero: Myth, Image, Symbol.* New York: World, 1969.

Pearson, Carol and Katherine Pope. *The Female Hero in American and British Literature.* New York: R. R. Bowker, 1981.

Pelous, Jean-Michel. "Métaphores et figures de l'amour dans la *Phèdre* de Racine." *Travaux de Linguistique et de Littérature* 19.2 (1981): 71–81.

————. "Une Héroine romanesque entre le naturel et la rhétorique: Le langage des passions dans les *Lettres portugaises.*" *Revue d'Histoire Littéraire de la France* 77 (1977): 555–63.

Picard, Raymond, ed. *Racine, Oeuvres complètes.* Paris: Gallimard, 1951.

Pot, Olivier. "La Mort d'Hippolyte ou la défiguration silencieuse du langage." *Papers on French Seventeenth-Century Literature* 23 (1996): 601–33.

Racevskis, Roland. "Generational Transition in *Andromaque.*" *Les Épreuves du labyrinthe: Essais de poétique et d'herméneutique raciniennes.* Ed. R. L. Barnett. *Dalhousie French Studies* 49 (1999): 63–72.

————. "Solitary Pleasures: Creative Avoidance of Court and Convent in *La Princesse de Clèves.*" *French Review* 70.1 (1996): 24–34.

Racine, Jean. *Oeuvres.* Paris: Hachette, Les Grands écrivains de la France. 1929.

————. *Oeuvres complètes.* Ed. Raymond Picard. Paris: Gallimard, 1950–66.

Raglan, F. R. S. *The Hero: A Study in Tradition, Myth and Drama.* New York: Vintage, 1956.

Relyea, Suzanne. "Se Manquer ou se prononcer: Presence and Self-Possession in the *Princesse de Clèves.*" *Papers on French Seventeeth-Century Literature* 10.18 (1983): 35–46.

Rousset, Jean. *Forme et Signification: Essais sur les structures littéraires de Corneille à Claudel.* Paris: Corti, 1962.

Schérer, Jacques. *Rodogune.* Paris: Droz, 1946.

Scott, J. W. "The 'Digressions' of The *Princesse de Clèves,*" *French Studies* 11 (1957): 315–22.

Shepard, James C. *Mannerism and Baroque in Seventeenth-Century French poetry: The*

Example of Tristan L'Hermite. Chapel Hill: North Carolina Studies in the Romance Languages and Literatures, 2001.

Shor, Naomi. *Breaking the Chain.* New York: Columbia University Press, 1985.

Spitzer, Leo. *Essays on Seventeenth-Century French Literature.* Cambridge: Cambridge University Press, 1983.

———. "*Les Lettres portugaises.*" *Romanische Forschungen* 65 (1953): 94–135.

Stamato, Doreena Ann. "Le Renversement symétrique des rôles masculins et féminins dans les pièces *Rodogune* et *Horace.*" *Papers on French Seventeenth-Century Literature* 16 (1989): 529–40.

Stanton, Domna. "The Ideal of Repos in Seventeenth-Century French Literature." *Esprit Créateur* 15 (1975): 79–104.

Stone, Harriet. "Exemplary Teaching in *La Princesse de Clèves,*" *The French Review* 62.2 (1988): 248–58.

———. "Les Voiles du pouvoir." *Ordre et contestation au temps des Classiques,* I. Eds. Roger Duchêne and Pierre Ronzeaud. Paris: Biblio 17, 1992. 225–33.

Sweetser, Marie-Odile. "Les Femmes et le pouvoir dans le théâtre cornélien." *Pierre Corneille.* Eds. Alain Niderst and Georges Couton. Paris: Presses Universitaires de France, 1985. 605–14.

Tiefenbrun, Susan. "Blood and Water in *Horace:* A Feminist Reading." *Papers on French Seventeenth-Century Literature* 10 (1983): 617–34.

Tobin, Roland. "Les Trachiniennes et Phèdre: D'un poison à l'autre." *Ouverture et Dialogue.* Ed. Ulrich Doring, et al. Tübingen: Narr, 1998: 421–27.

Tretheway, Jean. "Anti-Judaism in Racine's *Athalie.*" *Seventeenth-Century French Studies* 18 (1996): 167–75.

Tristan l'Hermite. *La Mariane.* Ed. Jacques Madeleine. Paris: Nizet, 1984.

Ubersfeld, Anne. "The Space of *Phèdre.*" *Poetics Today* 2.3 (1981): 201–10.

Varga, Kibédi. "Romans d'amour, romans de femmes à l'époque classique." *Revue des Sciences Humaines* 168 (1977): 517–24.

Verdier, Gabrielle. "Gender and Rhetoric in Some Seventeenth-Century Love Letters." *Esprit créateur* 22 (1983): 45–57.

Valincour, Jean-Baptiste de. *Lettres à Madame la Marquise ***sur le sujet de La Princesse de Clèves.* Paris: Sébastien Mabre-Cramoisy, 1678.

Virmauz, Odette. *Les Héroïnes romanesques de Madame de Lafayette.* Paris: Klincksieck, 1981.

Vuillemin, Jean-Claude. "Troie/Buthrote: Problématique de l'origine dans *Andromaque.*" *Australian Journal of French Studies* 27 (1990): 3–16.

Wadsworth, Philip. "Artifice and Sincerity in the Poetry of Tristan L'Hermite." *Modern Language Notes* 74 (1959): 422–30.

Wagener, Guy H. "*Horace* ou la pièce cornélienne des fondations: La Guerre entre Albe et Rome aura bien lieu." *Papers on French Seventeenth-Century Literature* 14 (1987): 745–80.

Watts, Derek. "A Further Look at *Rodogune.*" *Ouverture et Dialogue.* Ed. Ulrich Doring, et al. Tübingen: Narr, 1998. 447–63.

Wells, Byron R. "The King, the Court, the Country: Theme and Structure in *La Princesse de Clèves.*" *Papers on French Seventeenth-Century Literature* (1985): 543–58.

Yashinsky, Jack. "'Pourquoi ce livre saint, ce glaive, ce bandeau?' Commentaires textuels sur *Athalie.*" *Lettres Romanes* 38 (1984): 65–75.

INDEX